Benjamin P. Howell, M.D.

THE Book of John Howell & his Descendants

With Supplementary Accounts of the Families Related to them by Marriage

Collected from various sources

by

Frances Howell

of Woodbury, N. Y.

VOLUME I.

NEW YORK: Published by Frances Howell

M D CCC XCVII.

THE BOOK OF JOHN HOWELL
AND HIS DESCENDANTS

The Winthrop
Press

New York

Inscribed

to the memory of

MY FATHER

Frances Howell

Contents

LIST OF PLATES

PREFACE

SECTION I. *Concerning John Howell II. and Katharine Ladd, his wife.*

CHAPTER I. The Ladds 1
CHAPTER II. The Ladd Property 34
CHAPTER III. John Howell I. · . . . 60
CHAPTER IV. John Howell II. 64

SECTION II. *Concerning John Ladd Howell and Frances Paschall, his wife.*

CHAPTER I. John Ladd Howell . . . 117
CHAPTER II. Frances Paschall Howell . . . 132
CHAPTER III. Letters 134

SECTION III. *Concerning Joshua Ladd Howell and Anna Blackwood, his wife.*

CHAPTER I. Joshua Ladd Howell 215
CHAPTER II. Anna Blackwood Howell . . 224
CHAPTER III. Fancy Hill and Letters . . . 242

SECTION IV. *Concerning Children of Joshua Ladd Howell.*

CHAPTER I. Samuel Ladd Howell . . . 353

CHAPTER II. Paschall Howell 366
CHAPTER III. Frances Howell and Benjamin Betterton, her
   husband 389
CHAPTER IV. John L. Howell 398
CHAPTER V. Anna Maria Howell . . . 414
CHAPTER VI. Joshua Howell, Richard Washington Howell,
   Thos. James Howell, Abegail B. Howell, Rebecca
   Howell 418
CHAPTER VII. Brig. Gen. Joshua Howell . . 423
CHAPTER VIII. Benjamin Paschall Howell, M.D., and
   Rachel Lewis Howell, his wife . . . 460
ADDENDUM TO CHAPTER III. Benjamin Betterton
   Howell 484

SECTION V. *Concerning families related by marriage to the descendants of John Howell.*

CHAPTER I. The Collins Family . . . 513
CHAPTER II. The Clement Family . . . 518
CHAPTER III. The Blackwood Family . . 526
CHAPTER IV. The Harrison Family . . . 531
CHAPTER V. The Paschal Family . . . 536
CHAPTER VI. The Dodge Family . . . 571

APPENDIX

I. William Howell's Account of Ancestors . . 577
II. Letters to Jos. L. Howell . . . 582
III. Genealogy 583

INDEX

ERRATA

List of Plates

Benjamin P. Howell, M.D.	Frontispiece
Pages from Account Book of John Ladd, jr.,	35
Howell's Cove, Fancy Hill,	40
Marriage Certificate of Frances Howell,	132
Col. Joshua Ladd Howell,	215
Anna Blackwood Howell in Early Womanhood,	224
Anna Blackwood Howell at the Age of Forty,	230
Fancy Hill House, facing Inland,	242
Fancy Hill House, facing the River,	246
Samuel Ladd Howell, M.D.,	353
Paschall Howell in Boyhood,	368
Frances Howell and her Children, Lewis and Henry,	389
John L. Howell,	400
Richard Washington Howell,	418
Brig. Gen. Joshua B. Howell,	423
Friends' Meeting House, Burlington, N. J., 1683	514

Preface

A comparatively brief family chronicle written by Benjamin Paschall Howell, in familiar letters to his son, forms the nucleus of this book. Unfortunately Dr. Howell did not begin the records of his memory and researches till a time when they were frequently interrupted by his last illness; his death abruptly closed them.

Much, therefore, that his accurate genealogical knowledge would have enabled him to tell, much that is invaluable, in point of fact and interest, must remain a sealed book.

However, partaking of his enthusiasm, his daughter has grouped a mass of papers and data around what he left. The object is to make the lives and aims of the forefathers more real to the present generation, to many of whom they are but names.

While much of this matter antedates the Revolution, it has been difficult to learn much of the family prior to their emigration, because records in early times were not properly kept.

This is to be regretted, but not to be wondered at.

It is known that several branches of the family were impoverished by fines, confiscations, and imprisonments as

" Quakers," and fled from England, "persecuted for Truth's sake." The all-absorbing struggle with the difficulties of a rugged life allowed little time for retrospect, which, to say the least, could not have been wholly pleasant. Time had not for them cast about their hard experiences the romantic interest they hold for their descendants. If they looked away from the hardness of their present time, their glance was more likely to be to the future than to the past.

SECTION ONE

CONCERNING JOHN HOWELL, II. AND KATHARINE LADD, HIS WIFE.

CHAPTER I.

THE LADDS.

John Ladd, sr.—Samuel Ladd—John Ladd, jr.—Mary Ladd—Katherine Ladd—Hannah Ladd—The 'Pass' Given to Hannah Ladd by John Cooper—'John Ladd and John Ladd, jr.' by John Clement—Letters.

IT seems appropriate that a record of this kind should commence with the time and circumstances, as far as they are now known, attendant upon the arrival, in this country, of our ancestors, the first of whom was JOHN LADD, who with other Friends arrived at Burlington, New Jersey, in 1678.*

He was one of the Council of Proprietors.† He assisted William Penn in laying out Philadelphia. The compass and chain used on that occasion are now the property of the children of the late Samuel Harrison Howell, having been left to their grandfather, Samuel Ladd Howell, M.D., by Samuel Mickle, of

---

*See Smith's History of New Jersey, pages 109-10.
†Ibid, p. 551. See address to Governor Burnett.

Woodbury, who received them from his aunt, Hannah Ladd, widow of John Ladd, jr.

Connected with the laying out of the City is the following traditional anecdote : William Penn offered John Ladd property, probably a square in the city, or some £30 in consideration of his services. John chose the cash, upon which Penn remarked : 'John, thou art a Ladd by name and a lad by nature—dost thou not perceive that this will become a great city ?' John, 'could not see it,' or else he deemed the ready money of more immediate importance than the prospective value of the square.

Soon after his arrival he must have fixed his residence at the 'Old Homestead' known since as 'Candor Hall,' one mile northeast from Woodbury.*

John Ladd had five children: Samuel, Jonathan, John Ladd, jr., Mary and Katherine. He must have conveyed to his children during his lifetime, large tracts of land. His wife's name was Elizabeth ; she must have died—

---
*See old title papers.

according to Samuel Mickle's record of the event—on the 13th of March, 1734, as on this date he made a codicil to his will, in consequence of her death, leaving to his surviving children—John, jr. and Katherine—what he had willed their mother in lieu of dower. John Ladd's will was proved March 12, 1739, which, by new style, would be 1740, as the 25th of March was then, by the calandar in use, from, say 1450 to 1750, called the first of the year. This calendar was in use in this province, and doubtless gave rise to the custom here of moving on the 25th of March.*

John Ladd, sr. must have attained to great age, supposing him to have been twenty-one years old when he came to this country. In corroboration of this, his will, made some eight years before his death, commences thus: ' I— John Ladd, sr.—being at this time praised be God; of sound and disposing mind and memory, but far advanced in years, do, etc. ' This will was proved before Gov. Lewis Morris, April 4, 1740.

*See Smith's History.

SAMUEL LADD—spoken of in his father's will as his ' eldest son '—left five children : Matthew, Joseph, Sarah, Deborah and Katharine. ' He owned 400 acres south of Timber Creek and fronting on the Delaware River,' purchased of the widow of Samuel Carpenter, of Philadelphia, in 1714. This tract embraces the farms of W. A. Newbold and Elizabeth Githins, and the present hamlet of Westville and beyond. Deborah Ladd was second daughter of Samuel Ladd. She married Charles West. They had two sons, Charles and Joseph, to whom she gave the West Point Fishery. Charles had three daughters, Deborah Lee, Maria Tatum and Elizabeth Whitall. Joseph had two sons, Thomas died ; Joseph was a physician, and with his three cousins, Deborah, Maria and Elizabeth, sold the West Point Fishery to my father, late Col. Joshua Ladd Howell in 1811, for $9000.*

Samuel Ladd died intestate, and his widow, Mary Ladd, administered to his estate. John Ladd, Jr., in an old account book makes this

*See title papers.

entry: 'July y⁰ 9th, 1725—about 2 in y⁰ morning—then Samuel Ladd died.'

JONATHAN LADD, second son of John Ladd, sr., owned the property, some 600 acres, still owned by his descendant, Samuel H. Ladd of Woodbury, New Jersey. His will is recorded in Lib. 3 of Wills A 182, Secretary of State's Office, Trenton. He had two children, Samuel and Elizabeth, born 9th mo., 1724. He must have died in March, 1731, as his will was proved on the 5th of April, then called the 2d month. His wife's name was Ann. His will reads: ' I, Jonathan Ladd being somewhat ill of body, but of good memory and understanding, for which I am thankful, do etc.'

JOHN LADD, JR., third son of John Ladd, sr., and named in his father's will as his ' youngest son' was quite a prominent man in the county of Gloucester, and held the office of Clerk of the County of Gloucester for forty-three years, so said his nephew, Samuel Mickle, deceased. December 1, 1739, council recommended to Lewis Morris, governor, that John Ladd, jr. be appointed to the commission of peace and pleas in Gloucester county in place of Mr. Harrison. The Governor ordered his secretary to make out the commission. The system of rotation in office had not then been introduced. He died five o'clock A. M., December 20, 1770, his will being proved February 4th of that year. (In about 1754, March, ceased to be reckoned first month.) He left a very large estate in lands, amounting to some 6000 or 7000 acres. The great bulk of this he left to his widow, Hannah Mickle Ladd, 1600 acres at her death he bequeathed to his nephew, John Ladd Howell; she having outlived the nephew some twelve years it descended to his son, Joshua Ladd Howell, in 1797.

MARY LADD, elder daughter of John, sr., married Joseph Parker, of Delaware county, Penn. The nuptials must have been, for those days, a grand affair; I have heard my mother, Anna Blackwood Howell, speak of the account handed down, of Mary Ladd's wedding. The guests were so numerous that ovens were built out of doors to cook and bake for them.

Twenty couples on horseback attended them
to Haddonfield Friends' Meeting House—
many of the guests crossed the Delaware River
from Philadelphia.

' The Family Bible, late belonging to the
two John Ladds [father and son] is intended by Hannah Ladd, as she tells me,
to be given to Mary Parker Norris, in
Philadelphia, 11, 2d mo., 1791. She left the
above said Bible with Elizabeth Fox in Philadelphia, requesting her to give it to Mary P.
Norris, and which I am informed was since
done.' *Samuel Mickel.*

KATHERINE LADD, younger daughter of John
Ladd, sr., married John Howell, 1st mo., 25,
1734, son of Jacob Howell, of Chester, Penn.,
and grandson of the John Howell who came to
this country from Wales in 1698.

John, after his marriage, settled in Woodbury, N. J., removed thence in 1739 to Philadelphia, and afterward to Georgia, and lived
in the parish of Christ Church in that State.
He died at John Ray's, near Savannah, Ga., in
1765.

John and Katherine Howell had two children, viz.: John Ladd Howell who married Frances Paschall, daughter of John Paschall, M.D. and Frances, his wife, of Darby, Penn., and Sarah, who married a Sparks. Katherine Ladd Howell died in Philadelphia previous to May 9, 1764.

HANNAH LADD, wife of John Ladd, jr., was a Mickle; her husband as before mentioned left to her the bulk of his estate, and left a few hundred acres directly to his nephew, John Ladd Howell, and some 1600 acres to him at the death of his widow. She gave her consent at one time to her nephew to clear the fisheries, since known as the Fancy Hill Fishery. Consequently he arose very early one morning to go to Philadelphia to make the necessary purchase of twine, etc., with which to construct his seines, when he met the old lady coming from her bedroom, who told him she must revoke the permission, as she remembered a promise she had made to her kinswoman, Deborah West, daughter of Samuel Ladd, and who owned the West Point Fishery,

that no fishery should be established immediately below, as it might interfere with and
injure hers above. This was a most unjust
and unwise pledge, as John Ladd Howell, the
prospective owner of the contemplated fishery,
and Deborah West stood percisely in the same
relation to her husband; the one being his
brother's daughter, the other the son of his
sister Katherine.

The consequence was most unhappy, John
Ladd Howell was justly hurt and indignant
and never spoke to his aunt afterwards, though
living in part of the same house. Some eight
years after John Ladd Howell's death, about
1793, she was prevailed upon to yield a reluc-
tant consent that her grandnephew, Joshua L.
Howell should clear the fishery. This fishery
proved to be for many years a most lucrative
one, and did not materially injure the one
above, or West's Fishery.

Hannah Ladd made her will October 5, 1792,
bequeathing to her niece, Frances Paschall
Howell, $50; to her grandnephew, Joshua
Ladd Howell, an oval dining table and eight

silver spoons marked J. E. L., initials of John
and Elizabeth Ladd; to his wife, Anna Blackwood Howell, a bureau and looking glass. The
1600 acres which by John Ladd, jr.'s will became the property of John Ladd Howell, now
descended to Joshua L. Howell. The rest of
the estate was divided among her own relatives,
the Mickles and Hopkins.

The foregoing brief account of one of the
oldest families in that part of the State known
as West Jersey, may excite interesting reflec-
tions in the minds of some of their descendants.
To me every incident connected with them is
deeply interesting.

Among the papers of the late Samuel Mickle,
now in possession of Miss Martha Mickle, I
found the following 'pass' for Mistress Hannah
Ladd, given her by Hon. John Cooper who,
at that time was a very prominent man, and
was, I believe, a member of Council, the upper
branch of the Colonial Legislature. He owned
and I think built the house in Woodbury, N. J.,
now occupied by Miss Sarah Campbell and
Mrs. Barton daughters of the late Amos Camp-

bell, esq.* This house was the headquarters of Lord Cornwallis, while here with six regiments of British troops in November, 1777.

THE PASS.

The bearer Misstress Hannah Ladd,
Neither very good, nor bad,
 Aged as appears to me,
 Not far short of thirty-three.†
 With stocking tied below the knee ;
Of complexion rather fair
Flaxen colored is her hair ;
 Her stature neither great nor small,
 Her eyes, perhaps, you'd hazel call ;
A traveler from here to there,
And may be let go any where ;
 Has permission, with her man,
Her horses and her carriage,
 To travel all New Jersey o'er,
If well she pays her ferriage.

JOHN COOPER,

Gloucester County, July 1, 1777.   *Coun. C.*

---

*Now owned by Dr. Clarence Abbott.

$$\dagger\text{Born}\ \frac{1777}{1715}$$

Say 6₂ years.

George Fox had enjoined upon his followers kindness toward the aborigines. It appears that Hannah Ladd obeyed this injunction, not only in its spirit but in letter, for Anna Blackwood relates that Indians often came to Hannah Ladd's, at the 'Old Place,' and would make this demand for food 'Hann Ladd more Souk!'* and after partaking plentifully of this, they would turn their saucers upside down on her clean tablecloth and then say 'Hann Ladd more meat!' She made no remonstrance against this aboriginal inelegance, but submitted with a true 'Friendly spirit.'

BENJ. P. HOWELL, M.D.
Woodbury, N. J., 1879.

---

*Soup.

JOHN LADD AND JOHN LADD, JR*

BY JUDGE JOHN CLEMENT.

THE 'Plantations in America,' were the only place towards which the followers of George Fox turned when they found that neither their persons or estates were protected by the laws of England as then administered. . .

The concessions and agreements were published in London in 1676, and attracted much attention especially among the members of the society of Friends. Of these was John Ladd who arrived at Burlington with many others in 1678. His interest was evidently with the London owners, for his first settlement appears to have been within the territory of Arwaumus where the London people first proposed to have their town, but were persuaded to go higher up the river to Burlington.

This territory extended for several miles along the river, above and below where Gloucester City now stands, and was the Indian name for that locality, but soon lost sight of after the English came. Although his name does not occur among the original lot owners of Gloucester as laid out by Thomas Sharp, yet among the earliest deeds of record in which JOHN LADD is named as a party, he is mentioned as of Gloucester River, but subsequently called Timber Creek. He was a practical surveyor, and acted

*From ' The Constitution,' Woodbury, N. J., January 25, 1888.

as deputy for the Surveyor General of the Western Division for several years. .   .   .

In 1688 with Jonathan Wood and Samuel Toms, he located a large tract of land in Deptford township, extending from the river on the west to the Salem road and beyond on the east.   He soon after purchased Samuel Toms' and Jonathan Wood's interest, and built a dwelling for himself on the tract and where he resided until his death.   In 1721 he located an adjoining tract along the river shore, and where the fishery was established and used to the present time.   For many years a portion of this tract has been known as the Howell estate, coming into that family by the devise of John Ladd, jr. to John Ladd Howell, a son of Katherine Ladd who married John Howell.

There is abundant evidence to show that John Ladd was a member of the society of Friends, and there is but little doubt that he was an attendant of the meeting at the mouth of Woodbury Creek before the erection of the house by the south side of the King's road and west of the before named stream.   He was the first person named as one of the grantees in the deed from John Swanson in 1715 for one acre of land whereon to erect a house of worship, and although the purposes of the trust are not therein set out, yet it appears in subsequent conveyances of the same premises.   .   .   He came to New Jersey a young man, for about sixty-two years of his life were spent within the province and where he was a prominent and influential citizen. He was a man of considerable estate and of good education, as is shown by his operations in land and the places of responsibility he was called upon to fill.

It appears by the old minute book of the Gloucester County courts that John Ladd occasionally figured as a grand or petit juror, once as constable and occasionally as litigant. The first entry was made May 28, 1686, when the court sat at Gloucester and the next term at Red Bank. This alternation continued until about the middle of the next year when the latter place of meeting was abandoned

John Ladd soon became interested in the properties of the western division by purchase from several persons, and among others, finding that the increase of immigration into the province and the consequent sale of land so multiplied the labors of the commissioners that a new system was found necessary. To bring this about a general meeting of the proprietors was called at Burlington, March 14, 1687, when it was agreed that a council of proprietors be established, consisting of seven members from Burlington County and five members from Gloucester County, to represent the original owners of the soil. John Ladd was present at that meeting and helped to arrange the details of the council. This body is in existence at the present time, a period of two hundred years, with all the papers, documents and records in good preservation. Although never a member of that body, yet he was much interested in its proceedings, for his holding of properties was large.

At the first meeting of the council (1688) he, for Col. John Alford, of Boston, (a large owner) and himself with many others signed a protest to Gov. William Burnett against the repeal of the law providing for the running of the dividing line between East and West Jersey. . . .

Among the curious things pertaining to the times and applying to the subject of this sketch, is a libel duly signed and of record in the proper office. Copied here entire, it needs no explanation :

> This may certify all persons whom it may concern, That, whereas I, Samuel Taylor, of Gloucester River, within the province of West Jersey, lawyer, have of late publicly reported several false, scandalous, reproachful and detracting speeches of and concerning John Ladd of ye same place aforesaid yeoman, and Sarah*, his wife, which were of infamous import and tending to prove ye said parties to be of unjust dealings, and evil and dishonest lives and conversations; therefore, I, ye said Samuel Taylor, being moved to ye said report by my precipitate and unadvised passion and anger against ye parties above said, do hereby certify that I herewith repent of and am unfeignedly sorrowful for my speaking, declaring and publishing any report of such evil tendency aforesaid, and do freely and voluntarily own and acknowledge that I have grossly abused, traduced and wronged ye said John Ladd and Sarah his wife by means of ye false, slanderous and defaming reports and speeches above said.
>
> In testimony whereof I have hereunto put my hand this 24th of June, Anno Domini, 1690.   SAMUEL TAYLOR.

No such proceedings are now had and to the present generation of the legal fraternity this has many odd features. The science of the law has provided other means

---

*Ladd's wife's name was Elizabeth.

when an individual considers himself damaged by the sayings or writings of his enemy.

John Ladd died in 1740, surviving his wife Elizabeth about seven years. Their children were Samuel, who married Mary Medcalf in 1712; Jonathan, who married Ann Wills in 1723; Mary, who married Joseph Parker in 1730; John, who married Hannah Mickle in 1732; and Katharine, who married John Howell in 1734.

Samuel died in 1725, leaving five children : Matthew, Joseph, Sarah, Deborah and Katharine. Jonathan died in 1731, leaving three children : Samuel, Elizabeth, and a child unborn. Mary died in 1731, leaving one child, Mary. John died in 1771 without issue surviving him, and Katharine died, leaving two children, Sarah and John Ladd Howell.

As disclosed in his will dated in 1731, with a codicil dated in 1740, John Ladd survived his wife and all his children except John and Katharine. He devised his homestead estate of 500 acres to John and gave other parts of his property to Katharine and his granddaughter Mary Parker, having as he says in his will provided for Samuel and Jonathan while they were living. At his death he was one of the largest holders of real estate in the colony, and his selections prove him to have been a man of good judgment in such matters. He established the fishery where his land fronted the river and which was for many years known as ' Ladd's Cove. ' The exact date of this has been lost, but as he located the flats in 1722, that may be about the beginning of his fishery. Its particular situation on the shore always made it one of the best in those waters.

John Ladd was not a negative character, but his opinions were his own and freely expressed. He held a prominent place in the Society of Friends, and although he adhered to plainness of dress and simplicity of habit, yet about his home could be seen evidence of things generally attendant on wealth and liberality. His slaves, his plentiful board and his well-appointed household would convince any one that the creature comforts were not neglected.

JOHN LADD, jr., during his youth and until he attained to man's estate, had advantages that seldom fall to others. His father's wealth assured him of the benefits of education, which at that day could only be had at much cost. The society that enjoyed the freedom of the homestead gave him examples which if followed must inure to his benefit in riper years, and the precepts to which he listened were not wasted on him, as his after life abundantly proved.

From the time of his marriage (1732) to the death of his father (1740), John Ladd, jr., resided at Gloucester, and managed the ferry between that place and Philadel_ phia. This he purchased as the property late of Richard Welden, deceased, in 1735, and obtained his charter from William Cosby, then Governor. This was an exclusive privilege, and was the most important water transportation on the river. In 1721 it was taxed at thirty shillings while William Cooper's ferry was taxed at ten shillings, showing their relative value in the opinion of the Legislature at that time.

In 1740 he took an active part in suppressing the making and circulation of counterfeit coin within the colony. . . In 1747 he was appointed Clerk of Gloucester County by John Hamilton, Governor, and continued in the same office in 1762 by Josiah Hardy, the then Chief Executive of the Province. Five years after that date he was commissioned as Surrogate of the same county, evidence of his qualifications for such places and of his popularity with the Governors and with the people.

October 1, 1754, John Ladd and Samuel Clement appeared at the bar of the House of Assembly of the province of New Jersey, sitting at Perth Amboy, and presented their credentials as members elected from the county of Gloucester, and asked to be sworn in. They were there met by a petition from a number of voters of that county complaining that 'an undue election' in the choice of representatives had been held and praying for suitable redress in the premises. Samuel Shivers appeared for the petitioners and asked that the sheriff (John Hinchman) be summoned. A day or two afterwards the sheriff appeared and denied all the allegations made by the petition. After several adjournments a vote was reached October 11th, and John Ladd and Samuel Clement were seated as members of that body. It appeared that the members were

elected for an indefinite term, which depended on the
pleasure of the Governor who had power to prorogue the
Legislature at will.   Upon the receipt by the sheriff of a
writ from the Governor directing an election, it was his
duty to give public notice of the days and places where the
same was to be held.   He was required to select one Clerk
and one Inspector for each candidate, who attended every
day during the election and acted as Judges.   The elector
gave his vote by voice which was recorded by the Clerk,
and the sheriff could only change the polling places or
close the election by consent of the candidates.   This exposed him to much censure and the defeated candidate was
apt to complain that the poll was removed from a particular
place before his friends could have opportunity to record
their preference.   In 1716 the same difficulty occurred in
Gloucester County between John Kay and Daniel Coxe,
and William Harrison, the sheriff, was reprimanded by
the Speaker of the House of Assembly for removing the
poll to the injury of John Kay who had been defeated.
In this may be seen the latent seeds of dishonesty in elec-
tions and which crops out occasionally in these latter days.

   During his term several attempts were made to procure
a law to cut the dam at the mouth of Woodbury Creek.
Petitions and remonstrances numerously signed were
presented to the Legislature, one party claiming that it
stopped navigation and injured the health of the neighborhood.   The bill, after much contention, was defeated,
and the dam stood for many years after.   He remained a

member until 1760 when the Legislature was dissolved by
the Governor, but had been previously recommended
(1758) by Gov. Francis Bernard to the Lords Commissioners of trade and plantation, as one of the members of
his Council. This request did not reach the King, but
when William Franklin was appointed Governor he re-
newed the request in a letter dated May 10, 1763, in
these flattering terms : ' Mr. Ladd is a gentleman of fortune and unblemished character ; was formerly in the
Assembly where he was always on the side of the admin-
istration, and is now one of the principal magistrates of
Gloucester County, which office he has long executed with
ability and credit to himself. He, I think, has likewise
been recommended to your Board by a former Governor.'
This reached His Majesty, and he was pleased to approve
the appointment in the same year, and John Ladd became
one of the advisers of His Excellency the Governor . .

In a letter of Gov. William Franklin to the Earl of
Hillsborough, dated July 14th, 1771, he announced the
death of John Ladd as having occurred on December 20th
last past, and requested that Daniel Coxe be named to fill
the vacancy . . .

John Ladd, jr., took an active part in the proceedings
of the Council of Proprietors, he being interested in the
location of land within the province. In May, 1729, he
was returned as a member of the Board, and so continued,
excepting one year, until 1760. From 1751 to 1756 he
was Vice-President. In 1758 he was defeated, but the

next year returned and chosen President of the Board. In 1760 his name does not appear in the minutes, but the next year was elected and continued a member until his death in 1771. From 1762 to 1767 he was President and again from 1768 to his decease.

The Council of Proprietors during, and for many years after his membership, was a most important body, controlling the titles to the soil and the dispenser of the choice localities. Controversies constantly arose between rival parties as to boundaries and which had to be settled by the Council. The election of members was an event among the Proprietors and called together annually at Gloucester Green (where the voting took place) quite a concourse of those who favored or opposed certain candidates. Like many others, John Ladd, jr. had his enemies as will be seen by his defeat at several times   .   .   .

*[After the lapse of another half century, John Ladd, the son, appears to have been traduced by one of his neighbors in some of their political or religious controversies, and not resting very comfortable under the same, he required of William Ives a legal admission that he had said some ugly and untruthful things about him. This admission was spread upon the records over his own signature, done in open court, and witnessed by the judges thereof.

'A Knight of the Post,' implied that John had been convicted of some petty offence and had been punished at the whipping post, or set in the stocks, a means much in

*From History of the Early Letters by John Clement.

use at that time to vindicate the honor of the common-
wealth and to preserve its dignity.

The insinuation that he could not be trusted as a sworn
witness, perhaps touched John's pride quite as much as
the first charge, and led to the arrest of William Ives and
his admission to the falsity of the whole.

Like the first, the entire record is copied that the reader
may draw his own inference therefrom.

WILLIAM IVES' ACKNOWLEDGEMENT, MADE IN OPEN COURT AT GLO's-
TER :

Whereas, I, William Ives, of the township of Gloucester, in Gloucester, in the province of West Jersey, yeoman, in the presence of divers
creditable persons, inhabitants of the same county, sometime since did
falsely and without any cause or reason, speak and say that John Ladd,
of the said county was a ' Knight of the Post, ' and that I did not know,
but I might sue one Henry Sparks, but that I could not trust to the
said John Ladd's testimony, and I acknowledge likewise, that I spoke
and said sundry false, scandalous words touching and concerning the
reputation and character of him, the said John Ladd :

Now, I do hereby acknowledge and publickly declare that I have
wronged and injured the said John Ladd's character by the uttering and
speaking the said false, scandalous words and sayings, having not the
least shadow, colour or foundation for the same; and I do hereby desire forgiveness of the said John Ladd, for the injury done.

Gloucester, ye 28 October, 1744.

WILLIAM IVES.

Witnessed by Jas. Hinchman, one of ye Judges of the Court of
Common Pleas at Gloucester, Wm. Harrison, Daniel Mestayer.

Recorded, February 8th, 1745.

CHARLES READ, Sec.]

John Ladd, the younger, executed his will March 10th,

1760, and which shows him to have been a man of fortune and the owner of much real estate. Among the lands directed to be sold by the executor was one thousand acres on Absecon Beach (Atlantic City), and eight hundred acres on Brigantine Beach, now of great value. He gave his slaves to his widow and made numerous bequests to his relatives. He died without issue, and his estate passed under his will to the collateral branches of the family.

The will of Hannah Ladd (the widow of the younger John) is a noticeable paper. It bears date October 5th, 1792, with a codicil dated November 27th, 1796. She died the next year. Beside showing that she was the owner of a large landed estate and much personal property which she gave to her nephews and nieces, it is a genealogical document as showing many of the Hopkins, the Mickle and the Howell families. It contains much valuable information and can be depended on.

Chefter, May 8th, 1731.

To John Ladd, sr. at Gloucester These

Dr Father

After my Duty to thee with kind refpects to Brother and Sifter thefe come to inform You that my Dear Wife has given birth to a Daughter laft Night about Nine minutes after one in the morning to our Great comfort and Satisfaction She has been very weak but is much Recovered and by opinion of our friends wee hope will do well, The Child is a lovely promifing Child and very lively. My Dear Gives her love to thee & longs to fee thee, alfo brother and Sifter, Mother is well & Gives her very dear love to thee with Brother & Sifter. She thinks t'will be a convenient time for thee & Sifter Katharine to give us a vifit next Seventh day & if my Dr Wife recover well She thinks to go home with thee & leave Sifter to accompany us a little, My Dear wo'd not be prevailed upon to name her daughter but left it to me and I have named her after her mother. This with my Duty to thee & love to Brother & Sifter & all our other friends that may Enquire is the needful at Present from Dr Father thy Loving Son

*JOS. PARKER.**

---

*Husband of Mary Ladd, elder daughter of John Ladd, sr. Mary Ladd Parker's death followed soon after this event.

Chefter, Oct. 21, 1731.

To JOHN LADD, JUN., THESE PER Wᵐ MAY

Dʳ Brother

Thine wee Received laft night pr Wᵐ May & was Glad to hear of your welfare. Growing somewhat Impatient I Sho'd have feen you ere now but the weather being rough and unfeasonable deterd us & hearing yᵗ you were well made us well fatisfiede and more eafy than otherwife wee Should have been.

Wee are all well Sifter Katharine Gives her kind love to father Mother & thy Self & Jntends to be drawing towards you about the beginning of the next month or Soon after at which time I Shall take Care (Jf in being) to fee e'm well up. Little Molle thrives bravely & the nurfe is well. Sifter & Molle being here have added a Great deal to my Comfort & to my health too wᶜʰ has been much better then before, tho' J Expeft a decay in their abfence. J. S. has Sold all his land that was between him & mee & pay'd Me in One hundred pounds & J have lay it on Mortgage upon a plantation with a Quarter part of Naamans Mill wᶜʰ I look to be Good Security. John Salkeld, Jun. goes to yᵉ Monthly meeting next Second day wᵗʰ his ffriend & has given me and Sifter an invitation. (Yefterday J was waiting upon our Governor, he being going to yᵉ Assembly at New Castle wᶜʰ begins to day) Jf nothing prevents J think to be at Philadᵃ next Seventh day & if thy Occasion Called yee there shall See thee.

Pray Give my Duty to ffather & Mother & my hearty
refpeƈts to Thy Self is yᵗ needfull at present

Ffrom thy Loving Brother

JOS. PARKER.✱

July 10, 1741.

To My Friend John Ladd, Esq.

Of what vindiƈtive Power ſhall I complain
That makes my viſit and Intention vain
I Came unaſked yet hop'd my friends to pleaſe
And hop'd the ſlaughter of large Amphibes
Alas ! my Friends from home and all the Race
Of noiſy Croakers keep their Native place
They found their Trumpets fearleſs of their foe
Spring thro' the Reeds and wanton dive below
A Stranger I to their Canals and Cells
And too far off to hear their daring yells
Safe in their Sports and Clamours they remain
And ſo may live till I return again

✱Joseph Parker who was a nephew of the eccentric Quaker preacher, John
Salkeld, came to Chester from Cumberland, England, at the age of twenty-five to be
near his uncle. He entered the office of David Lloyd and after Lloyd's death he
succeeded him as Register and Recorder of Chester Co. In 1758 he was commissioned Justice of the Peace, a position of much dignity in colonial times.

Mary Parker (his daughter) married Charles Norris, of Philadelphia, 1759,
in the Old Quaker Meeting on Market street. On the death of her husband she
returned to Chester and resided in the parental mansion until her death 1799. She
was the mother of three sons and one daughter, *Deborah*, who was a small child
when she returned to Chester.

Deborah married Dr. George Logan, grandson of James Logan, Penn's secretary, and intimate friend. Her remarkable store of antiquarian information justly
entitled her to the appellation of ' The Female Historian of Colonial Times.' Her
manuscripts were published by the Historical Society of Pennsylvania. She is
spoken of familiarly in the notes of Anna Blackwood Howell.

Then by my fpear and with my friend to guide
The big mouthed Nation will be forced to hide
Or fall a prey and be like Chickens dreffed
But to their Greater praife a nobler Feaft.
And yet to be without fo Choice a Difh
Is the leaft Difappointment of my wifh
My dear Friend's Abfence is the Greateft Lofs
And I unfortunate deferve the Crofs.
Invited kindly often heretofore
To fee the produce of the Jerfey Shore
Partake with him a hofpitable treat
And view the Profpefts all around his Seat
But I neglectful made too long delay
And for my Crime with Juft Repentance pay

J. B.

To the Gentleman Esq. : John Ladd, Justice of Peace
and Proto Notary in the New Jarseys at Gloucester These 1752

Philadelphia 14th of May 1752

Dear Efquire

Having appointed feveral times and meetings with thofe
5 gentlemen of Gloucefter County in the New Jarfeys,
which bound themfelves over laft year unto me in 70 Pounds,
thereof to pay me 35 from the members of the Congregation at the head of Great Timber Creek, and finding that
they never would as yet meet me in a body in order to come

and finally fettle the accounts much lefs to pay me the reft of
my money, altho' they fome times have very fairly promifed
it. I hereby therefore humbly defire you to favour me with
your kind affiftance and to fummon in unto your houfe the
following gentlemen to fettle with & fatisfy me in order to
refume their Bond. Meffrs Thomas Chew, Jeremiah Chew,
Nath¹ Delap, Geo. Morgan, & And^rw Jones.

I know that your loving perfuafions will go the fartheft,
My Dear Efquire, that they fhould not hinder my voyage
another year and reduce me to the uttermoft ftraits, for that
I have ferved them faithfully as their own Teftimony and
Difcharging me in writings evidenceth it

I cannot expeft but they will agree to this way in the
amiableft manner poffible, I on my fide taking this kind
courfe out of real love to them all.

Next my humble refpefts to Your Dear Lady, I am

Dear Efquire
Your moft humble Servant
GABER^L NESMAN.

———

To JOHN LADD, JR.

New York
Aug 10 1758

Letters from Albany by laft night's poft inform us that the Bofton
Poft came in there on Sunday laft and brought Intelligence that Cape
Breton had Surrendered to the Englifh on the 22d of July, this News
was Brought to Bofton by a twenty gun fhip fent Exprefs thither, fhe
was not arrived at Bofton Harbour but her defpatches were fent up
from the place where fhe did arrive & that letters from Albany don't
mention tho' It is Generally believed here

,P. S. The Bofton Poft declared further that when he was five miles out of Bofton he heard a great many guns fired, which he believed to be cannon fired on Bofton Caftle on account of the fuccefs. A fiherman fpoke a man of War at Sea and got into Bofton before her, and there made oath of the information he got from the Captain wch was to the foregoing purpofe.

Philad Aug 12 1758

Honored Uncle

The above is an Extract of a letter from New York brought by the Poft this morning, which is pretty generally believed here, I got it from the Coffee Houfe Book. Mother is bravely & Defires her love to Aunt, thyfelf & Sifter Sally, for want of time I conclude

Thy Loving Nephew

JOHN LADD HOWELL

¶ Letters from John Ladd, jr., to John and Katharine Howell who at this time were living in North Carolina.

Gloucefter 15 April 1750

Dear Brother & Sifter

I wrote to you the 6th of Feb. Laft, but Capt Flower Sailed fooner than I Expected, the letter with the box of tea & Chocolate were Left at Philad both which I hope you will receive. I Got three letters from John & Sally Laft fall Late, and two days paft I rec'd another from John which I Take kindly and am glad to hear that you are all well which will always give me pleafure to hear. Brother Parker was

here 2 days agone & Molly was, he said, very well. I
shall write to you by all opportunities, I call and defire you
to do ye Same. My wife joins in kind Love to You, John
& Sally   I am your Loveing Brother

J. L.

———

Gloucefter County March 1st 1753

Dear Sifter

I could not Learn what part of the Country you had
moved to before Laft Week when Brother Jofeph Parker
brought me two letters which his daughter Mollie had received from you ; and that you take it very hard & unkindly
my not writing to you, as you think, But I have wrote letters to you which have not Come to you, and it is much of
a miftake to think that I do not think it worth while to
write to you, for I have been difappointed Several times before you removed from Newborn, and I knew not to
whome to direct any thing there, after you went from thence,
but Since receiving information of the place at which you
Live, you may Expect to hear from me oftener.

———

Glos^tr March 24 1753

*Dear Brother

I have the pleafure to acquaint thee now that I have got a
tenant for the place on Timber Creek that I believe will fuit
much better than any have yet done, he began work on the

———

*This muft have been addreffed to Jofeph Parker who married Mary, sifter to
John Ladd, jr.

place last week ; he Comes from Burlington Co. & has the
Character of a very hard working and good farmer, with
oxen & cows, and intends to follow the Market & keep
ftock, for which he has hands to Go on with his Bufinefs
without depending on hiring workmen Much.   He is to
have the place feven years from the 25 of March inftant at
£20 ℔ year rent—and is to build a Good Stone Cellar
adjoining to the House 18 foot fquare with a Ceder Log
houfe over it, for which he is to be allowed Ten pounds out
of the Firft years rent & Ten pounds out of the Second years
rent ; which he complains will be a poor price for doing ;
he is Likewife to Clear 30 acres of Land adjoining to the
place and is to maintain the Banks & leave them in Good
Order with the place at the end of the term ; His name is
Timothy Middleton ; he is very defirous to fee thee up in
the fore part of April when he will have all his Family on the
place.   I fhould be glad to fee thee about ye firft of April if
it fuits.   My wife gives her Kind Love to thy Self & Molly,
pleafe to accept the fame from thy Loving Brother

JOHN LADD, jr.

To Mary Parker Norris.

March 9th 1769

Dear Neice

John Hopkins & my Self have viewed the place and find
the Banks & drains have been very much neglected by
Daniel the Banks very full of Leaks & the drains filled up,
we have had them meafured and find 186 perch of the Bank

and 186 perch of the drain, which muſt be repaired &
scowered out before the meadow can be got in good order,
we have Computed that the Bank will coſt 1/9 ℔ perch
and the drains 9d ℔ perch ; we think we could not Get it
done Cheaper if it was our own, which will come to £35
however if thee can have it done for £30 it will be very
Cheap. This morning I hear Daniel is gone from the place
to Phila^d or some were over the River. If there is any
proof of the Bargain you made as to keeping the Banks &
Ditches in repair he ought to be compelled to perform it.
Some time agoe he told me he had taken a place about Germantown. As to what thee mentions of the Leting y^r place
to Saml Skill I think it will be beſt to guard ag^nst ſelling large
quantities of hay off the place by which Daniel had very
much hurt the upland ; it will be proper to allow no cord
wood to be ſold by any means, and avoid having any Sapling
or young wood made uſe of as much as poſſible. My Wife
gives her beſt reſpeẛts to thyſelf & the children. (She is
bad with being poyſon'd with Swamp Shoemack.) pleaſe to
accept the ſame from thy loving uncle.

JOHN LADD.

CHAPTER II.

THE LADD PROPERTY.

Description—The Fisheries—The Gilling Seines—Shad—
    Sturgeon—Herring—Salmon—Commissioners of Fish-
    eries.

THE road, which was the southwest
    boundary of the old 'Candor Hall'
farm, is called the Hessian Road from the fact
that the Hessian troops—variously estimated at
from 1200 to 2000—under Col. Count Donop
in their attack on Fort Mercer at Red Bank,
October 22, 1777, marched along this road.
They were signally defeated by some 400
Americans, mostly negroes and mulattoes,
under Col. Christopher Green. They passed
thro' Haddonfield, crossing Timber Creek
over Clement's bridge, full of confidence, but
returned completely demoralized and panic-
stricken. I have heard my mother, Anna
Blackwood Howell, then a child of nearly nine
years of age, describe the appearance of this

Teguingo .... Dr

1724
8m 2
9m 11

	£ s d
To a hatchet and Tobacco ----------	£0 : 4 : 8
To 1 pr stockins ----------------	0 : 2 : 8
To 2 knives ------------------	0 : 1 : 8
To 2 flints & steel --------------	0 : 0 : 6
To 1 ... lead -----------------	0 : 0 : 9
To 4 flyps to pay of a blankett ------	0 : 4 : 0
To Tobacco and paint entertainmo ----	0 : 8 : 4
To ... bushel Indian Corn 1 falb Ditto -	0 : 2 : 3
To 1 hatchet -----------------	0 : 2 : 6
To ... tobacco ----------------	0 : 1 : 8

Contra

Cr

9.m 11 — by 3 Gn.s Orerider — £0 : 4 : 0

9.m 17 — by 2 g.nº Ocnu.t Do. of Brakeno — 0 : 1 : 4

by 3 Deecons to do 1 per piece — 1 : 3 : 0

by 2 Loo.s to do (6d) kitle — 0 : 8 : 0

by 4 Deecons — 0 : 3 : 9

picked body of Hessians. Their Commander, Count Donop, was a very tall man of
elegant build and appearance. He fell in the
assault mortally wounded. The small stream
that takes its rise in the meadow just back of
the Old House, crossing Hessian Road and
emptying into Woodbury Creek, was called
Hessian Run from the fact that the retreating
soldiers there slaked their thirst, and many
were there found wounded and dead. On the
west side of the Hessian Road the embankment and ditch of the ' Deer Park ' are still
very distinctly visible. It embraced some 400
acres, and upon the embankment stood an eight-
rail fence. The ditch being on the inner side,
the wild deer could leap into the Park but
could not leap out. Game of all kinds must
have been here exceedingly plentiful in early
Colonial times. Account books kept by John
Ladd, sr., and John Ladd, jr., now in my possession, are of interest as showing the interchange of various kinds of commodities with
the numerous Indians who, even within my
childhood's memory, lived in their cabins in

the woods—deer, bear, otter, beaver and their skins, and wild turkeys, etc., being enumerated. The wild fowls, until within the last forty years, would cover acres of water surface on the Delaware in front of Fancy Hill. The small ponds in the woods adjacent to the river used to afford resting places for wild ducks when either driven from the river by sportsmen or the numerous steam and sailing craft, or when disposed to enjoy a siesta during the interval between feeding times.

While residing at 'Candor Hall' Farm, from 1843 to 1859, I frequently shot ducks in such ponds. One notable instance is worth relating. It occurred in the fall of 1852, and on a pond of my own making by hauling the swamp muck out as a fertilizer. It is on the east side of the road leading from the Old Farm to Fancy Hill, and about a hundred yards from said road and between the lane gate and Crown Point Road. This pond is nearly always well supplied with water. On the occasion named I was driving in my carriage and had stopped to investigate. On approaching it, I discovered an immense flock of teal. Retracing my steps, I drove back to the house and loaded my old silver-mounted double-barreled gun with No. 6 shot. The calibre of the gun, too, was so small as to take only a No. 20 cut wad. Calling to one of my workmen, I directed him, when I should fire, to fasten my horse and come to the pond. The product of the first discharge was twenty-one ducks. After two other shots I sent him to my house with twenty-nine ducks, and I took four to my mother at Fancy Hill. In the afternoon I killed ten, on the following morning, shot eight more, making a total of fifty-one ducks.

Another old road is historic, it is a continuation of the 'King's Highway' from Woodbury to Cooper's Ferries, now the City of Camden. Leaving Woodbury it crossed a stone one-arched structure, probably a hundred yards below the present covered wooden structure; thence running in front of a brick house, now plastered and modernized, owned by our Surrogate, Harrison Livermore, and

continued on the westerly side of the present
turnpike, running through the old John Ladd
tract which extended from the Hessian Run
Road to Westville, till it reached the lane
thro' the Old ' Candor Hall ' Farm, where it
took a north-easterly course crossing the head
of the mill pond near Westville, thence to and
by the hotel there ; then following the bank of
the creek and crossing the same at and passing
between the two brick houses owned and occupied by the late Isaac Doughten and Joshua
Scott recently deceased ; thence by the east
front of the Browning house, crossing little
Timber Creek east of 'The Two Ton Tavern';
continuing its course, it crossed Newtown Creek,
east of the present turnpike bridge.   The
road, where it enters the wood opposite the
lane of the old farm, is still distinctly visible.
It was on this road that Earl Cornwallis
marched with six regiments of British troops,
after his encampment at Woodbury in the fall
of 1777, having been ordered by Sir William
Howe, then in possession of Philadelphia, to
cross the Delaware River below Fort Red

Bank (from Chester to Bilingsport) and if necessary to reduce that Fort which had so signally defeated Col. Count Donop, in his effort to do so.

In 1797 the present road leading from the Old Farm to Fancy Hill was laid out by my father, Col. Joshua Ladd Howell. The old ' Candor Hall' consisted originally of what is now the back parlor and room above, of brick, and two wings built of hewn logs and shingled to the ground, with mansard or hip roof. At the end of the wing at the north side or end of the back parlor, stood also a large brick kitchen. What is now the front parlor and several steps higher than the back parlor, was built in the time of John Ladd, jr., and was used for a sleeping room. The brick kitchen was torn down in 1825, and in 1843 when Benjamin P. Howell removed them from Philadelphia, the wooden wings were torn down and cellar and drain put in. The latter of which was a very necessary improvement owing to the fact that very much of this old farm land had to be reclaimed by expensive underdraining, from the swamps which at that time were very extensive.*

¶ On the settlement of this country, our river teemed with shad, herring and other fish, as did the forests with deer, bear, foxes, beavers, otters and other wild animals. The shad and herring fisheries must have grown into importance gradually as the demand for these fishes increased through the growth of population. By my father's resurvey of 1797, I find that John Ladd, sr., had ninety-eight acres of the flats in Cork Cove—what was soon after called Ladd's Cove, and later still Howell's Cove—surveyed to him in 1721, and in 1743 his son, John Ladd, jr., had 221 acres of flats surveyed to him. In 1714 Samuel Ladd, oldest son of John Ladd, sr., purchased 400 acres of land south of Timber Creek, fronting on river Delaware as previously stated. When he established a fishery there, I do not know, but his daughter, Deborah, who married Charles West, was the owner of what has since been

---

*Old Surveyor's descriptions of the Ladd property are in the possession of John S. Jessup, Woodbury, N. J.

called the West Point Fishery, for a long while the most valuable fishery on the Delaware. This fishery, my father purchased of her descendants in 1811 for $9000. The Eagle Point Fishery was fished from Eagle Point Bar, part of the ninety-eight acres of flats surveyed to John Ladd, sr., in 1721. This and West Point Fishery were cleared and fished long before the middle or Fancy Hill Fishery was.

As previously stated my grandfather, John Ladd Howell, obtained the consent of his Aunt Ladd to clear and fish it; when upon recollecting a promise made to his cousin, Deborah West, that no fishery should be made there, she revoked her consent, and it was not till 1791-3, that she reluctantly consented to my father's establishing one there.

These three fisheries were fished with seines of only from 150 to 200 fathoms in length, and only during the ebb tide. Two nets at the Fancy Hill and only one at the Eagle Point, and one, or it may be two, at West Point, were used at that time. It was the custom to

wait till the tide had fallen, say to about one-
third ebb, when the landsmen were put out to
their middles; then 150 to 200 fathoms of
line was paid off till the edge of deep water
was reached; then nearly the entire length of
net was laid off, still diagonally up stream,
when a short hook was given to the water-end
of the net, down stream, and the 400 fathoms
of water-line paid off till shoal-water was
reached, and the crew at both ends hauling in
as they dragged the net down through the
channel. So numerous were the shad that
immense numbers were taken even by these
short seines. The late venerable Michael C.
Fisher, whose first wife was my mother's
sister Rebecca, told me that on one Sunday,
'after meeting' when he was lessee of the
Eagle Point Fishery, at a single haul they
landed 5000 shad. The late James B. Tom-
lin, of this city, a few days before his death
told me, that at the Fancy Hill Fishery, when
he fished there for my father, between 1807
and 1811, a dapper haul was taken, which is
the last haul of the ebb tide, the Brothers

Hampton, captains of water and land end of one of my father's nets, caught 5000 shad. There were no drift nets in operation in those days !

This mode of fishing was continued till 1816 a very cold season, when it is said there was frost in every month of the year. Owing to the cold and backward season fishing was less remunerative than usual. It was then that Capt. Augustus Sooy suggested to my father that the two nets should be joined and a haul taken at the slack or turn of the tide at high water, the net sweeping the channel in an opposite direction to that it had ever done before. The result was that 1200 shad were landed. The two single nets had not taken in a tide much over 300 ! My father not willing to make so important a change on one trial, directed Capt. Sooy to hang in the lines another net of 200 fathoms, and to let another captain (Sitley) fish the double net. Captain Sooy did as he was directed—but he told me that when Sitley began to lay off the big net, he dropped his needle to watch him and he soon read his fate. Starting too early in the tide, and probably not grounding the land end sufficiently to hold it, and not running off down stream sufficiently, the tide ran away with his net, and before he could recover it, it was carried nearly to Newton Creek, above Gloucester City.

The next day the small net was used in the old way, with like result. Sooy then took the following *high water haul* and landed 3000 shad. The little net was ordered to be cut out and the new mode adopted and continued till 1875, when Samuel Rice and John Bake-oven* becoming the lessees (after Francis and Rotan's three year's occupancy), have adopted the plan of fishing the two fisheries, Fancy Hill and West Point, with one net of about 500 fathoms, with a crew of over thirty men, and four horses; with this force they take from five to six hauls a day—high water, two ebb-hauls and first flood-haul—instead of the two high water and one low water haul as

*Corruption of Beethoven.

practised previously by myself and those before me.

On adopting the new mode in 1816, it became necessary to use capstans placed at convenient intervals along the shores. My father died January 10, 1818, when my oldest brother, Samuel Ladd Howell, one of my father's executors, then residing on the elegant farm up Timber Creek, carried on the fisheries for five years, from 1818 to 1822 inclusive; during this period immense numbers of shad were taken.

From 1823 to 1826 inclusive, my mother became the lessee of the fisheries. In 1827, she purchased at sheriff's sale the Fancy Hill property and the Fancy Hill and Eagle Point Fishery.* Captains David Ward and Augustus Sooy continued to be the captains of her crews. They both had been in my father's employ. The former as a laborer, marketman and tenant; the latter as fisherman, from 1800 till he died at the fishery in 1853. Cap-

---

*The former properties for $31000. The West Point Fishery for $3000. See Sheriff's Deeds among our title papers.

tain Ward was with my father some years before Sooy. He fished till the end of the season of 1841, and died July, 1842.

These two men were, in their spheres, remarkable men. Ward was a powerful man, six feet in height. Though of very limited education, he possessed great native intelligence and originality, and would be looked up to as a leader among men of his class. The following is from the notes of Anna Blackwood Howell, mother of Benjamin P. Howell:

July 17th 1842

Departed this life David Ward, after fuffering great bodily pain for more than a year. David had been in the employment of my family for nearly fifty years—in different capacities and confequently felt very near to every furviving member of it. He lived to perform *the laft* forrowful offices, to many precious members of my family, who were born after he was in our fervice, and was a moft faithful, and ufeful perfon in feafons of trial & affliction.

Sooy was from Egg Harbor, and when not engaged at the fisheries, commanded a coasting schooner. He was a quiet unobtrusive man of great integrity. They were both thorough fishermen.

Notwithstanding the introduction of and rapid increase of the gilling seines, both in numbers and length, the fisheries were, with a few exceptionally poor seasons, very profitable till 1873, which proved to be a very unremunerative season. The next season 1874 was better, but attended with loss. In 1875, the fisheries were leased to William and Samuel Rotan and Jacob Faunce for three years, for $2100 per annum. The seasons of 1876–77 did not pay well, and they asked and were granted an abatement of rent. In 1878, Messrs. Samuel Rice and John Bakeoven became lessees for five years at $1500 per annum.

THE GILLING SEINES OR DRIFT-NETS.

These seines were introduced on the Delaware about 1821—in length about forty-five to fifty fathoms ; six-and-a-fourth to six-and-a-half-inch mesh ; and some fifteen in number. They have increased to about eight hundred in number from the three states, Pennsylvania, Delaware and New Jersey, and to one hundred to nine hundred fathoms in length ; and the mesh reduced to five and one-eighth inches, and until the last ten years, to sixty meshes deep. Consequently the web suspended from a cork-line did not fish deeper than about twenty-two feet ; and as the water in the channel, at low tide, is from four to six fathoms deep, the shad had below the lead-line, a chance to reach the spawning grounds *above* the *head of tide*. Hence the decrease in their numbers was not so rapid as it has been in the last ten years that the floats have been used, whereby the lead-line reaches nearly to the bottom—the upper margin of the web being sustained by cords of from four to ten or fifteen feet long, attached to corks or floats.

This arrangement places the web out of danger from vessels of light draught, in passing over it, and puts it where, experience has shown, the great body of the shad swim. To show the comparative decrease in numbers, even before the float-lines were adopted by the drift-net men, I give the catch, at the two fisheries, in three cycles of five years each, and one five years after their introduction :

Prior to introduction of drift-nets.....1818 to 1822 total 656146 shad
When fairly established................1845 to 1849   "   332450   "
After they had assumed the present
    size, etc...........................1865 to 1869   "   303699   "
Since adoption of floats...............1870 to 1874   "   210945   "

The largest number taken in one season, of
which we have record, was in 1820 when the
catch at the two fisheries amounted to 170570.
The largest haul, too, was in that season at the
West Point Fishery, high-water haul of
10800; and at the Fancy Hill Fishery, high-
water, 6000.

GROWTH AND SIZE OF SHAD.

From the testimony of the two late octoge-
narians, Benjamin Wilkins and John Mickle,
and other reliable sources of information, the
largest and oldest shad have been fished out.
Mr. Wilkins, ten years ago [1871] told me
the shad caught averaged seven pounds, and
John Mickle said he carried shad to market
for the Messrs. Reeves and Hopkins from
Eagle Point Fishery from 1818 to 1822, five
seasons, and that in a boat load of shad he
could always find shad of ten pounds weight.
Mr. Wilkins, too, said one of sixteen and a

half pounds was once taken. This statement has since been confirmed by Gen. James Wall who told me in 1872, that there was preserved in the City of Burlington, the scale taken from a shad, many years ago, that weighed sixteen and a half pounds. George Moore, a Kensington fisherman, told me he once took a shad that weighed fifteen pounds ; and Isaac Reeves and Benjamin Sparks each had seen one that weighed fourteen pounds. I have been thus particular because by excessive fishing of late years shad of over six pounds have seldom been taken, and by the reduction in size of meshes to four and a half, large numbers of small sized male shad are annually taken that should be allowed to escape, as they formerly did through the large sized meshes, to return the next year, marketable shad.

Being anodomous, these fishes run to fresh water to spawn when sufficiently mature to do so. This occurs with the male at two years, and with the female at three years, as conclusively proved by the experiment of Seth Green when he placed in the head-waters of the Sacramento River, California, 5000 young shad hatched in the Hudson River and transported across the continent in 1871. Twenty males of these were taken in 1873, he wrote me, measuring about thirteen inches in length and weighing from one and a fourth to one and a half pounds. The females were taken the next year, weighing three and four pounds. The good effects of the weekly close-time from sunset Saturday till twelve at Sunday night, having been enforced by our State Fish Wardens on the Delaware, for the past few years, is shown in the fact that shad, the past two seasons [1879 and 1880] have been caught weighing seven, eight and nine pounds.

STURGEONS.

These fishes once so numerous to head of tide at Trenton, are now almost exclusively caught in the sturgeon gilling seines, below Pennsgrove, Salem County.

In the absence one day of Captain Joseph Budd, I took command of the Fancy Hill crew, and landed 1200 shad and seventy sturgeons. The next day Captain Budd landed 900 shad and 117 sturgeons.

Since the increase of the sturgeon gill-nets below, scarcely ever are there over sixty sturgeons taken at those two fisheries, the entire season. Formerly more would be taken than sold. Of late years they are sold to the fish-hucksters who give from fifty cents to a dollar and a half apiece for them.

HERRING.

These, too, by excessive fishing, are decreasing in numbers. These—unlike the shad whose spawning grounds are in the quick or running water above the head of tide—spawn, it is believed, on the grassy flats, as few of them are taken in the Delaware above tide-water. Great numbers of herring have been taken, either by having the small-meshed net hung to about ten feet depth in the centre of the shad-seine or by a small-meshed net laid around the shad-seine when it is nearly landed, the herring making no effort to escape through the shad-mesh till they find themselves in shoal-water or cooped up.

SALMON.

In 1871 a few thousand ova of these fishes, artificially hatched, were placed in the Delaware or its tributaries above tide. In 1877 some nine, weighing from ten to thirteen pounds, were caught from latter part of May till October. In 1878 quite a number, over fifty in all, weighing from ten to twenty-nine pounds, were caught. In 1879 only one was caught, and that at Fancy Hill near the close of the season. In 1880 none were known to be taken during the fishing season or summer; though late this fall some six or seven are reported as having been taken above Trenton, N. J. Since 1873 many thousands of ova presented by the United States Commissioner of Fisheries, from the Government Hatching Establishment under Livingston Stone, on the McCloud River, California, have been hatched out at Mrs. Dr. Slack's Hatching Establishment at Troutdale, Warren County, in this State, and turned into the River Delaware. As it takes several years before these fishes mature sufficiently to spawn, we cherish the hope and belief that they will in due time return to our river for that purpose.

Benjamin P. Howell, M.D., of Woodbury, N. J., appointed 1870.

John Hamilton Slack, M.D., Bloomsbury, N. J., appointed March 29, 1870.

Jacob Shotwell, of Rahway, added in 1873.

Dr. Slack, while engaged in hatching out shad ova on the Delaware in August, 1874, died of pneumonia. His brother-in-law, Geo. Allen Anderson, esq., of Trenton, was appointed by the Governor Parker, and afterwards confirmed by the Senate to fill the vacancy. These three continued to serve till expiration of their terms, when Messrs. Jacob Shotwell and George A. Anderson declining reappointment, Benjamin P. Howell, M.D., of Woodbury; Major Edward A. Anderson, of Trenton; Theodore Morford, esq., Newton, Sussex County, were appointed by Gov. George B. McClellan, and confirmed by the Senate, to hold the position for five years from April, 1878.

The duties of the commissioners were to in-
spect the rivers and bays of the State, and to
suggest legislation. Under them Fish Wardens
were appointed, at first for each of the counties bordering on the River Delaware, afterwards for each county in the State, whose
duties are to enforce the fishing laws and to
report annually to the Commissioners of
Fisheries.

These duties are no sinecures, especially on
the Delaware Bay and River, as against the law-
less class found among the drift-net men. The
Wardens of Camden, Gloucester and Salem
counties, in compelling these outlaws to observe
the weekly close-time from sunset Saturday to
twelve o'clock Sunday night, as well as from the
lawful close of the shad season from June 10
to July 10, are compelled to use tug-boats.
Before the employment of Fish Wardens the
owners and occupiers of the shore fisheries
were compelled of themselves to protect their
rights. From 1843 to 1874 inclusive, while I
carried on the Fisheries, I was compelled to
have patrol boats out at night at the slack or

turn of the tide. These boats from 1843 to 1859, while residing at the old farm and at Fancy Hill, I personally, for the most time, commanded. Sometimes I was compelled to have the seine-boats out with their full crews, so determined had these men become to get possession of the fishing grounds. At other times, in a batteau with a couple of men, I have watched the grounds. By one means or another I have in those years captured many of their nets, had them condemned and sold by order of the magistrates.

Sometimes these captures were made at great personal risk. On one occasion in particular, I went out with two of the crew in a batteau, captured one very large net and chased two other boats off, when two other skiffs hove in sight and hailed those in the three other boats, to know if I had taken any net. On an affirmative reply, they surrounded my boat, with the intention of recapturing it. I desired my two men to keep perfectly quiet, but each to take his oar in hand for self-defense. For some time these ten drift-net men, with up-

lifted oars and volleys of oaths, threatened us.
To convince them that we did not mean to be
coerced, I directed one of my men to cast our
anchor overboard. This act produced a quiet-
ing effect. They rowed off to some distance,
to hold a council of war. I took advantage
of cessation of hostilities to order one of my
men to slip overboard, for it was low water,
and go to the cabin and arouse the crew.
Soon lights gleamed from every window, and
Captain Budd and his crew of over thirty men
came rushing down, manned the boats and
came to my assistance, my assailants making
off as fast as possible.

Another occasion, by a little strategy on my
part, terminated in an amusing manner, what
threatened at first to be attended with serious
results. It was in the spring of 1855 or 1856
while I resided at Fancy Hill, after the decease
of my excellent mother. Capt. John Turner
from Egg Harbor commanded the West Point
crew. Noticing, as usual on Saturday evenings, when the tide suited their purpose, a
number of drift-net boats congregating at the

Horse Shoe Buoy, for a slack-water drift, I told
the captain, with his assistance, I intended to
break up the custom. Accordingly the captain and I, with four oarsmen, manned a skiff
and proceeded to the buoy. I then remon-
strated with them on their intended violation
of a law meant for the benefit of the fishermen
as well as for the public. They took it all in
good part at first. At last one said, ' Doctor,
if we lay off our net, you wont interfere, will
you ? ' I said I hoped they would not do so,
but if they did, I certainly should capture it.
Feeling so strong by numbers, one boat's crew
began to pay off their net. I at once directed
my men to pull for it and to take it on board.
With that, all the drift-net boats got in motion,
and their crews began to call to their fellows
who were, by that time, laying off their nets.
By this time it began to grow dark. Recollecting that these marauders held our seine-
boats, with their crews of twelve men each,
with their long oars of over twenty feet, in holy
horror, I sprang on one of the seats and called
to Captain Budd to bring out his seine-boat.

In an instant, perfect quiet reigned, and the men in their several boats could be seen taking up their nets and hurrying away. Captain Turner, knowing as well as I did, that, it being Saturday night, Captain Budd and all the men had gone to their homes, could scarcely repress his mirth, which, had he given way to, might have given our opponents a hint which would under the circumstances have proved inconvenient to us. He almost laid himself down, saying in an undertone, 'Well, that beats George Washington.' We took on board the captured net and went ashore. It proved a salutary lesson to the drift-net men for a long while.

BENJ. P. HOWELL, M.D.

CHAPTER III.

JOHN HOWELL I.

Jacob Howell—Friends' Meeting Houses.

JOHN HOWELL, widower, with three children, Jacob, Evan and Sarah, emigrated from the ancient walled city of Aberyswith, Wales, and settled near the centre of the City of Philadelphia in 1698. He died January 26, 1721, and was buried in Friends' Ground, southeast corner Fourth and Arch streets.

JACOB, son of John, born in Aberyswith, March 18, 1687, was a tanner. Removed to Chester, Penn., 12 mo. 23d, 1707. He built the first three-story brick house there—still standing [1881], with J. H. cut in face of a stone in wall of back shed. He was an eminent Quaker preacher. He married—6 mo., 1709, at Chester Meeting—Sarah Vernon, daughter of Randal and Sarah Vernon.

BENJ. P. HOWELL, M.D.

That Jacob Howell was born in Aberyswith, and did not merely sail from that port,
as some seem inclined to believe, is proved by
the following old paper found among the
family records :

IN MEMORY OF JACOB HOWELL.*

Our dear and worthy friend, Jacob Howell, son of John
Howell, was born in a little town called Aberyswith, in
Cardiganshire, in the principality of Wales, in the 1st
month (called March), 1687. He came with his father
to Philadelphia, who settled near the centre of the City,
1697. He was afterwards placed an Apprentice to a Tanner in the Northern Liberties of that city. At the expiration of his apprenticeship, he settled himself at Chester,
which was about the year 1707. *Copied 3rd March,
1801.*

FRIENDS' MEETING HOUSE.†

Richard Townsend, after giving an account of his
voyage in *The Welcome* states : ' Our first concern was to
keep up and maintain our religious worship, and in order
thereunto, we had several meetings at the houses of the inhabitants, and one boarded meeting house was set up where
the City was to be. ' This ' boarded ' house was situated
at Chester. The History of Pennsylvania states that ' the

*From an old piece of manuscript.

†Notes from Ashmead's History of Chester.

Quakers had three houses for public worship—one at Chester, another at Shackamaxon and another at the Falls of the Delaware.' In this temporary building the Friends held their meetings until 1693 when their first permanent meeting house was completed. The frame structure was located on ground which Joran Keen sold to the Society— for he, the 6th of 1st mo. 1687, conveyed to John Bristow, Randall Vernon, Thomas Vernon and others—a lot on the west side of Edgmont avenue, south of Third street, to the use and behoof of said Chester, the people of God called Quakers and their successors forever.

The meeting house, built in 1693, was sold in 1736, and in this year the Society found it necessary to erect a large building to accommodate increasing membership and, April 18, 1736, Caleb Coupland conveyed the southern part of the lot on Market street, with that of Third street, on which the meeting house now stands, to Jacob Howell, John Salkeld, John Sharpless, Thomas Cummings and others, and they the same day executed a declaration in trust setting forth that they held the land as trustees, and for the use of the members of Chester meeting.

In 1682 the Society of Friends purchased and enclosed a suitable lot located on the west side of Edgmont avenue, above Sixth street, for a burial place, and on the 5th of 9th mo. 1683, the Vernons and John Hastings were appointed 'to fence the burial grounds as soon as may.' Within this ancient Godsacre, lie the bodies of almost all

the first settlers of the old family names of Chester. They
sleep in that plot where the remains of hundreds of men
who fled hither to escape persecution in Europe, lie forgot-
ten because of the prohibition by the Society, of stones to
mark the graves of those who slumber within the burial
grounds belonging to their meeting.

CHAPTER IV.

JOHN HOWELL, II.

Letters—Joshua Howell—Sarah Howell.

AFTER pursuing in Woodbury, N. J., the business of Tanning, as his father, Jacob, had before him, John Howell removed to Philadelphia in 1739 where he continued it. He later removed to Johnston County, North Carolina, whence he writes, September 2, 1753, to his son that he has 'gott to Taning.' By a letter October 9, 1758, we find him still in North Carolina. The next letter, dated June 18, 1760, finds him in 'Charles Town, S. C.,' where he lived for a few months. This letter mentions 'Instruments of Writing' needed to transfer his interest in a tract of land 'in the Jerseys' to his wife and children, which transfer was accomplished in 1764. On the 18th of August, 1760, he arrived in 'Savanah Town,' and went into business with William Francis. Several of his letters lead to the impression that his family had been with him for awhile in Newbern, N. C., and had then returned to Philadelphia, leaving him there.

His business prospects never seemed very bright, and he regretted his unavoidable separation from his wife, but was always hoping that his business would improve so that he could rejoin his wife in the North and live there without being dependent on his friends. This hope was destined never to be realized, as his wife died without his ever seeing her again. In his letter of July 21, 1764, to his son, he acknowledges the receipt of his letter of May 9, informing him of his wife's [Katharine Ladd Howell] death and speaks very tenderly of her.

John Howell died at John Rays [or Raes], near Savannah, Ga., previous to October 15, 1765, as we have a letter of that date from William Gibbons to John Ladd Howell, stating the above as a fact. This letter, which mentions certain assistance given John Howell by Robert Bolton [or Boulton] as well as the letters of John Howell, throws a very pathetic side-light on his career.

John Howell's frequent and thankful allusions to his state of health and his good wishes for that of his wife and children, are not to be wondered at, as malarial fevers of a malignant type were very prevalent at that time all through the colonies.

There has been so little known of John Howell that a number of his letters are here given, as throwing a clear light on his life and warm affectionate nature, and making a living reality of what before was shadowy and uncertain :

To John Ladd Howell In Philadedphia These
Johnston County 3rd Sepr 1753
JOHN HOWELL.

—

north Carolina Johnston Countey September ye 2d 1753
Dear Johnney

I Receiv'd thine of the 30th of June the 17th of Auguſt with thy mothers & Salleys which was a Great Satisfaction to mee in Hereing of your Safe arivel and that you were ſo Kindly Received by our friends thee tel's me that thee art going apprentice to thy Uncle Joſhua, which I hope will do well and be to thy advantage.

I have nothing perticular to write att preſent but Shall be Glad att all times as oppertunity preſents to here from thee.

my Dear Love to our frd.   In perticular to thy Dear mother
& Salley, wth. the Same to thy Self Dear Child I Conclude,

Thy Affectionate Father

JOHN HOWELL.

P. S. I have gott to Taning I have young Freeman to
help me who doth very well.

Bill Rembers his Love to his mafter Johnney.   he Is a
good boy doth beter than I Expected.   he is often Differ-
ing with Lyon becaufe he wont follow him willingly when
he goeth of Errands   *J. H.*

To JOHN LADD HOWELL IN PHILADELPHIA THESE

Johnfton Co. Sepr 25th. 1753

JOHN HOWELL.

—

North Carolina Johnfton Countey Sept ye 25th 1753
Dear Johnney

I Receiv'd thine of ye 2d of Auguft by Tho. King the
9th of Septr. by which the tel's me that thy Dear Mother
is gott a good deal better wch. I am glad to hereof, thee
allfo tel's me that thee art Bound to thy Uncle Jofhua &
go's to School to Alexander Seaton & Boards att thy Uncle
Jones &c.   Dear Child make the beft Ufe of thy time dont
Lett the Company of new acquantanc Draw thy mind
from thy Larning by any means but be as Induftrious as
poffiable, I have no perticular Reafon to think thee will be
negligent but haveing a Great Concern on my mind for thy
future advantage cant avoid but put thee in mind to be

Carefull in Every Oppertunity that it Pleaſeth the Allmighty to favour thee with, allſo not forgeting to be thankfull for them. the Letter from thy Dear mother wch. thee tel's me thee Rec'd from her by thy Siſter with orders to copey and Send me bearing date yᵉ 4th of Auguſt I Rec'd yᵉ 15th of Sept. Dear Johnney Give my Dear Love to thy mother & Siſter to thy Grandfather & all thy Uncles & Aunts wth. our friends that may Enquire of thee after mee as if perticularly named. I Conclude dear Child affectionatly with the Same to thy Self thy

Loveing Father

JOHN HOWELL

P. S. I have my helth as Uſeual Rembering dear love to Alexa. Seaton & Spouſe & tell him I ſhall take itt kindly if he will ſend me a news paper by wch means I may know who are the Repreſentatives of that province wch. thee may Incloſe in thy next to me.   *J. H.*

To John Ladd Howell to the Care of Samuel Howell Hatter att Chester In the Countey of Chester Pennsylvania ᵽ favour of John Wiggins

Johnſton County 13th. Sepr 1754

JOHN HOWELL

To John Ladd Howell

North Carrolina Johnſton County Septr. ye 18th. 1754
Dear Johnney

I Receiv'd the Letters thee Sent by the way of Cape fear &c. Some time paſt, and thine of yᵉ 5th. of June by

Capt. Tarner y° 20th. of Auguſt, In wch thee tells me that
thy mother & Salley wth thy Self are In health, wch I was
Glad to here, thee dont tell me where they are wth. wch.
I ſhould have been allſo pleaſed, Dear Johnney thee mentions to me in one of thine that thy Uncle Joſa. & Aunt
Salley are Very Kind to thee (deſiring me to write to
them) wch I do Aſſure thee gives me much pleaſure in my
thoughts on thy Acct., hopeing (as Indeed I have ſome
Reaſon to believe) that thou will Endeavour to beheave
towards them Reſpectfully, & with gratitude, and in perticular to thy Uncle Joſa. as thee tel's me thou art bound
an Apprentice to him &c., when Ever thou art Directed
or Inſtructed in his buſineſs, beſure that thou be not
Neglegent not Letting him, nor any Elſe have it in their
power to blame, or Even Suſpeɛt thee wth. any breach in
thy Conduct, wch. if thou art Carefull in thou will be
clothed wth. that Inoſent Boldneſs the Truth, wch. will
allways Proteɛt thee, and dear Johnney I hope yt. thou
will be Very Carefull what Company thou keeps, Lett them
be Such that thou may Receive Some good Examples from,
and allſo in thy Leaſure hours that thou will be diverting
thy thoughts, with the Reading of Some good books, of
wch. I would thou Should have the Bible In y° Greateſt
Eſteem, and beſure keep to meetings let no oppertunitys
Slip. thee mentions allſo that thee heard from me by the
friends and that thee Expeɛted to have Some letters but
was diſapointed, had I known In time I Should have
write by them, I did not here of them till Seventh day In

yᵉ Evening, and they went away allmoſt Emediately after
meeting on the firſt day following, towards Tar River,
Accompanied by Caleb Hughs & Tho. Hughs, (men thee
Knew Very well I believe) as guides from falling Creek
meeting; I went after meeting wth them as far as Tho.
Mc. Clendons that night, had I known in time I would
have gone to have ſeen them through the deſert between
here and Tar River, and Endeavored they Should have got
over better then they did ; Either through Neglegence or
Something Like it, In Takeing Katha : Baton's horse into
the boat, they Litt him fall into ye River with Sadle on
and baggs &c. wch. were all much wett, and in takeing
Mary Peaſely's over they were but half as Carefull, I beleive them two Worthy women and am Sorrey they had
not had better guides, they had a great meeting here,
(their Service allſo as Great I beleive) theire never was ſo
Large a one, the houſe would would nott hold near the
people, theire was Several Came many miles to here two
women preach (as I Said) were well Satisfied, have Since
Expreſſed they never heared Such preaching, from any
men ; Meaning their preachers.

   Dear Johnney It is not for want of Love and Reſpect to
thee nor thy Uncle & Aunt &c., that I have not write to
them, and hope their Reſpect will not be the leſs to thee
on that Acct. till I do wch. I intend, and dear Child tell
them from me, that I am much obliged to them as brother
& Siſter Indeed ; and If Greatefull Expreſſions dear
Johnney would do, and it was for thy good where they

are due, they Should not be wanting, and was it in my
power to do for them, or theirs ; much more good then
they do for mine, It would I do Affure them, be much
pleafure to me in doing. the allfo mentions thy Aunt
wch. I take to be thy Uncle Jofa. wife, defired to be
Rembred to me, whether it was or not, I Receive it
kindly be it from wch aunt it may, and defire thee that
thou give my dear love to her ; thy Uncle Jofa. Wife, and
tell her ; that I wifh her all the Hapinefs She Could defire,
or Expeét to defire, in a Married State. I was in great
hopes of Seeing thy dear mother before now by her letter
of ye 7th. of march, but Shall Endeavour to make my Self
Content til Shee Come, keeping Batchelers hall as before
I have told thee ;

I intend to Convey this by they hands of my friend
John Wiggins by whom I Defire thou would Endeavour to
write back to me, he tels me he Intends to Come by water
In November next if poffiable ; Dear Johnney Affift thy
dear Sifter in writing to me. Give my dear Love to thy
dear Mother and Sifter, thy Uncle Jofa Howell, & Aunt
Sarah Jones, and all other friends and Relations that may
Enquire after me (More perticularly thofe whom have
Shown you all perticular Refpeét when Neffitey) a fheare
of which dear Johnney take to thy Self from thy Affectionate
Father

JOHN HOWELL.

P. S. I Receiv'd thee books Inclofed in the Letter by

way of Ceape fear wch. were Very Exceptable If thee did
not break that Letter open after the firſt Sealed it twa's
broken & Sealed again after it Came from thee, of wch.
let me know, I intend that bill Shall Gether Chinkinpines
for thee (Salley to have a ſhare) wch Indeed he promiſeth
to be very Carefull about, and allſo to ſave his Ground
peas or pendors wch. he has growing to ſend to maſter
Johnney & miſtres Salley he often Saith Speakeing of you
with Great Reſpeẟ but Suppoſe it will Require ſome ot
my aſſiſtance to forward them wch dear Johnney I intend
Shall not be wanting, I dont think him any better of his
Sight then when ſhe left this, he deſires to be Rembred to
you all, Send me by the Next good oppertunity a coppey
of thy Indenture.

J. H.

I may Give thee a Little of the Carroline News wch.
Indeed Is hardly worthey of place in apoſtcript.   Att the
Laſtt Seſſions of Aſſembley att Willmington by an Actt
then paſſed for the Emiſſion of Many Thouſend pounds
proclamation Money for good Serviſes In the province to
be done, as Mentioned by yᵉ ſd Act, Twelve thouſend
pounds of wch. was to be Aplyed to the Aſſiſtance of Virginia in the Ohio Expedition, (as tis here Caled) accordingly four hundred men was Reaſed, & Sent Under the
Command of Collonel Lieutenants Captains wth. their Inf . .
Officers &c., wch. tis Said Drew pretty well of the tw . .
Thouſend pounds, out of the Treasurey before the went.

Are now moft of them Returned after being Difcharged Officers & Men, without Seeing Ohio, or Engageing wth their Enemy as they Intended, before they went (they faid) for to be poffeffed of it before theire Return here Again, and that Emiffion of proclamation, Is in a bad Credit. amongft Some of thofe that are Efteem'd the Greateft treaders they will not take or Receive it in any payment for goods I doub not but thou may have heard of the other Extraordinary parte of that Expedition wch I need mention nothing of

J. H.

FOR JOHN LADD HOWELL TO THE CARE OF JOSHUA HOWELL MERCHT IN PHILADELPHIA.

From John Howell (my Father) rec'd 5th Mon: 17th, 1756 p Jno. Mc. Ilvain Johnfton Co. April 26th, 1756 Sloop Sufannah Capt. Durell

---

North Carolina Johnfton April ye 26th 1756

Dear Johnney

thine wth. thy dear Mothers of y° 5th of Novemb; I Receiv'd y° laft of February, one of decembr. y° 6th, a few days after, in March, with a Copy of thy Indentuers, wch was left at Newbern by Ifaac Greenleaffe, thine of Januy. y° 12th a few days after. I may Acquaint thee allfo yt. that letter of Salley of y° 23d of Januy. 1756 Came to hand y° 24th. of Februy, wch. thou Mentions Came too latte to

thy hands to Inclofe with thine to me—It happened to fall
into they hands of a friend who made Ufe of yᵉ firft Oppertunity to Convey itt, wch has not often happened with thy
Letters to me——

Dear Johnney, It Gives me a Great deal of pleafure to
hear from thee So perticularly, when thy letters Comes to
hand, Should be Glad to have ym. Sooner after they arive
att Newbern, which If thou defires I Should, Inclofe ym.
Under Cover & direct, To Richd. Cafwell Esqr. In Johnston County North Carolina to the Care of Samuel Cor-
nell Marcht. In Newbern, they are Men I Know whofe
friendfhip may be depended on where they Profefs itt——

If thou Chufe to Corispond with yᵉ Widdow Moore* or
her Sons that need not prevent.——dear Johnney I have
notthing Very perticular to write thee tis a Remote part
on Accot. of publick news Indeed I have none at prefent
only that ti's Reported yt. the Seat of Government will be
fixed Either att Atkins banks on yᵉ River Neufe, or near
the Plantation where James Mc. Ilwean Lived, wch yᵉ
Governour hath purchafed (wch will be then but about
five miles from me) If it Should be fix'd att Either of thofe
places I beleive thou'l oftner here of the Publick News of
North Carolina—Should Indeed been glad if thy Mother
Had thought itt beft to have Come to me but but by her
writeing I think her Inclinations are Greater to Stay where
She is, Shall Indeavour to be Content, I have my Helth as
well I think as Ever I had in my life for wch. I am Thank-

---

*Mary Moore of Trent River, N. C.

full. Continue Keeping batchellers hall as I Call it but Intend Soon to gett a Negro woman to Keep yt. houfe for me, Bill I Expeᵉᵗ to do a Great deal of work for me in the tan Yard this Sumer———

I have purufued the Coppy of thy Indentuer, as before I advifed thee I had Received, I have no Other Objection to them then One, to witt, yᵉ words (or Affigns)———

I have a better oppinnion of my Brothers friendfhip then to think them words Ever were put in with any Intention to make Ufe of them—dear Johnney I hope theire is no Ocation of puting thee In mind of thy duty &c. to thy Uncle & Aunt Remember my dear love to them both & Other frds. that may Enquire of thee after me a Large Shear thereof Receive to thy Self from thy Loveing and Affectionate

Father

JOHN HOWELL

P. S. the friendfhip of Richd. Cafwell is very perticularly Shown me, hope I Shall allways be greatefull Enough to Acknowledge ym., Ineed not say much to thee of his good Charactor (thou Knew itt in part when thou was here) butt only obferve to thee that he is now as much Efteem'd and as well as any man of his Age In North Carolina———

Thofe Letters Inclofed wth. thine are Recomended (Dear Johnney) to thy Care (handed to me by Richd. Cafwell wch. are from his mother &c. to her Brother &c.

In Maryland) thou'l be kind enough to have ym. Con-
veied as directed If it wou'd not be too much trouble thou
art defired to write a few lines Inclofing ym. all to Wm.
Dellam in Baltemore County wch may lett him Know if
they Send theirs to thee in Philada thou'l Inclofe ym. as
oppertunity Prefents wth. mine Direct as before have defired.

J. H.

Newbern Mar. 26tb. 1757

To JOHN LADD HOWELL

Dear Son

This day Receivd thine of Febry. 25th by Coufen John
Wharton, Who was so Kind as to Write me line Letting
me Know of his being arrived att Newbern, Where I
Came this day on purpofe to See him and to heare from
you all by him, he tel's me he Saw my Dear Fathr.*
and Brothers a few days before he Sailed, and thy Self the
day before, I am Glad to here from You So Perticularly
as I do by him.   I have Receiv'd thofe Books thou Mentions Brother Jacob Intended to Send, thy Letter (thee
Mentions) of y° 29th of Janry. Under Cover to Saml Cor-
nell he has not Yett Receiv'd.

Dear Johnney I have not forgot You—Notwithftanding ti's fo Long Since I write to thee You are Often in my
Thoughts, I Shall not Enlarge on that Subject at this time,

----

*Jacob Howell, sr., of Chester, Pa.

give my Dear Love to thy Mother and Salley, and all frds.
that Enquire of thee after me, I do Intend to Write to my
Dear Father to my Dear Wife and Dear Salley &c. In a
few days By an Oppertunity which I Expect going by
Land,

Thy Loveing Father

JOHN HOWELL

P. S. deare Johnney Lett James Hill's Sons Know yt
theire Father is Weel Lives wth. me yett and wants to
here from

J. H.

_____

To Katharine Howell

North Carolina Johnston County Janry. y' 24th. 1758
My Dear Wife

I Receiv'd thine of Septr. y° 26th by our Dear Brother
Isaac Howell y° 22d of this Inftant Wch is of Great Satisfaction to me in Receiving and In perticular by yt hand I
Receive it His Stay here being but Short and So much to
Converse on that I have not time to write to thee fo full
as I Could defire Must Only let the Know by this that I
am In helth and Intend to write by Some friends (wch my
Brother tels me he Beleives will be this way Soon) more
perticularly and full therefore, at this time must Refer the
to him for Perticulars, Concludeing with my

Dear Love to thee thy Loveing

Husband *JOHN HOWELL.*

To Sarah Howell

Johnston County Janry, y 24th. 1758

Dear Salley

I have Received thine by thy dear Uncle Isaac Howell at the Same time wth. thy dear Mothrs wch. Is Very Exceptable. I have not time to Enlarge for the Reasons Mentiond above but Shall I hope by an Oppertunity Soon, Desireing my Love Rembrd to all friends, Conclude thy Affectionate Father

JOHN HOWELL

To John Ladd Howell In Philadelphia By favour of Isaac Howell

Johnsion County Janry. y 24th. 1758

No. Carolina January 24th 1758

Dear Johnney

I have Received thine of Septr. 26th & of Octobr. 6th. By thy dear Uncle Isaac Howell His Stay Being but Short here and So many Subjects to Convers on that I have not time to Enlarge But hope to have an Oppertunity with Some friends as I have Mention'd to thy dear Mother (wch. Oppertunity I hope to be Prepared for) I Conclude wth. Dear Love

Thy Affectionate Father

JOHN HOWELL

P. S. I Refer thy Self and Dear Salley to your Uncle Isaac for Perticulars.

J. H.

To John Ladd Howell att Joshua Howells Marcht. In
Philadelphia by Favour of Tho Taurance.

North Carolina October 9th 1758
JOHN HOWELL
rec'd 24th. October

—

North Carrolina Johnston October y 9th. 1758*

to John Ladd Howell

Dear Son

I have Juft time to Advife thee by this Oppertunity of
Receeveing thy Letters of May the 27th & June 15th and
the Other of Augft y° 22d wch. were all Very Agreeable.

I am Juft Recovering from a Very Severe Spell of the
fevours wch. hath Reduced me Low and Weak but hope as
the Coole Wether Comes on I Shall Again Enjoy my
health.

Dear Johnney I have not time by this oppertunity to Enlarge but Intend Indeed am Determined In a few days to
have Letters write wch. I will Send by the firs Oppertunity
to thy Dear Mother thy Sifter & Self to whome Give my
Dear Love

Concluding with the Sa ·. . . . to thy Self and all friends
thy Loveing & affectionate Father

JOHN HOWELL.

P. S. The Bearer Tho. Taurance now on his Jorney for
New York Is a Man of Good Character Kept a Store

neare here for Some time paſt Is now Removed & Enterd in Trade wth a Relation of his in the South Government.

J. H.

————

To JOHN LADD HOWELL
Received from Jno. Howell June 30th 1760 p Capt. Dyare
Charles Town So. Caroline 18th June.

—

Charles Town South Carrolina June 18th. 1760.

Dear Son

I have now Before me thy Letters of June yᵉ 25th 1759, of October. 25th. 1759 of Febry 11th. 1760 & of Febry yᵉ 22d. 1760. which gives me Pleaſure in the peruſeing from the Idea I Conceive of thy Good Prinſiples &c.————

I have not time to anſwer ym fully as I wou'd but In anſwer to part of thine of Febry yᵉ 11th. 1760 I do Aſſure thee thou hath not droped any thing In Any of thy Epiſtles that hath Ever Given me any Diſrepeċtfull or Undutifull Opinion of thee————

Thou Mentions thou has not Received any Intelegence &c. Since October 1758 I have write to thee Several times tis Evident yt. mine have been Intercepted————

Now Dear Johnney I hope this will not wch. is to Adviſe thee that tis Agreeable to me to Confirm what thou Mentions may be Advantageous to thy Self &c

In thine of the 25th of June 1759 by Prepareing the Inſtruments of Writing to Convey my Right of yt Traċt of Land in the Jerſey wch. I will do thy Self or any Other way Agreeable to thy dear Mother & Siſter

If thou'l get prepared proper Inftruments of Writeing for yt purpofe and Send them by Capt Dyar who Intends here Imediately, or any Other hand I will wth pleafure do whats in my power to Confirm my Right wch I hope will be agreeable & attened wth. Sucfefs——

I Shou'd have write by John Bartram had I had the oppertunity wch. I had not neither did I Receive thy Letters till a Confiderable time after he left Newbern, After Receveing of ym at Newbern where I Staid & at Wm. Herritages Ten days haveing an Inclination to Return home as Bufinefs where you Left me doth not Prove Advantagious, But Reflecting on the Subject I Concluded to See more of the South part of the Continent and not willing to Return altogether Dependant when the wheel may turn tis Uncertain but am Yet Poffeffed with Hopes I Shall meet wth. frds.——Dear Son I Shall not at this time Enlarge but Draw to a Conclusion wth Telling thee that tis more Concern to me than Is Convenient to Exprefs that I am the Hufband that's Obliged to be Abfent from my Dear wife and the Father from his Dear Children and When it will be Otherwife I Know not, till it is (as I now am) hope to Keep poffefed wth that Sincere Gratitude that's due to your frds. for the Great Obligations I am Under to ym on your Acct. I have nothing Elfe to make Return wth. wch I hope they will Except——

Dear Johnney I have Reafon to beleive thou art not Unfenfeable of ym. allfo, to whom I Recomend thee Under Providence for Direction and Conclude with my Dear Love to my Dear wife and Dear Salley with Sincere prayers for all Your Happinefs thy Affectionat Father

JOHN HOWELL.

P. S. I wou'd have Sent thee a power of attorney by Capt. Dyar but was fearefull yt it wou'd not be Suffitient Let me have a line by the firs Oppertunity Direct for me to the Care of Edward Bullard a friend yt Lives here thy Mother may Remember that he Accomppanied Mary Wefton from here to Virgina when we Lived at Newbern I have Inclofed thee y⁰ two Laft papers I have been here but a few days and tis but a few hours Since I found this Oppertunity had I had time Shou'd write more fully

J. H.

Charles Town So. Carolina July 20th 1760

Dear Brother & Son

I Write by Capt Dyar In Anfwer To a Letter Regarding the Tract of Land held by my Wife and me in the Jersey that I was willing to Convey my Wright that it might be Applyed to the Ufe Defired I now Again by Capt. Rivers Advife that I Still Continue in the Same Difpofition, and In Order to have it Compleated would have you Send the Inftruments of writeing for yt purpose, To John Remington Notery Publick In Charles Town So. Carolina who will take Care of them, and Advife me allfo, So that they Shall be Confirmed. My Scircum-ftances are So at Prefent that I Could not do with out Some affiftance which Capt Rivers has been So Kind as

to Suppley me with have therefore Drawn on You for
Ten Pounds—Philadelphia Curriancey wch I hope and
Defire that you may Anfwer and Shall be a full Consideration to my wright in the Land above mention'd (I Shoud
have Defired none if my nefecety had not Obliged) Capt.
Rivers has been a perticular friend to me here and by his
Intereft Am Like to Get into Good Bufines In Georgia
where he has Been a Small time paft Obliged to be to
Settle Some Afaire of Confequence to whome I Refer You
for Perticulars Conclude with Great Refpeft to all frds.
&c Your Loveing Brother and father

JOHN HOWELL.

Georgia Savanah Town Sept y° 26th 1760

To KATHARINE HOWELL

My Dear Wife

I write to Johnne from South Carolina the 18th of June
by Capt Deyer and by Capt Rivers the 20th of July, by
wch you are advifed of my Leaving the Place where you
Left me &c. and yt by the Affiiftance of Capt Rivers
Friendfhip &c. I Believed Should get into good Bufinefs in
Georgia where I now am, having the Profpeft Agreeable
to what I then write, wch is in Joyning in Partnerfhip wth
William Francis a man here in good Scircumftances has a
Tan yard Conveniantly Situated on the River Savanah,
about Six miles above Savanah Town, wth whom Intend
to Stay one Year perhaps Longer if nothing Prefents more
advantagious

I have met wth many Difagreeable paths to Travel fince you Left me. My dear it is not the moft agreeable one, our abfence from Each Other, when it will be otherwife is Uncertain, But notwithftanding the Gloomey Profpects, I hope we Shall Spend Some of our days together Agreeably Yet, by the Laft Advife I have I underftood that thou was at our Dear Fathers wch I hop'd wou'd be agreeable to thee as we are Scircumftance'd I Shall be Glad to Reeeive a line from thee by this Opportunity Hopeing yt thefe may be Receeved by thee in the Enjoyments of helth as at prefent I am for wch I am thankful——

With Dear Love to my dear Father &c and all frds. Concludes me at this time as at all others

thy Loveing Husband

JOHN HOWELL.

——————

Savanah Town in Georgia Septr y^e *26th 1760*

To John Ladd Howell.

Dear Son

I Hope thou has Receiv'd mine of June ye 13th by Capt Deyer, and of July the 20th. by Capt. Rivers, I Drew on Brother Jofa. Howell and thy Self for Ten Pounds Philada. Currencey, wch I hope Brother Jofhua anfwer'd Capt. Rivers for me, my Scercumftances at yt time were Such yt Obliged me againft Inclination, I hope to have it in my power to Reimburs him before it is Very Long, I Defired Allfo yt thou Send the Inftruments of

Writeing that I might Convey to thee my Right of yt
Land in the Jerfey's, or as you may think proper wch. I
am Willing to do y* firft Oppertunity I have——

I mention'd to thee in mine by Capt. Rivers the Prospect I had in Georgia, I Arived (in the Scooner Barrington from Charles Town into Savanah River in fourty
Eight Hours we were Obliged to Lay Quarantee in Sight
of y* Town Ten days on Acct. of y* Small Pox being at
Charles Town from where we Sailed) the 18th day of
Augst. at Savanah Town, Staid theire two days, where I
met wth. Wm. Francis (which is the perfon Capt. Rivers
his Friendfhip &c. Recommends me to) a Man of Good
Scircumftances, Lives on the River Savanah, about Six
miles above the Town with whom I intend to Stay in
partnerfhip in the Taning one Year, Perhaps Longer if
nothing Offers more to Advantage.——

I have nothing New to advife thee of Soposeing You
have heard of Capt. Paul Demere being Obliged to Surrender Fort Lowden to the Cherokee's and yt Since as it
here Reported, they have Killed Capt. Demere & as many
more as makes the Number Equal to the Cherokee's Killed
Some time paft at Fort Prince George allfo yt the Remainder of y* men &c are Ufed Very Ill not Regarding
their articles of Capitulation Signed Augft. y* 7th 1760
we here we here that William Wright Efqur. of Charles
Town South Carrolina Lately Arived there from England,
Is to Sucfeed Governour Ellis in the Government of this
Colleny

Dear Johnney Remember me to all frds. as Ocation
offers In Perticular my Dear Love to thy Benefactors Dear
Brother Jofa. Howell and John Ladd Sincerely wifhing thy
Health and Happinefs at this time as at all others, Conclude thy Affectionate Father

JOHN HOWELL

P. S. Edward Somervelle from whome I have Receiv'd Peculiars favours of friendfhip In Charles Town In
Our Paffage here &c. as allfo in this place, Is a Gentleman
of Good Character here, the Owener of the Scooner Barrington by wch. I have this Oppertunity, any thing yt
Happens in thy way Refpectfull towards y* Captain &c.
for acct of my frds. Intereft Shall note it as done to my
Self

Let me here from thee by the firs Oppertunity favour me
with Some of your Lateft papers as Ufual Direct thy Letters for me to the Care of Capt. Edward Somerville In
Savanah——

J. H.

I Expect to be more Acquainted with this Colleney then
at Prefent wch I hall Advife thee with as Oppertunity
prefents, now can that the Town of Savanah is Butifully
Situated on the River Savanah the Bank about fourty foot
high (above Water) neare a Mile fronting the River tis a
fine Level on wch y* Town Stands hath the Greateft Sime-
letude of the City of Philada. of any Place yt I have Seen,
In the Streets Alleys and Convenient for Shiping a Hand-

fome Market and tis Said theire trade Increafeth which tis allfo Said Governor Ellis hath been a great frd, to Leveing this Government with a Good and Indeed Great Charter in General.   Dear Johnney Take an Oppertunity to Remember me to Capt Rivers and Let him Know yt I am there &c.

J. H.

To John Ladd Howell Marcht. in the City of Philada Pennsylvania p Scooner Barrington Capt. Jos. Howard
Savanab 26th Septr. 1760
JOHN HOWELL

—

Savanab in Georgia Novr. ye 16th. 1760.

Dear Son

I hope thou has Receivd mine of Septr. y° 26th Before now by the Scooner Barrington Capt. Howard, who Sailed from hence Bound for Philada. the 6th. of Octobr. By them I Advifed where I was and what Profpect I had &c which I hope will be Advantagious to me while I Stay here

I Hoped to have heard from Some of You by a Brigantine arrived here the Other day from Philada. Capt. Thornton But after Enquire found She was Bound for Cape fear when She Sailed, my hope thereof was no more, I had the Perufeal of Several of y° Philada papers to y° 23d of October, thou art Capeable of Judgeing what by ym I may be Advertifed.

Dear Johnney one Paragraffe in thine of Feby. Laſt I believe I Said nothing to thee off Regarding thy Cosen Polleys
Conduct Since a Wife towards thee &c. &c. I am well As-
ſured yt She is Under Great Obligations In Gratitude Both
to thy dear Mother & Uncle Ladd, I would Judge as Favour-
able as Poſſiable, In her favor for I think it muſt be more
Owing to the Conduct of ye Perſon yt Married Her then
Her Own Will, I Sopose yt he wants to be Poſſeſed of all
yt he Married, I Know the Man Well I am, However
Pleaſed with thy Conduct In Returns thereof, as thou
Repreſents it in thine, and Sincerely Hope that thou'l Never
Steer So as to Streeke on the Rock of Ingatitude, Young
People when the mount the Stage in Life, two often Looke
for Nothing more then Companions to Encounter &c. &c.
thoughts of Greater Conſequance ar Steped over, Therefore
Deare Johnney Let me adviſe thee not be Haſtey, In too
much haſte I mean wth. thoſe thoughts, I did I did Intend
to Adviſe Dear Salley In mine to her of Septr. Laſt that
Polley Caſwell has Been Some time Married (and has a
Son) to Simeon Bright Jr. the Son of Simeon Bright Esqr.,
that was known to You when we lived in No. Carrolina
By the Wigg Jeſtiſe, Her Siſter Chriſtian was Married Is
Since dead Left a daughter I am Tould that Polley dont
think her Self Very Happey as She Looked for a Higher
Seat then She has Got, tho Some perſons are Never Con-
tent Let ym be in what Situation Soever I Sopoſe you to
Rember the Dispoſition of yt Famely.

I have nothing Perticular to Adviſe thee Had I had Time

I Shou'd have Several Letter to Thy friend &c. By this Oppertunity wch is Sudden to me, therefore make Ufe of it Juft to Let the Know that I am in Health and to Convey my Dear Love to my Dear Wife and Salle and all Others Your frds &c. A Large Share of which take to thy Self from thy Affectionate Father

JOHN HOWELL.

P. S. Direct to me at Savanah In Georgia to the Care of Capt Edward Somerville yt a Liver there as I advifed thee In mine of Septr. yᵉ 26th. I intend this by Capt. Martin who has tould me yt he wou'd Endeavour Carefully to deliver it by whom I hope thou'l have an oppertunity to write to me

A Mallencholey peice of News, I have from Capt. Thornton wch (has much Effected my thoughts) Happend In I. P. family of Jos. Jordan's Stabbing Young Smith wch. I Sopofe to be Ifreal Pembertons former Wifes Sifters Son thou'l advife me of the Perticulars in thy Next

I Have Inclofed one of the Laft Papers that's Come to Hand here Excufe this Rent in the Paper I have not time to Copey it anew thine as allways

J. H.

Savanah Novr. 15th 1760
JOHN HOWELL

Savanab in Georgia Jun ye 22d, 1761.

To KATHA. HOWELL

My Dear Wife

It is Long Since I had a Line from thee, from Johnney I Beleive as often as Opportunity Prefents to him, I here from thee Very Refpectfully

By his Laft wch was dcembr 20th. I was Glad to here of thy being then Better in helth then for Some time before, which I much defire may Continue

Our misfortunate abfence so Long muft Lay thee under great Inconveniances, which gives me as much concern, tis' not in my Power yet to alter tho, hope it will not All-ways Remain fo I fhould be glad of a Line from thee by this Opportunity

I hope I Shall do Better here then where thou Left me, Sopofe I Shall in a few months Know & agreeable thereto Intend to Advife thee.

Dear Johnney Advifeth me by his Laft wth his Inten-tions of Entring into the Matrimoniel State which I hope will do well, to whom by this .Opportunity I write as allfo to Dear Salley, hope they will all Come Safe to hand, and by the Same Shou'd be as Glad to here from you all——

I have the Enjoyment of helth beyond what I Could have Expected for which I am very Thankful for, and Conclude thofe few Lines who Remaines

Affectionately thy Loveing Hufband

JOHN HOWELL

P. S.   I Shall be Glad that my dear Love Be Rember'd
to my dear Father Perticularly Johnney frequently advifeth
me of his helth &c. wch I hope may Continue   *J. H.*

———

Savanab In Georgia June ye 22d. 1761.

My Dear Son

I Receiv'd thy Letter with dear Salleys Inclofed By
Capt. Howard and thine By Capt. Martin allfo thine of
October y° 23d wch. Came to hand but a few days paft
forwarded from Charles Town By Peter Mazyck a Gentleman there yt. I am not Acquainted wth. therefore
taken the more kindly.   All of them are Very Acceptable
to me, one of y° Greateft Enjoyments that I am Poffef'd
wth Is hearing from you and the Pleafure with Hopes that
your Conduct (my dear Children) may be and Continue
to be, Such that Draws down the Blefling of a Kind Providance wch. is Often, my Ardent Prayer.

It Gave me Concern thine of the 18th. of Novbr. In
hereing of the Indifpofition of you and frds. wth the Dis-
trefed Scircumftance of Brother Sa . . . Familey at
that time. thine of decembr. y° 20th A . . . me of
the Recovery of Several and Other Like . . . Recover I hope they all have and Now Enjoy h . . .

I am Well Pleafed to here that there . . . good
Harmony Like to Subfide wit . . . and Your Cofen
Polley, there is But . . . you Decendants of the
Ould Stock of John & . . . Ladd (wch. may Be
Called as in One Clafe)   It may Long Subfifte

Dear Son thou Advifeath me of many things Dutifully,
The moft Worthey of my Notice an Concern is, thy En-
tring into the Engagments of Life &c.   In Regard of
Changeing thy Scircumftances Endeavouring to make thy
Self Happy In a Vertious Companion, I have no Objeftion
(Shou'd Be glad was it in my Power to make the more
Capeable to Engage in the affaires that attend Life.)   I
have Some Reafon To Beleive thou'l Endeavour to Acct
Confiftant with the Advice of thy friends, and thofe good
princeaples of Gratitude Virtue and Truth, all things will
then I hope do well.   I have no Objeftion to the Young
Woman or Famely but am Pleafed as thou Chofe Allfo to
Engage in yt State of Life thou art Likely to fall into
Union wth. So good a One, I Sopofe it is So before this
time wch if it be (or not) I hope you will do Well and
that as Great Bleffings Attend and Reft on You As a
Parent with Scincerety Affeftionately Can defire

I Cant well Omit Advifeing that Capt. Rivers Spake to
me Several times Very Refpeftfully on thy Behalf I hope
thou'l Allways as Juftly deferve that Good Charraftor he
gives thee

He Sailed to Sea from this Port the 17th. of may For
Tortolo Laden wth. Lumber & Live Stock—

The Remainder of that Fleet that Sailed from Charles
Town Since the Storm Under Convoye Have Had the
Misfortuene of Meeting wth. a Voilent gale of Wind a few
days After Sailing at Sea wch. Has Parted them tis thought
Some are Loft the Scooner Barrington Capt. Drummond is

Blown Back on this Couſt to the Southward the Veſal Loſt
her Bow Sprit met with Other Conſiderable damages as
allſo her Cargo is much Damaged

dear Johnney I have my health In this Southern part of
the Continent Byond what I might have Expeƈted, In
which I Conclude to the at this time as Indeed allways
with ſincere Prayers for thy helth and Proſperity thy
Affeƈtionate Father

JOHN HOWELL

P. S.   Remember me Reſpeƈtfully to all friends

J. H.

To John Ladd Howell Mercht. In Philadelphia
By Favour of Capt. Martin In the Sloop Kingstone
John Donbar Comander
recd. 4th July 1761 Savanah 22nd, June 1761 John
Howell recd. 4th July

Savanah In Georgia Sept. 5th. 1761.
To John Ladd Howell
Dear Son

have Receiv'd no Adviſe of thy Receipt of mine, which
Adviſe thee of my Receiveing Severall of thy Letters all of
wch. are Agreable, And In Perticular Expreſſing my Con-
ſent In thy Choice In A Companion, and Alliance with
Doctr. John Paschall's Famely, In thy Marrage with his
Daughter, which I hope will be Attened with the Bleſſings
of a Kind Providance, I have Some Reaſon to hope thou

has Receiv'd ym, I Conclude it muft be by Some Hurrey of Buffines &c. and not Knowing when Capt. Donbar Sailed, that I have Receiv'd none, However Let this Affure thee that thou'l allways Act Agreeable to me while thou Conduct thy Self Confiftant (I have no Reafon to Beleive Otherwife) with the Advife of thy Dear Mother and Uncles John Ladd and Joshua Howell (thy Great Benne-factors) which I am Senfiable Dear Johnney will be De-fined for thy Advancement &c. Shou'd be Sorry Any Deficulty attend for want of a Scrole from me, on any Subject &c. that might be for thy Good, As I have Pre-ferd their Advife to thee being as I Sopofed Under their Perticular Notice.

Have Nothing to add More Perticular then Expreffing that My Sincere Concern Is for thy Happinefs, Defireing thou'l Convey my dear Love to thy Mother and Sifter wth. Others thy frds. a Large Share of which Receive to thy Self and friend

From thy Affectionate & Loveing Father

JOHN HOWELL

P. S. I was pleafed to Receive So perticular an Acct. as I have by thine how Jordan's Unhapy afaire Ended In the Law. *J. H.*

—

Savanah In Georgie Septr. ye 16th 1761

To JOHN LADD HOWELL.

Dear Son

Thofe Letters by Capt. Donbar are Coppeys of wch. I

Sent to Charles Town to the Care of Peter Mazyck to forward, as this Oppertunity Prefents make Ufe of it Allfo,
have nothing here now Worth noteing.   My Dear Love
to thy Mother and Sifter with all Others &c.

I am with Great Affection thy Loveing Father
                                JOHN HOWELL

---

*Savanah Septr. 1761 John Howell recd. 10th Octr. p
Savanah in Georgia Febry. 19. 1762.*

To John Ladd Howell
Dear Son

I Receiv'd thine of Novbr. 2d with dear Salleys for
Company y° 23d Inftant which are Very Accptable

I am Well Satisfied hearing of the Accomplifhing thy
Marrage with a Young Woman So agreable to thy Self
and friends as I am Well Affurd of She is I have Allfo a
Very agreable Charractor of her Handed me by thy dear
Sifter,

I Sincerely hope you'l Poffes much Happinefs as
Affectionate Parents are defireing yt their Dutifull Children
in Perticular Shou'd Enjoy

I have Much Pleafure in hearing from You, So Perticularly and Often as I do by thine &c I hope it may Continue
tho I am not doubtfull as time permit & Oppertunity Prefent——

am Glad to here of thy dear Mother's Receiving Benifit
by Medicines wch. I hope may be Sucfesfull and affiftive to
the Recovering her helth, I Shou'd Allways be pleafed

with a Line from her, the Reasons dear Son thou Give me are Sufficient. I Very Kindly Accept of her Affectionate Regards for me Expressed by thine, Desire thou'l hand my dear Love again with Sincere Affections hopeing I Shall yet have it in my Power to Express them more agreable then by Pen Ink & paper——

I Acknowledge Benja. Trotters friendShip &c. as Very Kind, as oppertunity present thou'l Oblige me In returning mine, I had when Personaly Acquainted the Same Good Oppinion of him as thou Expresseth, am Glad it is thine,

Tis Reported here as Scertain that Martinceo Is In Posfesion of the English Forces &c—that a Spanish War will be and that Soon I expect the Certainty thereof you'l have before the Receipt of this——

I Expect an Oppertunity by a Small Brigg Capt. Olliver whose to Sail in a Month for Philada which Intend to make Use of therefore now Conclude with dear Love to all riends not forgeting my Dear Father In Perticular a large Share thereof Receive to thy Self and Spouse, from Your Affectionate & Loveing Father

JOHN HOWELL.

P. S. thou need not Recomend mine now to the Care of any one In Perticular

———

To JOHN LADD HOWELL
*Savanah 21st Mar 1762   John Howell
recd. 3rd May 1762 Answd. 26th follwg.*

—

Savanah In Georgia March ye 21st. 1762

To JOHN LADD HOWELL

Dear Son

I write to thee by Capt. Martin who Sailed from here the Laſt of Febry. Copey's of which thou has with this—

I have nothing Perticular to advife thee more then I then had—I Expeft thou'l Receive a Caſk of Rice by Capt. Oliver Shiped by Jofeph Wood, Marcht, here free from Any Expence &c.—which thou art to do with as thy dear Mother K H Shall think proper which Concludes me as Allways with dear Love to my friends Generally and in Perticular to you my dear Children

Your Affeftionate Loveing Father

JOHN HOWELL.

· P. S.   Excufe me to thy mother In the above as ti's But Little &c.   I hope to have it in my Power to Enlarge on yt Subject &c

J. H.

P. S.   I have Defired my frd. wood to give the news if there is any there is now a Ship Jeft Arived from Jamacai, Return him the Same Compliment &c.

Savanah In Georgia May ye 8th. 1762.

KATHA HOWELL

My Dear Wife

I wrote to thee by Capt Olliver of March y⁰ 18th Advifing thee yt, Our dear Son I hoped Would Receive a Small Quantity of Marchantdise Shipped to him by a friend of mine for thy Use I hope by this Opportunity he will allfo Receive the Like Quantity Shiped by the Same Person wch is allfo for thee I Shall be glad to here of its Safe Arrival Small as it is———

I was Glad to here from thee by Salleys of April Laft that thou Continued in Better helth then Some time paft which I hope may Continue, with dear Love to all our friends &c. Concludes me with

Sincere Affection Thy Loveing
Hufband
JOHN HOWELL.

I may advise the I am at Present in h——*

To John Ladd Howell
Savanah 8th May 1762 John Howell

—

Savanah In Georgia May ye 8th 1762

To John Ladd Howell
Dear Son

*   *   *   *   *   *

Dear Salley Advifeth me by her's of April Laft of thy being in Bofton then & yt She had advife of thy helth &c. wch I was allfo Glad of——

I hope thou'l be Bleffed with Sucfes in thy Engage-

---

*Prefumable that he means health.

ments In Life With dear Love to thy Mother &c. Dear Children I Conclude Your

Affectionate Loving Father

JOHN HOWELL.

P. S. I have not any thing to advife thee with yt. I Can Sopofe News from here to thee *J. H.*

Dear Johnney

David Mounteufe a Marcht here Juft now advifed me he Shiped a Small Cafk of Oringes to David Francks by Capt Olliver for my accot he allfo tell's me he thinks he Orderd they Shou'd be dd. to Jofiah Howell In Stead of John Ladd Howell wch. Is a Miftake tho Wille be of no great Confequance thine as Allways

JOHN HOWELL.

Poftag 2-6

To John Ladd Howell Mercht. In Philadelphia Via of Norfolk Virginia by John Starr

Georgia Septr. 1st. 1762.

JOHN HOWELL

—

Savanah In Georgia Septr. ye 1st. 1762

To John Ladd Howell

Dear Son

Thy favour of may the 16th was forwarded from Charles Town So. Carolina by Peter Mezyck & was Very Acceptably Receiv'd the Eight of June

I have much pleafure hereing of thy Mother & Sifters

helth &c. and that thy Jorney to Bofton has Been Agreable,
more So that thou has Reafon to hope for future Advantage
from it; I muft note it's Very Agreable thy Perticular
Accot. of that Countrey and In thy Jorney finding People
So Hofpitable and kind with Some Other Ocurances Contained in thine thy Entring Into a Partnerfhip with a gentleman (who I doubt not but mus be Agreable) In a Trade
to London I Sincerely hope may Prove Sucfesfull to you
Both——

thou Advifeth me of Receiveing a Cafk of Rice from
Jos. Wood Marcht. here, by Capt. Oliver I hope thou has
Received another from the Same hand for my Accot. by
Capt. Jones which I Should allfo have been glad to have
heard on, am Sorrey that the Oranges proved Bad they
were Shiped in my Abfence, for wch. Reafon thou paid
freight if any Was, I Expefted an Oppertunity Long Since
by a Veffel wch. Was Intend to Sail for Philada. but on
the Arival of Capt. Jones from thince here there was not
an agreable accot. of the Markets for what they Intended to
Ship, Capt Jones Came away I Sopofe Unknown to thee
or I might have had a Line Jos. Wood tel's me he has
only one Letter & yt from yᵉ Gentleman he Sent her

Yefterday Morning by a Veffel from the Havanah in
nine days we have the Accot of the Reduftion of that
Place to his Bretaniack Majefteys Forces the Perticulars we
have not, But will Sopofe you'l have the Pleafure of hereing before this Can Reach thy hand, there was great Re-
joicings here on the Ocation Yefterday, Capt. Rivers His

Brig of 20 Guns with a Sloop Allfo Under his Comand of
10 Guns and a Sloop under the Comand of his Son of 12
Guns, Began the day with the Rifeing of the Sun, then
Other Veffels in the Harbour fired; the Guns on & in the
fort in their Order a Very Gentele Entertainment at the
Governours the Conclufion Elumanations &c. &c.

Dear Son Excufe me to thy Mother & Sifter I am Juft
now Recovering from a Small Spell of Sicknifs the fevour
which hath Obliged me In town Some days Paft to be
Near the Doctor to take Medefines the moft of wch. hath
been the Bark I intend out when my Buffinefs Engages me
at Prefent to Morrow— I have nothing at Prefent for-
ther to add which Concludes me with dear Love to thy
dear Mother and Sifter, with thy dear Fanney, and all
friends &c. Share thereof and Receive to thy Self from
thy Loveing and Affectionate Father

JOHN HOWELL

To John Ladd Howell

P. S. This Oppertunity is by the Exprefs Sent from
here to Oxford In Maryland to Gentleman there, Mar-
chants, that had a Large Quantety of Uropian Goods
Shiped in a Scooner from on Board a Ship at Norfolk in
Virginia which was to be Tranfported to Oxford aforefd.—

Which Said Scooner was Taken In Chefapeak Bay off
the mouth of York River (By a French Privateer Sloop)
and Is now here Retaken by the Mafter & mate of Said
Scooner as followeth wch. Information I Receivd this day
&c. The French Privateer put on Board the Scooner a

few of his men with one of his Prize Masters and Ordered
her for Augustine the English Notifing that the French took
no Care to put Provisions &c. on Board Equal for yt Voyage Expected the Consiquance might be theire advantage as
It Proves, the Soon Wanted Water &c. Some Days the
French Agread that they Sho in Shore to Obtain Some
Reliefe—

In her Return Tooke a New England Sloop and is gone
Into Agustine She put Some of the New England men on
Shore to the Southard of this the English Captains fell in
after being Several days Clofe on the Coft near this Inlet
the Pilots Went off brought him in and up here with a
faire wind, has made Report to the Judge of the Admiralty
Clames for the Oweners of the Veffel and Cargo wch
Clame is Said good and will be Supported.

thine as Allways

J. H.

the name of the Captain of the Scooner is Wm Greymes

———

To John Ladd Howell Marcht In Philadelphia.
Georgia Novr. 22nd. 1762
JOHN HOWELL.

—

Savanah In Georgia Novbr. ye 22d. 1762.
To John Ladd Howell.
Dear Son

I Wrote to thee of September y° 1ft. which I may
Sopofe thou has Received before this time as I am Advifed

it was forwarded to Oxford In Maryland, In wch. I Advised thee of my Receiving thine of the 16th of may &c. which is the Laft Oppertunity I have heard any thing from you by,

I Shoud be Glad to here oftener from you if Oppertunity prefented, which is one of the Greateft Comforts that I Enjoy hereing of your health &c. I have nothing perticular to advife thee Only make Ufe of this Oppertunity Beleiveing it allways agreable to thee hereing from . . . I have been Much Afflicted with the feavours Since I wrote thee, but am now Got pretey Cleare of them and Enjoy my helth Better then for Some time paft wch I hope may Continue

Dear Som my Dear Love wth. Sincere Affections to thy dear Mother & Sifter With the Same to thy Self and Spoufe I now Conclude as Allways thy Loveing & Affectionate Father

JOHN HOWELL.

P. S. Dear Son I dont for get but defire thoul Remembr me to frds. &c. as Opprtunity Sutes the &c.

J. H.

This Oppertunity is by Capt Grymes in a Scooner for Oxford in Mary Land—

Savanah in Georgia May 3d 1763

My Dear Wife Howell

It is now allmoft one year Since I had the Pleafure of heareing from thee, which was by Johnneys of May Laft, the Scene *neceffity** *t*hat we are Under of being abfent from Each Other Is Very disagreea*ble* I hope it will not allways Rema*in so* It Some Times Affe&ts me more *than is* agreable to Exprefs, I Shall be *glad* to here from thee by all opportuni*ties* and hope to have it in my Pow*er* to be more Affertive to Releive thy *nece*fliteys then Some time paft——

I may Let Thee know allfo yt I *have* Receivd much Friendfhips here, an*d* as to my prefent Situation &c. Dear Johnney I Sopofe will advife thee. Shall now Conclude as Allways with dear Love thy

Affe&ionate Loveing Hufband

JOHN HOWELL. · ·

———

To KATHARINE HOWELL THESE TO THE CARE OF JNO LADD HOWELL

—

Savanah In Georgia Auguft ye 5th 1763.

To KATHA: HOWELL

Dear Wife

I am Glad to here from Thee by all opportunitys and perticularly as by our dear Son's of Jun* 7th who advifed me of thy being in a better State helth then for Some time paft which I hope may Long Continue I have Allfo the Agreable advice of our having a Grand Son which I hope

---

*The words and letters in Italics have been supplied, the right hand margin of this letter being much mutilated.

will add Some Comfort to thee and be a Bleffing to his
Parents. I have Sent a power appointing John Ladd to
Convey all the Rights I have in the Jerseys by thee &c.
which I hope may anfwer the purpofe I Should have Sent
it Imediately to our Son, but my Counfil here thought thy
Brother the moft proper perfon But. if any other way
you think is more proper I Shall be Willing to Conform
to it

I Shall allways as Opportunitys prefent be glad to here
from thee. I hope thou'l be Blef'd with the Enjoyment of
Helth at yᵉ Receipt hereof as at this time I am, which
Concludes me with Sincere affections.

Thy Loving Hufband
JOHN HOWELL

————

To John Ladd Howell Marcht In Philadelphia By
favour of Capt. Jones.
Georgia Septr. 11th 1763
JOHN HOWELL

—

Savanah In Georgia September 11th 1763

Dear Son

Thine of Auguft yᵉ 8th I Receivd the Laft Evening by
Capt Jones with the deed of Leafe & Releafe as Mentiond
which I would have Executed and Sent thee by him (who
Sails from here by way of Edenton) But I had an Oppertunity the Begining of Augft. Laft which I made Use of
writeing to thee by James Haberfham Esqr Inclofed in

apacket Directed to thy Uncle Josa Howell which I Expect before now thou haft Received, thy mother Sifter &c with apower of Attorney to thy Uncle Jno Ladd which I Sopofe may Anfwer the End Defired as well if not Better then my Signing thofe deeds now fent, which is the Reafon I have not But if it Shoud so happen yt that Power Should not Come to hand or not Anfwer the purpofe defir'd, Advife me thereof by the firft Oppertunity and if you yt are Corcerned think it beft thofe deeds fhall be Signed they fhall and fent by the firft Oppertunity after.

I am Glad to here of thy wife Recovery thy dear Mother & Sifters helth· with others Our frds. I note some other paragrafs with Concern— the Miferies and Diftreffes of the poor People of your Country are Shocking and Indeed beyond the power of Language to Difcribe, We have fome Reafon to hope that the Indians Back here will Keep from Difturbing the Inhabitants of Georgia and South Carolina there is Advices from fome of the Nations Head men of their Affurance of being at the Congrefs which Is to be held at Augufta the 15th of October Next—

I will hope mine by James Haberfham is be fore this time in thy hands therefore Shall now Conclude with dear Love to all friends and in perticular thy Grand Father thy Mother and Sifter thy felf and Spoufe with your little Jofhua

thy Affectionate and Loveing Father

JOHN HOWELL

P. S.   I Shoud be glad of a Line from Brother Josa.—I have my helth as well as I Can Expect for the Seafon.   I Shall be Glad thou has it in thy power by the Next Opertunity to give more Agreable Accot. of the Savage Cruilty in Your Country

---

To JOHN LADD HOWELL
Georgia Novr. 22na 1763.
JOHN HOWELL

—

Near Savanah in Georgia Novbr 22d 1763.
Dear Son

Thine by Capt. Jones with the Deed of Leafe and Releafe I Received, the Reafons I did not Execute ym & fend by him I gave thee in mine with him·

Since I have Received thine of Octobr· 20th by Capt Bolitho Advifeing me of the Receipt of mine by James Haberfhome Efq &c. &c.—and defireing yt I fend thofe Inftruments of Writing Compleated Receiv'd by Capt. Jones, wch I have done and forwarded by this Oppertunity and Agreable to mine (by Capt. Jones) of Sept. Laft— The Reafons of my fending yt Power of Attorney was, that thou Long Since advifed me of your Intentions of fending yt I might Convey my Right of thofe Lands, as I now have done, was haveing fo Good an Oppertunity thinking it might have Anfwer'd the End Intended, and been Agreable, but if this is more fo ti's as Agreable to me

I hope that this Oppertunity may fafely Reach thy

hands, which Advife me with by thy firft.   I defire thou
Remember me to my friends which Concludes me with dear
Love &c as Allways to thy dear Mother & fifter thy felf
& Spoufe with Your Son

Thy Loveing & affectionate Father

JOHN HOWELL.

P. S.   I have nothing to advife the with as News but
the peafeable Difpofition of ye Indians here

———

Savanah in Georgia July.` ye 21st. 1764. .

To John Ladd Howell
Dear Son

   Thine of may the 9th.   I Receiv'd a few days paft
perufeing of wch.   Caufeth many Serious thoughts on the
fubject Relative to the defceafe of thy dear mother a Loveing wife and a tender Parent, whofe Change from time into
Eternety I Beleive a hapey One, I Sincerely hope we may
all live to fteer our Courfe throw the Changable Scenes of
Life, that we may arive att that defired Port and Heaven
of Reft, where all tears fhall be wiped from Our Eyes
where there Shall be no more death, Neither Sorrow nor
Crying, neither fhall there be any more pain, for the former things fhall then be paffed away.

   I Sincerely Acknowledge the Affectionate kindnefs and
perticular Refpect and care of my friends towards my dear
wife In the time of her Sicknefs, dear Son it was not for
want of affection that I·did not write to thee by yt. oppertunity thou advifed me of thy hereing from me, I intended

writeing. but yt. Veffel Sailed Some days sooner than I was Advifed She would, which was the Caufe——

Agreable to thine of Octobr. the 20th 1763 I Sent thofe Inftruments of writeing Executed as thou defired; Inclofed in my letter to thee of Novbr 22d. 1763 by Capt. Bolithe, I fhould be glad to here if thou hath Receiv'd them which I have not yet——

I am glad to here of my dear Fathers Helth and of his moveing to Chefter again, I hope thou'l have an Oppertunity of hereing perticularly the Cituation I am now In by Robt. Bolton, the Bearer hereof it is att his houfe yt. I Lodge &c when in Savanah, he is a Very Friendly man I dont Know many in this place in better Efteem with ym yt know him thou'l give my dear Love to my dear Father and daughter Salley with all other friends a Large Share thereof Receive to thy Self and Spoufe with your Little famely from thy Loveing and

Affectionate Father
JOHN HOWELL

———

To John Ladd Howell Marcht. In Philadelphia
Georgia July 24th 1764
JOHN HOWELL.

—

Raes Hall Near Savanah In Georgia July ye 24th. 1764
Dear Son

I was in Savanah the 21ft Inftant on purpofe to make ufe of an Oppertunity writeing to thee as I have by Robt.

Bolton to whom I deliverd m'ne for thy Self & thy Sifter which I am Advifed are miflaid, which advice Came too late to write Again by yt Oppertunity I now Send thee Coppeys of ym which I hope may Come safe to hand If the Other Shou'd not, which I Expeft will be by Capt. Frank Goff that I have heard Is bound for Philada. Comander of a Small Scooner of his Own, he is an Intimate Acquaintance of that Gentleman John Rae where I live and with whom I am Concerned in businefs who will be Kind Enough to acquaint thee of the Cituation I am at prefent Relative to Buffines—

att prefent I am in the Enjoyment of helth, with wifhes for thee and thines helth's &c. Concludes me as Allways
thy Loveing & Affeftionate Father
JOHN HOWELL

To John Ladd Howell
Georgia Auguft 13th. 1764.
JOHN HOWELL

—

Savanab In Georgia Augft. ye 13th 1764.

Dear Son

I Receiv'd thine of July y⁰ 23d forwarded to me by Chriftopher Pechin now in Savanah from Capt. Anderfons Ship by which I here perticularly from thee and friends, whis is very Satisfaftory, I . . . to thee and thy Sifter, of July y⁰ 21st & y⁰ 24th by Robt Bolton a paffinger in a fmall Sloop, and Fran Goffe Comander of a Small Scooner

bound for Philada. from hence which Before this time, or
the Receipt hereof, I Expect thou'l have Receivd,

I have not any thing perticular to Advise thee with, am
glad to here of my dear Fathers being moved to Chester
which I hope may be attended with agreable Confiquances,
Rember me perticularly to him, and my dear daughter
Sarah, as allso to frds. &c.   I hope she will allso have Receiv'd mine as I have mentioned above, I Shall   .   .   .
glad of a line from her, thine on her Accot. fully Excufed
till the next oppertunity—

I hope the Little Voyage &c. thou mentions with thy
Spouse and friends down to your Cape may be Agreable
and at your Return find yours &c, in helth, Shall att
Every Oppertunity, be glad to here from thee and thine,
with your Enjoying the Bleffings of helth . . . prosperety,
which Concludes me as allways your affectionate and
Loveing Father

JOHN HOWELL

P. S.   Anderfon that thou wrote to me to Enquire After
Came not in the Ship Chriftopher Puchin will advife thee
of him from the Enquirey he Made

I Shoud be glad if thou by Some Oppertunity foon fend
me a few Quarts of Timothy Grass Seed

J. H.

---

att Raes Hall Near Savanah In Georgia Septr. 16th 1764
Dear Son

thine of the 17th of Augft by Capt Hughes I Receivd

the 8th of this Inftant with Galloway and Dickinfon's Speeches, I am Sorrey that difputes are got to Such a hight in the Government of Pennfylvania from the Idea I have of Governments I think Dickinfon arguments are beft founded at this time—

ti's Very affecting to here of the Horrid Cruelteys of the Indians In your Settlements, tis to be hoped thofe misfortuines will not be here—

I have Inclofed a paper where thou'l See how thofe Indians that were in the French Intereft are beging for forgivenefs—

dear Son after advifeing thee of my being in helth defire thou Remember me to all friends, Concludes me as allways with dear Love to thy Self and Spoufe with your Little Famely thy Loveing and affectionate Father

JOHN HOWELL

P. S. my being so Short at this time the Veffels Sailes to morrow morning as I am advifed therefore write while the mate of her is here fearing I Shou'd mis the Oppertunity   *J H.*

Savanah October 15th. 1765.

To JOHN LADD HOWELL

FRIEND JOHN HOWELL

I find that thy Father died at John Rays Efqr.; the affiftance that he Recd. from Robert Bolton, was not in his laft ilnefs (as I am informed) but on this wife; when he had the management of Rays Tanyard, being frequently

obliged to go to Savanna on Bufinefs, Ray Recommended
a Private Lodging to him, which he took at this fame
Boultons, * * that while he was at his houfe, a Perfon from
South Carolina came with a note of £100 that Currency
againft him, which Bolton Paid to prevent his being dif-
treffed, this, & his Lodging with him is what he died indebted to him for.

I being but juft arived here, have not had time to make
any further Enquiry; but fhall take the Proper Care to get
a more Particular Account.

Interim Remain thy Affured Friend

WILLIAM GIBBONS

Joshua Howell, brother of John Howell,
and uncle of our common ancestor, John Ladd
Howell, was a merchant in Philadelphia at the
time when John Howell was writing to his
son from the South. The following, from old
papers, shows in bare outline the course of his
life.

Joshua Howell was supercargo for John
Reynall, 1748, to Barbadoes. There is exist-
ing an invoice of a Bill of Exchange drawn by
John Jordan and Messrs. Lucellas and Max-
well in favor of Wm. Sturge, and remitted by
Joshua Howell to John Reynall, merchant in

Philadelphia for account of said Reynall and Sam Run.

Philad. Oct 4 1759*

To Mr. Joshua Howell Commissary for the Army

There is in the barracks Jno William a private soldier of the 11 regt. incapable of joining the Corps.   He was left in my care and has an incurable disease, please to issue your orders that he may have provision out of the King's Stores

SAML ORMS

———

To Carpenter & Moore

Deliver the Sergeant this man's provision and keep acct thereof, and the sergeant or Doctor may give receipt for it hereafter   •

(signed)

JOSS. HOWELL.

Sarah, daughter of John and Katharine Howell, married John Sparks.

———

*From a paper of the old Joshua Howell.

SECTION TWO

CONCERNING JOHN LADD HOWELL AND FRANCES PASCHALL, HIS WIFE

CHAPTER I.

JOHN LADD HOWELL.

JOHN LADD HOWELL, son of John and Katharine Howell, born March 15, 1739, died August 30, 1785. He was apprenticed to his uncle, Joshua Howell, a merchant in Philadelphia, for six years and nine months, to learn 'the trade or Mystery of a merchant.' The indenture—binding him to a faithful service, and his uncle to provide him with food, apparel, etc.—still in existence, is dated 'the Twenty Sixth Day of June in the Twenty Seventh year of the Reign of our Sovereign Lord George Second King of Great Britain, etc., Annoque Domini One Thousand Seven Hundred and fifty three 1753,' and is signed by Joshua Howell with Katharine Howell [mother of John Ladd Howell] and Charles Jones, as witnesses. He evidently traveled for the firm, as is shown by letters from his uncle, directed to him in Boston and other places.

In April, 1760, he was 'one of his Majesty's Justices of the Peace in West New Jersey' as he is called in a letter to him from Richard Waln, jr., on the fifth of that month.

The opening of the War of the Revolution found John Ladd Howell a merchant of prominence in Philadelphia. His first connection with this conflict appears in a bid for supplying the troops with rations and other necessities, directed to a committee of the Continental Congress. It is signed, J. L. H., and is on behalf of John Ladd Howell & Co. This firm, as seems to be shown by old accounts, consisted of John Ladd Howell and William Govett, and was called Govett & Howell. William Govett was very intimate with the family, and wrote many very kindly letters to his friend John, in after years.

Both John Ladd Howell and Joshua Howell, his uncle, had business relations also with Joseph Allicock and a ship owner, one Capt. William Kidd, who was frequently mentioned in the correspondence between John Ladd Howell and his uncle. This of course was not the Captain Kidd of romance, since that worthy was hanged many years previous to these letters.

The papers of John Ladd Howell show that he was a Commissary of Purchases for the Continental Army, at various times during the war. The earliest of these, is a letter of instructions from Carpenter Wharton, dated March 1, 1776. It mentions the fact that 'John Ladd Howell has been appointed Deputy Commissary of Provisions to the Second Pennsylvania Battalion under command of Colonel Arthur St. Clair', then on its march to Canada, gives instructions in regard to returns for provisions obtained, and directs him to deliver up the troops to the Commissary General of the Northern Department on his arrival at Albany. This commission kept him occupied until after May 9, 1776.

His next service to his country is shown by the following extract from Colonial Records, vol. x., p. 579 :

In Committee of Safety 24th May 1776.
    Present

James Biddle Chair'n	David Rittenhouse
John Nixon	Joseph Parker
Daniel Roberdeau	Benja Bartholomew
John Cadwalader	Owen Biddle
George Ross	Samuel Howell
Sam'l Morris, Jun'r	Thomas Wharton Jun'r

To the Honorable the Representatives of the Freemen of ae Province of Pennsylvania in General Assembly Met:

The Memorial of the Committee of Safety of the said Province Showing:

That there being etc. etc.

Resolved etc etc.

Resolved, That Mr. Jacob Howell be employed to go to the different Powder Mills employed by this Board, in order to this Committees being informed of their state, and that Mr. Owen give him Instructions for that purpose. etc.

The committee or the clerk evidently confounded John Ladd Howell and Jacob Howell, as the former was ordered to make the inspection, and reported as below to Owen Biddle.

On May 26, 1776, Owen Biddle writes to John Ladd Howell as follows:

Philada May 29th 1776.

To JOHN LADD HOWELL

Sir

   The Committee of Safety requefts you to go the Powder Mills, of which you have a Lift, and examine the State they are in.   Stimulate the workmen to diligence and care in forwarding the making of Powder, and direct them to fend it in to Robert Towers, Commiffary as foon as they have made a Quantity, if you were to take a powder tryer with you and prove the powder that each of them have made, it would inform them of the Quality of their Powder.   If it is not fufficiently Strong they muft improve it or it will not be paffed by the Committee as Merchantable.

   You muft report to the Committee in writing on your return what State each Mill is in, viz: whether it has began to work, when it began to work, when it will begin to work, what number of Pounders they work, how many drying Houfes they have erected, what Quantity they can make per day, what Quantity of Salt Petre and Sulphor has been delivered to them, whether the conveniences at the Mill are good or otherwife, with fuch other remarks on them as may occur to you that are of any importance.

   If they have made any Quantity of Powder they fhould fend it Immediately in.   This being all that occurs on the Subject conclude with wifhing you a Pleafant Tour.

Your Friend &c
by order of the Committee of Safety
OWEN BIDDLE.

John L. Howell to Owen Biddle, 1776.

Philadelphia June 3rd. 1776.∗

Sir

Agreeable to your directions of, I have been round to the Powder Mills as mention'd in the Lift delivered to me, and find them in the following State, viz :

Doctr. Robert Harrif's on Cromb Creek, about three miles from Chefter began to Work about the 23rd. ult. The Dimenfions of the Mill Houfe, 30 ft. by 20 ft., Head of Water about 2½ ft., fall about 6 ft., Water Wheel, 12 ft.

The Shaft that Works (eighty Stampers of 2¾ by 3¾ Inches, & eleven ft. Length) is thirty-two ft. Long, five Mortars made of Two Inch Plank, about five foot each, one Stamper & Mortar for preparing Sulphur.

Drying Houfe 20 ft by 15 ft., neither floor'd nor plaftered. He has received one Ton of Salt Petre & five Hundred wt. of Sulphur, or thereabouts, expecting to deliver one Ton of Powder on the firft Inft., & the fame Quantity Weekly.

The fides of the Mill Houfe, & the Gable Ends of that & the Drying Houfe being enclofed by Boards not fufficiently feafoned, are very open & muft have a bad effect on the Powder, yet the Doctr is of a Different opinion.

The Dimenfions of the Powder Mill erecting by Meffrs. Cowperthwaite & Biddle on French Creek, about four miles above Moore Hall, 102 ft. by 31 ft. 8 Inches.

∗ From the Pennsylvania Archives, Series 1, Vol. 4, p. 795—7.

Two Water Wheels in the Center of the House, 18 ft. Diameter, four ft. Head & 9 ft Fall, each Wheel to work three Shafts 32½ ft. Length, Six Mortar Trees 28 ft. Length, 12 Mortars, each Tree 22 Inches Length. 12 do. Br'dth, 17 do. D'pth; Two Stampers, each Mortar 4 Inches Square & 12 ft. Length.

The Graining Mill, 37½ by 27½ ft., built of Stone, not yet covered in. Water Wheel, 10½ ft. Diameter, to work seventy-two Stampers for preparing Sulphur, 12 Seives for Graining Powder, & one Bolting Cloth.

One Salt Petre House for refining ready to set twelve Kettles, each Kettle capable of refining 150 wt. Four Drying Houses 27 ft. by 21 ft. each One end of the Powder Mill being nearly finished, can make thirty Hundred Powder p. Week, or perhaps Two Tons ; will be ready to work about the 25th Inst., the very extraordinary Fresh on the 26th May having fill'd the race, carried away the Dam (as it has most in that Part of the Country) besides other Damage in the Loss of Boards, Scantling, &ca., has put them back at least Two Weeks.

Thomas Heinberger's Powder Mill on a Creek which emptys into French Creek about five miles above the aforesaid Mill & two miles from Young's Forge, 36 ft. by 30 ft.

Water Wheel, 16 ft Diameter, over Shot.

Two Shafts, 22 ft Length, to work 18 Stampers, each 9 ft. Long, 4½ Inches Square.

Two Mortar Trees, 20 ft Long, 9 Mortars, each of 12 Inches by 9, & 16 Inches Depth.

One Drying Houfe, 18 ft by 20 ft, the Mill not floor'd nor the Drying Houfe Plaftered, expects to begin to Work in Ten Days.

His Dwelling Houfe not being yet in hand, I cannot think he will begin fo foon ; he has received one Ton of Salt Petre but no Sulphur; has not began to build a refining Houfe, what Salt Petre he has recd. he refines in this City; he expects to make half a Ton of Powder p. week.

Henry Huber is erecting a Mill in Lower Millford Towfhip, Bucks County, about four miles from the Great Swamp Meeting on Swamp Creek; he was not at home, which prevented my receiving any particular Information respecting what Materials he has recd for making Powder, or the Works he intended to erect; the following I got from Workmen then there:

The Houfe to be 23 ft by 15 ft., very little done to it, the dam nor race near finifh'd, & unlefs he has more Hands employed than I obferved, I cannot think he will begin to work before the firft of July.

I made ufe of every argument in my Power at every Place to pufh them on to diligence, & forward the making & Delivering the Powder when made to the Commiffary here; one circumftance I beg leave to mention, that is, Huber's erecting a Saw Mill under the fame roof with the Powder Mill.

> I am, Sir,
> 　　Your Humble Servt,
> 　　*JN. LADD HOWELL.*

John Ladd Howell evidently was anxious to serve his country, for on June 22, 1776, Jos. Reed wrote him that, when his letters came, he had already engaged an assistant, but suggested that there was a position in the Quarter Master General's office, that he might obtain.

On July 14, 1776, Clement Biddle directed a letter to Mr. Gustavus Risberg and Mr. John Ladd Howell, and signs himself 'D. Qur. Mr. Genl.'

It is an order to use the Presbyterian and Friends' Meeting houses on Market St. Philadelphia, as barracks for a body of troops expected from Maryland. On August 15, 1777, John Ladd Howell took the oath of allegiance to Pennsylvania, and to New Jersey, October 10, 1778. There are no papers to show that he was connected with the Continental Army in 1777.

These papers of the early part of 1778 are worthy of note here. The first is a copy of an order of the 'Board of War' dated January 1, 1778, signed Joseph Nowise, directed to

Ephraim Blaine, and gives instructions in regard to the seizing of supplies in counties of Lancaster, Bucks, Berkshire, Northamptonshire and Chester, Penn. Quakers 'and such other sects or individuals as have betrayed a disaffection to the cause' were especially to be levied upon, but nothing was to be taken that was essential to a family's sustenance.

John Ladd Howell received his instructions from John Chaloner dated January 12, 1778, and went with one of the parties sent by Col. Ephraim Blaine. John Laurens, aide-de-camp to Washington, encloses to Col. Blaine a copy of a grievance dated January 21, 1778, received by Gen. Washington from a Wm. Rodman. Rodman complains bitterly that George Kitts, with John Ladd Howell and a guard, came to his house, entered his cellars, and took half his pork and hams. 'But what added to the violence, was they refufed, tho' repeatedly follicited, to weigh any of it, but gave a Receipt for fcarce one half the Quantity they took. My Liquors they alfo took as they faw proper, & behaved in every Re-

fpect infolent & oppreffive to the higheft
Degree.' He goes on to say that he does not
want to bear more than his proper share of his
country's distress, and signs himself ' Thy Excellency's Affured Friend.' Col. Blaine mentions this matter to John Ladd Howell, and
then dismisses it as of no consequence.

During the two years, 1778 and 1779, John
Ladd Howell was kept actively employed collecting and forwarding stores of grain, pork,
flour, etc., from place to place, for the use of
the army. This period is fully represented
by a quantity of letters of instruction, directed
to him as Assistant Commissary of Purchases,
and of letters from him in reference to this
work. Appended are a number of these, in
order to show the character of the duties and
the activity and integrity of the man. During
the early part of 1778, he seemed chiefly occupied in collecting horses and cattle. The rest
of that year, and of 1779, he almost exclusively gathered grains, flour and pork. During 1778, he was very seriously hampered by
the lack of wagons to move the stores collected,

to places convenient for the army. His zeal and energy can be seen from extracts like the following, which is taken from a letter to Col. Ephraim Blaine, in 1778.

'I fhall ufe my utmoft endeavours to have the Stores & Provifions removed from this place & Chs Town as Speedily as Poffible. it is a Bufinefs fatiguing & expenfive & ought to have been done by thofe who pur-chafed them. I am forry that men of Under-ftanding fhould not cordially join in forward-ing the public Bufinefs owing to trifling Jeal-oufies too mercinary for Liberal Minds.'

A little grim humor appears in his letter of December 4, 1778, to William Govette, in which, in speaking of the evils attendant upon speculat-ing by public officials in the necessaries of life, he says that 'perfons in publick office fhould, under the fevereft Penalties, be prevented at leaft from fpeculating in the neceffaries of life—as from perhaps it may be an odd whim of my own, I think an Army cannot exift without fuch things.'

Febuary 10, 1779, John Ladd Howell in a

letter to Col. Ephraim Blaine, spoke of leaving the Department, but later in the year, and again in 1780 was still connected with it.

John Ladd Howell was Judge Advocate of a court martial held August 4, 1780, to determine the fines to be imposed on those men of Col. Joseph Ellis' regiment, who refused to march to Morristown when William Livingston, Governor of New Jersey, under orders from Gen. Washington, called for a detachment of troops to rendezvous them, August 1, 1780. The other members of the court were Major Samuel Kaighn, Pres., Lieut. Jacob Roberts, Lieut. Isaac Albertson, Ensign Joseph Morrell, and Ensign Charles West. The fines varied from one hundred to six hundred dollars. Some few delinquents were excused for various reasons.

He was Judge Advocate again on September 4, 1780, to assess the fines in similar cases. The rest of the court were Capt. John Stokes, Pres., Lieuts. Saml. Matlock, and John Marshall, Ensigns Jacob Albertson and Benj. Juskey.

Jos. Hugg, in a letter to him in the latter
part of 1779, addresses him as Col. Howell,
aide-de-camp to Gen. Ellis. The following
are the places where John Ladd Howell was
during his connection with the army: 'On
March of Col. Arthur St. Clair, towards Canada as far as Albany, Dover, Middletown,
Head of Elk, Sassafras River, Valley Forge
and Philadelphia.

Sometime in 1780 he made his home at
'Old Candor Hall,' the Ladd Homestead
where Hannah Ladd, widow of John Ladd,
jr., was then living. Here he resided till his
death in 1785, which was presumably caused
by gout with which he was a great sufferer.

He was a member of the 'Union Library
Company of Philadelphia,' being admitted
April 28, 1766, on payment of seven pounds.
Clement Biddle was the treasurer. On April
6, 1769, he was admitted to membership in
the 'Library Company of Philadelphia,' under
a law of that company, passed March 13,
1769, admitting members of the first named
company. Francis Hopkinson, the secretary,

signed the certificate of admission. The dues were ten shillings per year. Receipts for payment of the same are signed by Samuel Morris, jr., Samuel Sansom, and others. The latest found is dated May 10, 1783.

The kindly feeling and high esteem with which John Ladd Howell was regarded by his numerous friends, can be described in no better way than by letting their letters speak for them. Of these friends, William Govette, Joseph Allicock and Col. J. H. Cummings (afterward general) were the most regular correspondents, and the warmest in their expressions of friendship.

CHAPTER II.

FRANCES PASCHALL HOWELL.

JOHN LADD HOWELL married Frances Paschall, of Darby (or Derby), Penn., the daughter of Dr. John Paschall and Frances Hodge. She was born December 27, 1740. Their marriage certificate is reproduced herewith.

The Paschalls were prominent people of the Province of Pennsylvania, and belonged to the Society of Friends.

Judging from the contents of a few letters now in the possession of the writer of this sketch, there was frequent communication between them and the sister Frances who made her home in Jersey, at 'Candor Hall' near Woodbury. She continued to live at this 'Old Place' for some time after the residence at Fancy Hill was built by her son, Col. Joshua L. Howell.

Throughout the extensive correspondence maintained between her husband and his personal friends, there occur allusions to her, so kindly in their import that it is evident she largely shared the respectful esteem in which John Ladd Howell was held. As her years increased, she yielded to her son's wish, to make Fancy Hill her home, where her death took place, May 27, 1812. She rests in the Friend's Ground at Woodbury, with her husband, son and five grandchildren.

She is described as quite small in person. She must have had a strong character, to have won the unbounded respect and affection with which it has become traditional that Joshua Ladd Howell always regarded her.

CHAPTER III.

LETTERS.

Social—Military

                                    Trent Aug: 2 1755

Mafter John
   I received yours Sometime paft and tooke ker to Send your father his by Mr. Caswell.
   Your father was well the other day I heard as is all friend.   Pray Give my Love to your Mother and Sally tell them I hant heard one line from them Since I wrote to them I fhould be Glad to hear from them.   Nothing new to tell you but it is Reported * hear that our forcs art much hurt at Ohioah by the french and that our Governor's fon is poisened there by fom of them, but I hope it is not fo bad as it is reported

                   from your frind and humble Sarvant

                                    Mary Moore.

---

* Probably rumors of Braddock's defeat and utter rout by the French and Indians, the previous month.

To John Ladd Howell at Mr. Joshua Howells Merchant Philad.

—

Chester Aug. 11th 1759

Dear Sir

Your very kind epiftle of yᵉ 7th Inftant per Benj. Davis, Esq. I reced. the fame Evening—Upon receiving the Contents whereof I found you had put in my power to Oblige all my Neighbours with the moft agreeable News of the Surrender of Niagara to the worthy Sir William Johnfton, whofe prudent Conduct in that affair has gained him immortal Honour, and I hope, set him above the reach of Envy and Detraction I now take leave in Behalf of myfelf and of all the Inhabitants of Chefter, to fend you Sincere and hearty thanks for the early communication of fuch good news. I wifh it lay in my Power to Oblige you in my Turn, but as I have nothing at prefent (not even fufficient to raife a faint Smile) to communicate, I give you the affurance that whenever anything happens either Comical or Tragical I will think of you, and thofe thoughts fhall not die in Embryo but committed to Writing and fent for your Amufement. When you receive News of Importance think of him who is with the greateft respect imaginable

Your Much Obliged Friend
and moft Obedient and Humble Servt
*ELISHA PRICE.**

———

*Elisha Price, who became fo noted in the controversy between Penn and Lord Baltimore, was a lawyer of prominence in the last century, having been a student in

To John Ládd Howell

Philadelphia Alley in Bridgetown Barbadoes Aug. 4, 1759
Dear John

I have not had the pleafure to hear from thee fince my arrival, I prefume the ladies engrofs thy attention, I abfent am out of mind, that is not my cafe here I rather feem to have an averfion to the fex—whilft I am in this ftrain let me add in behalf and at the Requeft of my Friend and partner Clement Biddle, his love to Hannah Howell, and for myfelf my Refpects and not to curtail the matter whilft at it.   I beg thou wilt give my Refpects to Rebecca Hartley and defire her to Requeft the Same to Betsy Armitt, to Polly Richardfon & Hetty Defhler.   I have nothing worth writing thee & in order to tire thy patience add the fubfequent—There is a large number of Affes on this Ifland fome with four legs are imported from the Cape de Verdes, & fome with two legs, natives of this place—One the latter, came to our Store—the Negro fellow for want of proper infpection miftook it for a gentleman & gave us Notice according to his miftake (it will be neceffary here to inform thee that our Counting Houfe is above ftairs, we keep a Negro below to inform common people the price of goods &c, but when Gentlemen come we are informed accordingly and he is defired to walk up) this we defired to

---

the office of Joseph Parker. He frequently represented Chester Co. in the Colonial Legislature, and in the troublous times preceding the War for Independence, he was an unflinching Whig. He was an earnest Episcopalian, and from 1757 till his death in 1798, his name appears among the vestrymen and wardens of St. Paul's Church, Chester.

walk up, it feems he wanted fome flour we not having much for Sale nor defirous of felling. afked a price I knew he would not give, upon which he wheeled about and replied, ' You're a Quaker,' this was letting me know what I long knew before—to witt—that affes would kick, tho' not by felf experience for this is the firft I 'ere had, tho' I've frequently heard them Bray which is now become fo familiar to me that I'm not the leaft terrified by it. I long to come home which I expect to do with Capt Hutton whom I fhall look for from the Land my friend Biddle will accompany me. I hope our little Library ftill continues to flourifh.

I conclude with Sincerity—Thy Affectionate
RICHD. WALN jr.

To John Ladd Howell Merchant Philad.

—

New York, 27 ffeb. 1759.

Dear Johnney

I am favored with yours of 19 and 20 inft. your uncle Jofhua wrote me himfelf, and acquainted me of the death of poor Anna, and his apprehenfion of Sally's following fhortly, which is moft certainly a trying Circumftance, in which afflicted fituation I moft earneftly condole with him and all the ffamily I have made Enquiry for Baily in 2 vols. but no fuch thing to be had here at prefent—I can get Johnfon in 2 vols. which is a later and in my opinion a better Book for 30 s, if you incline to have them advife me in your next, my compliments to Bil'y Govett & Believe me to be with Truth Dear Johnny

Yours Sincerely
JOS. ALLICOCKE.

———

New York, March 28, 1759

Dear Johnny

My prefent hurry of Bufinefs prevents me from faying much to you but good manners (exclufive of the regard I profefs towards you) bids me anfwer your kind favour of the 20th which came yefterday by James Ennis, and it is with pleafure I congratulate you on your recovery from the Meafles which is a Diforder I know from experience to be very troublefome. Am glad you approve of my Choice in the Dictionary, I really think it the beft of any of the fize extant. Pray tender my Love to Hook & tell him I wifh he may be bleft with all the Comforts and social Blifs that matrimony is capable of Conferring on him. As for my part I am determined to wait until the Campaign is over, in the meantime I am not without hopes of having the pleasure of paying a Vifit to Dear Philad. where I may finally fix my Standard. I fhall at all times gladly receive and anfwer your epiftles being very fincerely yours whilft

JOS. ALLICOCKE.

Tell Billy it is my defire he will take Time by the fore-lock and not be rafh in taking a new wife immediately on burying an old one, which it feems he is fhortly to do—

I am in hafte yours unfeignedly *J. ALLICOCKE.*

New York April 1760

To John Ladd Howell
Dear Laddy

I duly recd. your kind Letter of 13 and thank you moſt heartily as it were—I'll buy you a Matrimonial Preceptor, look you, but ſee that you ſtudy it early and late and adhere thereunto religiouſly.   Be good enough to make me and mine civil to Mr. Howell and Spouſe—farewell, But ſtay a little, tell your uncle too, that Promiſes are to the full as brittle as ever. I   was promiſed a Bill of £250 yeſterday, laſt night I ſought for it & again got another promiſe and it a'nt come yet being (according to Mr. Knickerbocker's Watch) a minute after 10—Cordially yours

J. ALLICOCKE.

New York 18 Oct. 1760

Dear Johnny

The Bearer hereof Capt. Alberſon talks of ſailing Tomorrow—he has in Charge a barrel of the right kind of Oyſters for your Uncle Markt J. H. which pleaſe have conducted to his houſe with my beſt Compliments.   The ſaid Alberſon hath likewiſe in Care your Matrimonial Preceptor, which you'll be good enough to accept of as a Commiſſion for the Negociating a certain Piece of Buſineſs for me undermentioned—Being convinced of the great difference in the prices of Commodities between your City and ours I am induced to benefit thereof in the purchaſe of 4¼ yards of the beſt Women's Velvet to be had in 'Delphia & doubt not that you will accommodate me, the fooner the better, but be circumfpect in your choice, I want it for Patty—pray fend it by a friend you can rely on and I dare venture to fay Mr. Howell will advance the . . . . and debit me accordingly. I'll venture that Billy Govett advifes you to get the affiftance of fome She in the execution of this weighty matter

yours Deare Johnny
JOS. ALLICOCK.

New York, 22d Mar. 1762

D^r. Ladd

I received both your favours of 5th & 15 inft. Your Uncle wrote me concerning the Lofs of his daughter, which grieves me not a little, efpecially as another little one was taken ill fo fuddenly after the death of Sally: But join with you in Good Wifhes & Sanguine Hopes that his next letter will convey the glad tidings of the Baby's (Keaty) recovery.

We are ftill without news from Europe and our army to the Southward—but cannot long remain fo according to the rule of Thumb. My little Flock enjoys good health and joins me in owing Respects to you and hearty compliments to Friends Leddle and Kidd

With Sincerity Dear Johnny Yours
ALLICOCKE.

N. Y. 9th June 1762

Dear Laddy.

of your favours of the 29th & 31ft ult before me and the firft of 'em put me in diforder, but was greatly alleviated by the latter, congratulate both you and your Spoufe on her recovery from the unlucky accident which befel her on returning from the Banquet. A packet is now arrived from Falmouth in six weeks, which muft I prefume bring fome interefting Intelligence. If I can collect anything worth while it fhall be added before I deliver this into the care of friend Saunderfon. this event will moft likely create a Good Conveyance for your two Letters for London. For the love of Mercy have fome Compaffion on the Wax and Paper when you feal your letters, you have fo heavy a hand when you ufe wax that there's no poffibility of undoing your outward cover without utterly demolifhing the fame, which may be attended with inconvenience when the cover is compofed of a letter, as words themfelves oft go to pot.

Hurry makes me conclude wi.h Patty's and my Complts. to your Spoufe & Self

Yours Sincerely

JOS. ALLICOCKE.

New York 20 Decem 1762

Dear Laddy

Your gentle admonition under date the 16th for which **Thank You.** Now how does your fair Spoufe and the

Young Fellow—Mine are very hearty and join me in Compliments of the higheſt taſte to you and yours, little Jardine hath had the Small pox finely. I dare Say Uncle Joſhua has told you from time to time of my having you in remembrance—A quantity of 10, 12, or even 20 would ſuit this market admirably, I don't think there's o Caſks in Town, ſo there we're off, and am Sorry. I note what is ſaid concerning the Memorandum, the things will ſtill be of uſe So let them come to ſhield Yoſep from the inclemency of the weather—every one that ſees the young Lad, ſays that he's thee Hero of the Age, a finer Boy I ever peept at I vow. God keep you

Adieu   *JOS. ALLICOCKE.*

---

11 April 1776.

Y⁰ Favours you ſent encloſing one for London is before me, but that which was encloſed is gone into the Pitt Packet's Mail, She is to ſail tomorrow—If you wiſh to ſend a Duplicate there will be a good Conveyance in Abt 10 days. I ſend encloſed a Letter from the Gentleman who looks for his money at Stake in your City, be good enough to exhibit the Same to the other Gentleman concerned, and I dare ſay he comes you down the ballance. The Packets coming and a Packet going has obliged me to conclude with great precipitation & Abruptneſs—but neverthelefs with Sincerity and hearty Compliments your other half—Dear Laddy

Your Moſt Humble Servt   *JOS. ALLICOCKE*

To John Ladd Howell Marcht. In Philadelphia

—

New York, 12th Sept. 1763.

Mr. John Ladd Howell

My dear Ladd

I am favour'd with yours of the 8th covering two Letters for Kingſton in Jamaica, which go this day in the Ship Brotherly Love Eliſha Bell Maſſe· bound for that Port; I ſincerely wiſh them ſafe there, and ſoon—

I confeſs my Silence with ſhame, neverthelefs have no reaſon to think you can entertain the leaſt ſurmize of its being occaſion'd from want of reſpeet—

The Contraet ceaſes the 5th of next November; very ſoon after I propoſe me the pleaſure of ſqueezing your hand, and laying a foundation of ſuch Conneetions as will oblige both of us to addreſs each other very often, and that to advantage.

My Ribbs Compt. and mine go full tilt at you and yours, wiſhing you mirth and Proſperity

Adieu my good Lad

J. ALLICOCK

———

April 7 1766

Dear John

I ſhipt laſt week p Ferguson, as p Bill of Lading tranſmitted my friend your Uncle Joſhua, (you'll obſerve wherefore too, I don't love a great deal of writing if it can be avoided) a qᵗ caſk of the right ſort, value £16.10 Paid for Cask, Case, Casing, Carting & Clearing—19.6

Total £17.9.6

which be pleafed to notify in Conformity, and wish you may never have the Gout while you can lift a bumper of fuch to your lips. Its almoft a month fince I wrote to you and have been expecting very much to hear from you. I beg on receipt hereof, if convenient, & you have not fent off any Jerfey notes for me, you will make a payment of 5 Pipes of Wine your Uncle bo^t of Peter Reeve on my account & pleafe let me know concerning the fmall draft I gave you in poffeffion when here for negociation. My wife and I falute you and yours.   Adieu

JOSEPH ALLICOCKE

Montreal 14th January 1761

Dear John

I am here in Montreal in good health, and well condition'd, hope all my Friends in philadelphia are well—

I wrote Clem fometime fince in Regard to a fcheme form'd by me, I beg you'l get that Letter into your poffesfion.

Cannada is Cold but not more fo than philada in my oppinion, tho' the fevere cold lafts longer

My felf with eleven more of the _Principal_ Merchants of this City waited on his excellency the Governor with an addrefs on New Years day which I intended to have fent you but have not time tho' you'l fee it in the New York papers with the Governors anfwer, we waited on him in a

Body, headed by one Willfon— If I have a veffell in the Spring
fhall ftay till her Cargo is fold, then for philada but believe
Cannada will bring me back again I wifh you could come
here, when I get to Delphia fhall talk with you.

I have not time to enlarge at prefent, the mail fhutting
up at twelve o'clock.

Remember me to every Body, accquaint my Bror Joseph
of your Receiving this give my compts in Perticular to
Frances, to Bedales all and every of them, to pennock,
Casper, Bob, Isaac, Dan, Cale, etc etc etc

I am yours without ceremony

Wm. GOVETT.

_____

Joseph Rudolph I hope you are well, write Mr. Howell
will not, I'd write you by this oppty but have not time
Howell

there is one Dejean a French Man here who wants a
Letter Conveyed to Martineco, to a Bror. of his its in Regard to getting fome money from his Bror. to pay Genl
Amherft for cafh rec'd of him while he Dejean was prisoner in New York, if you can fend it to fome perfon in
the West Indies to be conveyed to Martineco it will much
oblige me. I'l give my Word there is no mention of
News or anything elfe but that of money in it, if his
Brother fends anything it will by fome means or other be
conveyed to you, if anything comes advife me of it

W. G.

_____

*Wm. Govett to Joseph Rudolph.

in that letter of Clem's that I mentioned to you there is one inclof'd for James Campbell I enclofe one for him now pray if will you my compts to him.

Reedy Island 21 Sept 1761

To JOHN LADD HOWELL

On board the floop Three Sifters

Dear Jack

As I had not the pleafure of bidding you adieu on my Departure from Philad I have began my Epiftolary Communications with you.   I cant help being a little melancholy on leaving the dear place of my Nativity especially to think I am out of the good Graces of the ladies there especially one Dear Girl, who this affair has prevented my telling my mind to & perhaps for ever will.   I fhould have been glad to have taken leave of your Frances to whom don't fail tending my refpectful Compliments as well as to her fifters.   As you are a friend in whom I confide & I believe you do in me.   I hope you'll not fail writing.   I am deftined for Monto Chrifto & you may inquire for an Opportunity of my father.   My Compliments to Jos Rudolph and all other friends.   As I am aboard fhip excufe everything that's amifs.

Your Sincere Friend,

CLEMENT BIDDLE.

To JOHN LADD HOWELL BOSTON
Philadelphia March 25 1762.

Cousin Johnny

I have thine of the fifteenth I have nothing very material to say to Capt Kidd—obtain what money you can of J. Sweetser for the payment of the veffel and then call on W. Whitwell to help out I have Letters from the aforefaid firms. I think it would not be prudent for Kidd to truft to one anchor & cable—therefore defire him to get another Efpecially as the difference of buying them there or Here will not be much, a good anchor here will come @ 8 or 9 pds and a cable at 70s. or 72s.6d.—Capt Harper brings an account of Martinico being ours. thou may fee it in the papers. Thee may tell Capt Kidd freights are very brifk and high to the West Indies, and if the veffel comes foon—we may have our choice of going to almoft any of the Iflands. I am with Refpect

JOSHUA HOWELL

—

April 5, 1762.

I did not write, becaufe I hoped the veffel might be in readinefs for Sailing and you would be on your paffage home but I learn that you are like to be detained. I admire at McKards wanting to be off his bargain. I think it is money enough for her and as there is a certainty of a Spanifh War. I think it will not make Veffels in New England the higheft priced

Thy mother is Here and quite well. She would as

leave thou waft come back by Land, but I fhall leave that
to thee.   I hope Kidd will take care and not let the
Spaniards or French come near Him.   We heard from thy
Uncle Ladd.   the Schoolmiftrefs was over the River and
fays they are all well.   I am not quite well myfelf have had
a dizzinefs and was let Blood laft night.   Simpfon &
Dougherty are come to light they were blown off to the
Weft Indies and Jos. Wharton's Brigg to the Bermudas all
fafe arrived in this Port.   My Refpects to Capt Kidd and
defire him to pufh in as foon as he can and run no Rifks
for want of Anchors and Cables

I am with Refpect

JOSHUA HOWELL.

Philadelphia Mar 22 1762

To John Ladd Howell, Boston.

Coufin Johnny

I wrote thee laft fifth day p poft I enclofed a letter from
Frances and one from thy Father which I Expect will reach
thy hands at Bofton.   As it will take fometime for Capt
Kidd to fit his veffel I may write again this week.   I would
have Capt Kidd fhip his hands for fome other voyage after
they arrive at this port, but where for He can tell as well
as I, as to Quebec I fhould like that Voyage but I Believe
there is no Great Encouragement yet, but times may mend
by the latter end of April.   Notwithftanding the Law offering a Bounty on Wheat Raifed in N. E. I believe they
muft be Obliged to Pennfylvania for the greateft part of

what they want.   I wifh thou may make it worth thy time
& Expence going this Jaunt.   Try if any good hands may
be had.   Jenny Hartly has taken Sifter Rawlif's Store.   If
any good Cranberrys to be had bring thy Aunt fome, or
any other matter worth bringing, we have got little Keaty
down Stairs again.   Give my respects to Capt Kidd.

I am thy Loving Uncle ´

JOSHUA HOWELL

Philad. 18th Feby 1762 .

To JOHN LADD HOWELL, BOSTON

Coufin Johnny

I received thine from New York laft evening p post Capt
Wm Kidd's namefake Kidd fat out Yesterday p the Stage.
I wrote by Him but I am thinking he will overtake thee at
N. Y. as you expected to fet out 3d or 4th day.   I faw
by the papers that two veffels were bound for Rhode
Ifland perhaps Geo. Kidd may be in time for one of them.
I have not feen Frances fince thy letter came.   She is now
at Jemmy Pearfons (married Mary Pafchall) Jofey carryd
her letter laft night.   No letter from Wm Kidd to this port
give my respects to him.   The Schooner that I mentioned
to Kidd in my letter, the Capt. tells me is owned by Himfelf & Wm Nicholls of Boston.   She is a fine veffel, Capt
Kidd may enquire if they will fell Her.   She will bear
another Deck without much coft.   is 54 ft. Keel, 22 ft.
Beam, 9 feet 8 inches Hold.

Frances received a packet from over the River yefterday.

Thy Mother & Sister were well, thy Aunt Ladd better &
Thy Uncle Ladd at Amboy.   Thy Aunt Keaty joins in
wishing the Health and a pleasant Journey & Safe back.
                    I am, Thy Loving Uncle
                         JOSHUA HOWELL

———

To John Ladd Howell To the care of Wm Whitwell
                    Boston
                         Philad. 8th march 1762
Cousin Johnny
    I wrote thee the 25 ult and therein sent one from Wm
Govett p Capt Duff who sail^d the next Mon^y but was
obliged to come back to get out of the way of the ice,
which yet continues very plenty in the River.   In that
Letter I mentioned Sally's illness (not thy Sister) she has
been very poorly ever since, and not able to walk about or
leave her Chamber these 12 days past.   Flour has been
very high at and no opportunity of Shipping thee any.
Thee Severity of the weather has unhinged the post.   he
did not come in till Seven day.   I sent the one Inclosed to
Darby for Frances, and here is one Inclosed in return.
                    I am with Respect
                         Thy Lov^g Uncle
                         JOSHUA HOWELL.

—

                         18 march 1762
    Dear little Sally died the 10th inst. we were in hopes
the worst was past, but she changed for the worse on third

day night and continued till morning, little Keaty has been
Ill Since her Sifter was buryed, is better and I hope will
be fpared us.   Frances was in Town laft Sixth day but returned home to Darby, her father was ill but is now Better, I sent her thy two Letters.   The weather is fo bad
this morning I do not expect any one will be in Town
from Darby.   I obferve Capt Kidd has bought a veffel, I
think fhe is quite large enough.   I would have him fit her
as frugal as poffible for I imagine fhe will come pretty High,
i: her Hull cofts £610 ster^ls.   Defire Capt Kidd to give
me timely notice of his failing to make Infurance.

I am thy Lov^e Uncle
JOSHUA HOWELL

To John Ladd Howell, Merchant of Philad.

Bofton 24th May 1762

Sir

This ferves to acknowledge the Receipt of & return you
my thanks for your Friendly Favour p laft poft, and am not
a little pleafed that your Journey proved fo agreeable.   I
rejoice with you in the profpect of a peace with Germany,
the confequence of wh^ch will induce France & Spain to an
accommodation, and as Adm^l Pocock is arrived in the Weft
Indies and part of the troops are embarked from Martineco
and Guadeloupe for Jamaica, that, that Ifland will be Se-
cured againft any attempt the French & Spanifh may make
to reduce it, and that we may turn the Tables by our endeavors for the reduction of Cuba.   We have likewife with

us an Embargo on provifions, but I, after being detained a
fortnight, thro' much difficulty by petitioning the Gov^{nr} &
Coun^d &c. have obtained Liberty to clear out near 130
Barrels of flour for Quebec, but they have obliged me to
take all my pork on fhore, however, I hope it will be attended with advantage to me.   I expeft to fail in about
three days.   You have a Return of the compliments of my
Father & Mother to yourfelf & Mrs. Howell, who heartily
wifh you every thing that may render the marriage State
agreeable, and in cafe He fucceeds at Jamaica, as he pur-
pofes a remittance from thence to Philad. you may depend
the bufinefs will pafs thro' your hands & is much obliged
for your kind care of the Letters which you propofe to forward by the firft oppor^{ty} after the Embargo is off.   You
may depend on a Line and price currt. from me p firft opportunity on my arrival at Quebec, and must beg you will
believe me to be your Sincere

Friend & Humble Servant

JONAS CLARKE MINOT.

New York May 27 1763

To JOHN LADD HOWELL PHILAD.

Coufin Johnny

We reacht here about 7 o'clock laft evening all well &
sup^{ed} at Allicocke's, have very agreeable Lodgings next
door, nothing Remarkable happened on the Journey, the
women had a fine time being Near Four hours crossing the
Bay with our wooden fails.   Our Carriage and horfes were

landed on Long Ifland at the ferry oppofite N. Y. and we intend to crofs the Sound to morrow for Flufhing, I need fay little about Bufinefs for I make no Doubt thou will do the beft for me and defpatch Shiverick's veffel.

I hope Jacky is a good Lad and carefully attends to affift thee Give mine and thy Aunt Keaty's love to Frances, Josa, Hannah Ladd, Polly Parker & Benny Swet, J. & H. Sansom and all friends & Relations who may inquire after us, our Journey fo far has been full as agreeable as we expected. I hope thou haft wrote a few lines and fent word how all our frds are & please to tell little Keaty her Daddy & Mammy fend their Love to Her. Tell Sally Hafmer & Meany that their miftrefs hopes to hear a good account of them on her return.

New York June 2 1763

Thine receiv^d which are full and quite agreeable and make no doubt of thy having done the beft in my abfence I can't fay when we fhall be at Home, for the women think now they are abroad its as well to take time as they may not have the like opportunity. We returned from Long Ifland laft third day and were well pleafed to receive thy Uncle Fifher's Letters with an account of our family—I have wrote fome little account of our tour to Uncle Fifher to which I refer thee. Capt Southcott was failed before I came to N. Y. Shiverich I hope will be difpatched & I would have Burrows get the Grape loaded as foon as poffible. Capt Kidd I make no doubt will take the neceffary care refpecting the Hannah.   I leave that affair Entirely to his management.

> I am with Refpect
> Thy Loving Uncle
> *JOSHUA HOWELL.*

To John Ladd Howell

> *New York December 20th 1765*

Dear Jack

I embrace this opportunity to refer you to a Letter I have wrote your Uncle, I muft not omit to inform you that I am ufing my endeavors to eftablish a weekly Club (of the true Sons of Liberty) by the Name, ftile, and Title of the Liberty Club who will ever be vigilant in difcovering & ready to prevent any attempt, that may be made to infringe upon the juft rights of ours and our fellow fubjects. I would have you propofe fomething of this kind in your City.   Such organizations being the beft means of keeping up the fpirit of Liberty, which now reigns in America.   I have but to add that Mrs Lamb Joins in kind Compl to you & Mrs Howell.   Dear Jack

> Your Affectionate Friend
> *JOHN LAMB*

To John Ladd Howell By the Brig Ranger Capt Pickles Horsley Down Eng.

> *Sherborn Lane No 16 Lombard Street, London*
> *22 Sept. 1767*

Sir Your letter to Mr. Kilby with whom I am in Part-

nerfhip, I have opened.   Mr Kilby is at prefent at Suffex.
I am acquainted with your name and have an efteem for
Joshua Howell with whom I had frequent correfpondence
during my refidence at Albany fome years ago.   If you
will call on me I will endeavor to Serve you and fhall rep-
refent you to Mr. Kilby.   I am Sir

Your Huble Serv:

JAMES SYME

To John Ladd Howell A. C. P. Head of Elk

Philad. July 24th 1778

Dear Confin

    Yours of the 18th received p your fon Jofhua.   I waited
upon Mr. Hollingfworth, in Confequence of it, he thinks
Jofhua is not fufficiently Qualified to enter into the Bufinefs
of a Store and as there is no School in this City fit to put a
young lad to.   He and Several others recommend Powell's
School at Burlington.   Levi Hollingfworth promifes he
will not take an Apprentice for fix or nine months if you
Send Jofhua to School.   As I expect to go to Lancafter in
a day or two, I fhall defire Mr Powell to fend an anfwer
to Brother Hugh who will acquaint you of its contents

I am Dear John

Yours Sincerely

JACOB S. HOWELL

To John Ladd Howell Head of Elk.

Philad. Aug 10, 1778

Refpected Confin

    When my brother Jacob went to Lancafter he re-

quefted that I fhould write to Mr Powell he (*i e* Jacob)
intimating that there would be the moft likely place for
thy fon Jofhua to get that knowledge in Mathematics which
you defired he fhould have, and which is requifite to qualify
him for the place intended. Mr Powell informs me that
he will take him and will do that Juftice by him that the
preference deferves. His prefent price is £80 p annum
which he fays " upon mature reflection you will fee is in-
adequate to £26 p ann. before the prefent troubles began. " I heard from Capt Howell Laft week, was well,
& at Head Quarters on White Plains

I am with Due Refpeft
Yours &c
SAMUEL HOWELL, jr

N. B.—Quarterly payments moft agreeable to Mr
Powell.

———

September 17th 1780

Dear John

My dear father bore his lingering diforder 'till laft evening about 8 o'clock. When he left this for a better world.
The time of his interment is tomorrow morning at half paft
9 o'clock.

You will inform coufin John Sparks & fuch others as you
think proper of it. Mother has fupported herfelf thro' the
fatigue of mind & Body much better than could have been
expected.

I am Dear John
Your affétionate Kinsman
JACOB S. HOWELL.

Philad. 1779

To JOHN LADD HOWELL

Dear Coufin

I enclofe a Letter which I have written to the Commis-
fioners & if thee thinks it will do, fhall be obliged to thee
if thee will feal and deliver it to them. I am very forry
to hear of thy indifpofition. I am obliged to thee for the
information about the fallen Timber, if they prove to be
mine I fhall be glad to difpofe of them, & fhall be obliged
to thee for thy affiiftance, unlefs they are fuch as will be of
ufe on the place if wanted. Pleafe to remember my kind
love & my children's to Aunt Ladd & Coufin Frances &
Jofhua

Thy Affectionate Coufin

MARY PARKER NORRIS

———

To JOHN LADD HOWELL CANTWELLS BRIDGE

Philad. April 26 1779

My Compliments to your little Widow and yourfelf—
I now inform you that I have purchafed for her one yard
& a Quarter of Muflin as near the pattern as I could pro
cure, alfo yard of plain black gauze, which I fend agreeable
to your defire by Mr Brown—and below you have the
amt., I could get none at a lower price.

1 ¼ Muſlin @ 6odls p yard... 75
1 yd Gauze @ 30 dols p yard. 30

———

105
Cash rec'd................ 90

———

15 dollars balance due to
SARAH GOVETT

The good Man deſires his compliments to frᵈ Howell &
acquaents him that there is nothing more new than what he
will find in the paper that envelopes the Widows Gauze &
Muſlin—except an account of a party of Gen. Lincoln's
Troops having had an advantage over a band of Indians
& Tories in Georgia,

———

To JOHN LADD HOWELL PHILADELPHIA

May 3rd 1779

Dear Jack

Incloſed you have a letter for my friend Which I flatter
myſelf you will deliver or forward—I have not taken any
notice to him of what I intend to do. you may therefore
act as you think proper and treat the ſubject with that deli-
cacy which I know you maſter of - I am ſenſible that Mr
S—— is anxious to have the matter ſettled as well as myſelf, therefore, hope you will have all the ſucceſs in this
ſmall Negociation which I have impoſed on you as I can
wiſh

Wishing you health & happiness I can only inform you how much I am your

Affectionate Cousin

JOS. HOWELL

———

Mr. John Ladd Howell Near Woodbury, N. J.

Trenton Oct. 4 1780

Dr Sir

I have been dancing attendance at Trenton since I had the pleasure of seeing you last and have at length accomplished my Purpose in getting the promotion which was my due and that of the Officers of Brigade I leave town at two o'clock P. M. News I have none—you no Doubt have heard enough of Arnold and let his Name serve instead of Treachery as the letters A-R-N-O-L-D have a much blacker cast than that of Treachery, Hell, Damnation or what you please. America is a fruitful Country—it has produced a Worthy Superior to a Cæsar, a Cato, or Cyrus and all the Tribe of Ancient Heroes and Patriots, it has likewise produced a Villain Superior to a Nero or Devil and all the Black infernal List. I have nothing more to say but that I am yours by Command Also by common Affection and Mystic Union

J. N. CUMMING

Major 1st Regt Jersey

To John Ladd Howell Gloucester Favd by Mr. Carpenter.

Morris Town Oct 10th 1780

Dr Sir

Thus far on my Way to Camp—A good opportunity offering I would not let it pafs although I have but little to write—Major Lee on Saturday laft took a Capt and fifty men on Bergen Point.

The Capt named Ward is a Deferter and without Doubt will be Andre-fied.

The Army are now returned to Lotowa about twenty miles from this Place I expect to join them in a few days.

> With Respect
> Your Very Hble Servt
> *JOHN N. CUMMING.*

To John Ladd Howell Gloucester County By L. I. Bloomfield.

West Point Novr 5th 1780

Dr Sir

This may inform you that your very humble fervt is in a very Cold Place, ware Old Boreas comes through the narrow Paffage of the River Hudfon guarded on each Flank by a very large Mountain, and pours forth his Vengeance on the Inhabitants of West Point, who thank God are three Thousand in Number, compofed of New england, New York and New Jersey Troops who are able at this Poft, to fight the whole Britifh Army and defeat them (provided they are well supplyed with Provifion and Clothes, the latter they are much distreffed for. This Poft has three Forts and twelve Redoubts and between or twixt you and I, it is the Strongeft Poft upon the Continent, and the Britifh well knew that Arms could not prevail and therefore had recourfe to Gold.

The Letter and Certificates figned Salley Warren directed to Gen Arnold you may be affured are real ; She is a Sutler and W——e at this Poft. The New Arrangement of the Army gives (I believe) general Satisfaction. Being the youngeft Major I fhall be under the unhappy Neceffity of retiring upon half pay unlefs Major Rofs or Hollingfhead choufe to retire which I much wifh for. If they do not I fhall spend Part of the Winter with you and endeavour to gain a Refidence in your County on account of the efteem I have for many of its Citizens and you Sir in particular.

I diflike the Part the Quakers have taken in the prefent Contest but love their Simplicity of Manners and Drefs I mean the lefs Rigid of them.

My best Respects and wifhes attend you Mrs Howell and Family with my particular Friends

I am Your Obdt Servt

J. N. CUMMING.

—

Either of the Members from Gloucefter will much oblige Major Cumming by forwarding the inclofed.

JOHN LADD HOWELL NEAR WOODBURY GLOUSTER COUNTY
TO YE CARE OF WM MILNOR AT OLD FERRY.

Camp Jerfey Hutts
Feby 24th 1781

Dr Sir

The hurry of Bufinefs and Confufion of the Times has
prevented my writing you for fome Time paft.

I am now ever with you in the Number of my Letters if
not in Substance. How are you my honeft Friends. I
hope you are well & expeft the Holyday Geese Turkeys
&c &c &c have fatened you to a great degree. I expefted
to have paid you a Vifit in the Month of April but at present am doubtful as the Marquis La Fayette with three
Regiments of Infantry will arrive at this Place tomorrow
when the Jerfey Brigade will be annexed to his command
for a fecret Expedition—We have much Converfation on
the Arrival of a French Fleet—Paul Jones we hear is in
your River—Keep up a good Heart better Times are
coming.

I Congratulate you on General Morgans fuccefs and hope
the Face of Affairs will be altered in that Department—We
live excellently in Camp upon a Variety of Difhes Viz :
Salt Beef and Ash Cake for Breakfaft. Do for Dinner and
the same for Supper provided there is any left.

Now I expeft provided I am not fled to the Elyfian
Fields that I fhall within fix months endeavour to partake
of fome of the Good Things from the bountiful Tables of

my very Good Friends in Gloufter County untill when &
ever after remember

I am Your Affectionate Friend and Obdt Hble Servt.

J. N. CUMMING.

---

from J. N. Cumming. recd. 20th March 1781.
To John Ladd Howell Near Woodbury To ye Care of
Charles Lyon

—

Jerfey Camp Mar 5th 1781

Dr Sir

I received your Numbers 8 9 & 10 and an honeft
Friend of theirs Coll Hilman—I was very happy to fee
four Companions fo cleverly intermixed and over a bowl of
Grog I perufed them. Whilft I was doing this a Letter
was put into my Hand which prevented my reperufing according to Cuftom—The Caufe was barely this it was from
a fine Girl who if something extraordinary does not prevent
I fhall make a Rib of.

She's virtuous fair fhes good and Juft,
To Wed her Ladd I furely muft.

Two Lines at one Time for a Lover may anfwer—I am
not married yet fo your Report is groundlefs—I wifh the
War was over fo that I might ufe every Effort to make up
the lofs of Men occafioned by it—You mention B. W. I
beg you would not fay any more about him for if he wont
take Pleafure in writing to his old Friend I wont be plagued
with seeing his name——Adieu yours

J. N. CUMMING.

I again attempt to write fomething More and hardly know what—You have heard all the News the Wor'd affords and I hope fhortly will hear better News than any heretofore. I am fomething of a Prognofticator—I have dreamt a Dream and Dreams may fomtimes prove true.

The purport was that Cornwallis was killed, his Army taken, Arnold delivered up and hanged—Peace declared— The United States Free and Independent &c.   I am entirely flabbergaftrated by a faternifous Brain which caufes my Ideas to be abunbulated and only remain as common

Your Affectionate Friend

J. N. CUMMING.

Remember me to thofe I love or ought to love.

———

JOHN LADD HOWELL NEAR WOODBURY GLOUSTER COUNTY.

—

Camp Dobbs Ferry July 23d 1781

Dr Sir

As yet I have had but little Leafure to write you and until now not a fingle opportunity in Confequence this will remain in poffeffion of the Author until one offers—Yefter-day a detatcht. of 5000 thoufand from the main Army went on to Morrifania the perticulars are not arrived They drove all the Britifh Heffians & Cow Boys after giving them a fine two & thirty Pounders burnt their Habitations and three fhips or veffels &c &c.   How comes on our Friends Mat-lack, Whitall &c.   I wifh they may not go to the D——C—— for my neglecting their Friends &c I have nothing more to fay except that I am with real Affection your friend

& Humble Servt

J. N. CUMINMG

Compliments &c to all Friends

JOHN LADD HOWELL NEAR WOODBURY TO YE CARE OF WM MILNOR

Chriftiana Bridge Sept 6th 1781.

Dr Sir

Yefterday when the fun was at high Merdian and all Nature feemed to rejoice at the glorious light thereof— When every Laborer was either cooking or repofing his Iron Limbs under the benign fhade of fome venerable Oak when the Cry the glorious Cry was made Count D Grafs with twenty eight fail of the Line was in the Chefapeak and that a part of the land Forces had landed in order to join the Marquis L. F. I am pitched upon by Gen Lincoln for to forward to the head of Elk the Military Stores which will amount to fixty waggons of Gunpowder and Shells & fhot in proportion.

The Mortars Cannon &c are gone on—God blefs you and yours with all the Friends and give into the Hands of G. W. the Lord of the South with his abandoned crew.

Yours Sincerely

J. N. CUMMING.

To my Friends in the County of Gloucefter

From J. N. Cumming Oct 12th 1781
Camp before York Oct 12th 1781

Dr Brother

This is the firft that I have wrote you fince the Allied
Army took this Pofition which was compleatly done on
the 29th ultimo. The 30th Coll. Scammel was made
prifoner and agreeable to Britifh Barbarity wounded after
he had furrended from this Time until the 6th of Octr
bufily employed in preparing Materials for the firft Parallel
which was opened on the evening of the Sixth within fix
hundred yds of the enemy's lines with the lofs of fix French
grenadiers—On the 9th we opened a Ten gun battery 10th
continued opening Batteries the fire from which was fo fuperior to that of the Britifh that, but few fhot are fired by
them except under cover of the Night when by their bad
Directions they are fcarce felt. Their Embraffures are
very much battered particularly by the French whofe main
Battery is oppofite to theirs ; in the Evening a hot fhot or
the explofion of a fhell from the French fet fire to the Charon
a britifh Ship of 44 Guns and confumed her with another
Veffel and on the Morning of the 11th a large Brig was
confumed by the French in the fame Manner.

The Cannonade and Bombardment increafes with us and
with the Enemy the Reverfe. This Evening we have
opened our fecond Parallel at the Diftance of 200 yds from
the Enemy's Works with the Lofs of only two Malitia and
one Regular killed. 12th The Bombardment more fevere
than yefterday. Twenty two Deferters came from the

enemy yefterday & laft night and 40 by their Acconts (which muft be imperfect) have been killed four (of which) were officers and two Commiffarys—Lord Cornwallif's Head Quarters is in a Cave—Our lofs very trivial—Camp Healthy. Provifions good. Army in high fpirits and do dutys with the greateft Cheerfulnefs—Hafte on thou God of Armies the happy Hour of the Surrender of the Lord of the South and give to thy injured Servants the American Whigge Joy of Heart in feeing the Pride of Brittain the declared Foes to Humanity reduced to proper Terms.——

My Duty, Affections Frendfhip, &c &c &c attend my neare folks, relations & Friends and as thofe of your county are well known I requeft you would communicate my Efteem to them

Intimately & Sincerely

Yours

J. N. C.

I intended to have wrote to many others of Your Vicinity but am called to Duty—I requeft you will fend either this or a Copy of the particulars to the Rev Wm Schenck at Pittfgrove informing him that I fhall write him by the earlieft opportunity.

¶ Extracts, General Orders, October 7th

Lt Coll Lawrens and Major Cumming are appointed to the Command of a Battalion of the Eight Infantry lately commanded by Coll Scammel.

JOHN LADD HOWELL ESQ. GLOUCESTER TO THE CARE OF
WILLIAM HUGG

—

12th April 1781

Dear Jack

I promifed to write you If anything happened below &
tho' Nothing extraordinary has happen'd yet I write—
What about you'll say—Why about myfelf I reply, for I
muft follow the fafhion

I often think of the fellow of Ephefus who burned
Dianna's Temple that he might be talked of through
futurity, defpairing of executing a Virtuous Act that might
Render him famous to pofterity. after Many hardy En-
counters through almoft four Years Service, I could Do
nothing to make the world to come my own (as Couley
terms it If I remember right) tho' I ardently panted after
fame, but faith like the Ephesian, either for Mifdeeds done
or fuppos'd to be done, I am famous at laft without hard
knocks or hungry Belly—By—— I write to you to Inform
you of the happy Difcovery of my Guilt by fome Ingenious
Gentlemen of the Neighborhood—I was lately but a bas-
cars'd Chriftian at moft & being modeft, would hide my
pofterior from Public View—So took a pair of Breeches to
a Tory to be made up, now sir altho' he would have made
them fooner than any other, yet thus ftands the Proof

Major. None but a Tory will give work to a Tory.

Minor. The Taylor is a Tory and I fent my work to
him.

Conclusive. Then I am a Tory   Then, a Tory would deal with the Enemy Maj.

Minor. I am a Tory. Conclus. Then I deal with the enemy. Thus you fee Ariftotle could not prove it better.

I have fent it by the ftage but this would not pafs without fpring.

(Nothing in the Boys as I hear of).

yrs   R. HOWELL*

NOTE—I put a feal to this of my own making therefore good for nothing & apply a fecond of a better kind.

R. H.

MR. JOHN LADD HOWELL NEAR WOODBURY GLOUCESTER COUNTY.

—

Philad. 14th October 1782

Refpected Friend

Your fudden departure from Gloucefter yefterday prevented my giving you an invitation to hunt this day as well as deprived me of an Opportunity of converfing with you on the fubject of the remonftrance intended to be handed in to the next General Affembly—and as I moft ardently wifh a repeal of that wicked Law I take the liberty of recommending it to you to procure as many figners as poffible, alfo your fending a copy of faid remonftrance to Col Brown at Sweedfborough, which I am fearfull has been

negle&ed & am apprehenfive it will give uneafinefs to that
part of the County fhould they be deprived of an opportunity of fhowing their difapprobation to a meafure calculated to abridge the freemen of the State of New Jerfey of
one of their moft effential privileges—Your complyance
with the above as well as writing a few Lines to Col
Browne on the Subje& I am of opinion will much oblige
the Inhabitants of Gloucefter County—I affure you it will.

Your Friend & very hble Servt

ISRAEL MORRIS junr

Mr. John Ladd Howell Philad Near Woodberry

Naffau Hall November 21ft 1782

Dr Sir

I expe&ed to have received a Letter from you before this
time which wou'd have opened a Correfpondence between
us, but as I have not, and am youngeft, think it my duty to
fend the firft ; fhould have written to you, when I wrote
to my Father and Mr (Thomas) Johnfon, but did not
know of the ftage going off fo foon, but can now have
an opportunity of writing every week. As it is necesfary to let you know how all my time is employed, fhall
endeavour to tell you in as few words as poffible.

I ftudy from about feven till ten o'clock and then recite
to Doctor Witherfpoon till about twelve ; every other Day
we have to attend on the Doctor at his own Houfe which
is about one mile diftant from this place which in good
weather is a very pleafant Walk, We Live exceeding

well, and I want for nothing, but fome good fruit, and to
hear from all my friends, there is no news at prefent.
You'll be pleafed to give my Compliments to Mrs. Howel
& Jos Howel

> I am yr. Humble Servt &c.
> WILLIAM HUGG iunr

Mr John Ladd Howell Near Woodbury

> Naffau Hall Jany 9th 1783

Dear Sir

Yours dated 29th of laft month came to hand laft evening, I was called away from a very diverting entertainment,
to receive your letter and fome others, which I was very
happy to receive, but am forry very forry indeed to hear
that you are unwell, but I am glad to hear that you are on
the mending hand, and I hope that Time, patience and
flannels, may reftore you to perfect health, and will fet you
on the little Grey mare (Fly) again, I meant to have told
you in the prior part of this letter, what entertainment I
was at, but forgot, tho' I muft tell you in the posterior part,
left you fhould think I was fomewhere, where I had not
bufinefs, but fir I have not been at any place, or in any
company, fince I have been here, that I am afhamed, or
afraid my friends fhould know of, and hope I can always
fay fo ; The Entertainment that I was diverted with was
in hearing the fenior clafs fpeak, which was really very
entertaining, there were a great number of Gentlemen, and
Ladies prefent, who faid that it was perform'd very well.

I hope that if you live till the next commencement your curiofity may lead you to come, and fee them fpeak I dare fay you would not repent your ride, there are no news at prefent. I am your friend and Hubl Servt

WILLIAM HUGG junr

Pleafe to prefent my compliments to Mrs Howell and Jofhua.

———

To Mr Benj. Paschall Henry B Paschall Ebenezer Worth & Margt. his Wife John Ladd Howell & Frances his wife The Legal Representatives of Mary Pearson dcd The Legal Representatives of Eliza Armitt dcd & The Legal Representatives of Ann Paschall dcd

Philadelphia Feb 1783

Pleafe to take notice that a Jury is fummoned to meet at the Houfe of Benjamin Paschall, Jur on Monday the 24th Inst. at ten o'clock in the Morning to make Partition or valuation of two pieces or Parcels of Land Situate in King-feffing Townfhip Philadelphia County part of the Real Eftate of John Paschall late of Darby in the County of Chefter deceafed at which time and place you may attend if you think proper.

Your Humble Servt

WM WILLS Shf.

To John Ladd Howell, in Philad.

Antigua May 5, 1767

Your Kind Letter I Received Dated Sep. 3rd By Capt Harper, & hopes your Goodnefs will Excufe my Long Abfence in not anfwering yours Sooner. I Received they Money for they Negro Boy and returns you many thanks for your Trouble. My fon Harry has been to the French Iflands and was the time he was there very ill but is now come to Antigua & is much better than he was there. This letter comes by one who is married to a Near Relation of Ours, whofe name is Henry Bryn, who Is come to fettle his children for they Benefit of Their Education. He is a very Sober Induftrious man and I fhould be glad if Some of Our Family would make themfelves known to him. I Shall write to my Coufin Frances Soon.

For my warning has been very Short By this opportunity.

My Son Harry joins in Love to You & Wife
I Remain with Hearty wifhes
for your Health & Welfare
ELIZABETH HODGE*

PASCHALL LETTERS.

To Frances Howell Near Woodbury

Darby Jan 9th 1781

Dear Sifter

Our Dear Mother has through a Long Fitt of illnefs ar-

---

*Elizabeth Hodge was a niece of Mrs. Dr. John Paschall, jr.

rived at length to her Defired port, though Great the lofs
to us yet her happinefs fhould be our Joy, yet Real Joy can
hardly overcome our Natural weaknefs, without a Steady
Attention to that Divine Principle which tells us fhe is
Really happy ; which happinefs we muft not envy by De-
firing her longer Stay in Mifery.   We have propofed to
bury her on Fifth Day at ten o'clock in the morning ; of
which pleafe to acquaint Aunt Ladd & who Elfe thee may
think proper.   The reft of us are in Some Degree of
health—All at prefent from

Thy Friend & Brother

HENRY PASCHALL

To John Ladd Howell,

Phil. Old Ferry Mar 10 1781

Dear Brother

   Having an opportunity by a ftranger I write to acquaint
you that our Sifter Ann continues very ill—I fhould be
glad to hear how you all are, and my little girl, I do not
know when I fhall go over again to See you & bring her
home ; pleafe to fend her by thy fon the firft opportunity,
I have began a Chimical Opperation which I cannot leave
this twelve days.   I fear fhe will be troublefome

Farewell

HENRY PASCHALL

To Frances Howell

Derby April 21 1781

Our Sifter Grows worfe daily and feems very uneafy for want of thee & would not be Satisfied Without my Sending for thee—I think it can't be long fhe will Detain thee here, if thee can any way Leave home a few Days—She often fays Oh I wifh Sifter Howell were here & feems fo diftreft for want of thee—If fhe contiuues and grows better I will fee to get the back again. All at prefent but Love

from

HENRY PASCHALL

———

Derby April 27 1781

Dr Brother

Our Siftter Ann Continues Very ill—She will Not Give up that her Sifter Should leave her, as fhe don't Expeét to be many Days before fhe leaves us, Frances would be glad to fee thee over & next Fifth Day we are to have a Vendue of the Superfluous Goods which our Mother left, if She our Sifter fhould not prevent it by a Deceafe which I am Doubtfull off—All at Prefent but Love—from thy Fr^d & Brother

HENRY PASCHALL

———

To Frances Howell near Woodbury

Kingfeffing 6th of 3rd mo 1807

Dear Aunt.

At laft I have taken up my pen to write to thee—When

I left thee 'aft Summer ᵀ a'moft expected to Spend a week or two with thee in the fall to affift at the foundation of the fhell work thee talked of doing for me, and tho' I did not come I hope thee did not forget it, I think thee faid I muft procure a handfome box to put the fhell work in, now I wifh to know the dimenffions that I may provide one, it will be delightful to have fuch a curiofity of thy making. Since I have feen you, the incidents that have happened in our family, and the addition of Young Joshua to thine, makes the time feem long—Margaret's marriage, which was an important change in our houfe—the birth of John's daughter and now the death of Wolton has kept us bufy and agitated, now we appear likely to have a calm.

The night before Wolton's death, he bid the man who fat up with him to burn his will, which he did, this was a difappointment to Lydia Rudolph for fhe with the reft of us fuppofed he had provided fomething for her—he certainly had the means. With refpect to writing to thee my Aunty I have been but a bad girl, and I believe I muft not promife to do better for the future left I fhould not be able to do fo and fo forfeit the little credit I have remaining— but I dare fay thee thinks when I do begin that I don't know when to ftop, fo I will afk to be remembered to you all and bid thee farewell

> Thy Affectionate niece
> *ANN PASCHALL*

¶ In connection with this letter, it will be fitting to introduce a note of ceremonious comment on Frances Howell's skill in arranging shell work—there is a specimen of her work still extant:

MONUMENTS OF PRAISE IS DUE.

This cabinet of natural curiofities was conftructed by the Superlative hands of Mrs. Frances Pafchall Howell of New Jerfey Gloucefter County—To whofe genius and induftry I humbly Subfcribe myfelf to with refpects and veneration for fo good a fpecimen of natural tafte performed in her 64th year of Age.

From her Moft refpectfully

W WOLTON

See how beauteous nature diffufe her various colours And art untutored arrange them in fet ordors.

———

To Frances Howell in Jersey Near Woodbury,
Bradford 21 of 7 mo. 1807

Dear Sifter

I received thy Letter with my Stays for by which I am much Obliged to thee. They are a Great Deal too big but that can be remedied—I am glad to heare of your Healths—My Hufband grows weak, but favoured with his fenfes yet, how long he is to be continued is not for us to know—I wifh that Patience may have Poffeffion—Sally's family is favoured with Good Health but fatigued with getting the Harvefts, the weather makes much work to fave the grain and they have a Great Deal of feveral forts,

Wheat, Rye & Barly—before they get it Dry enough to Draw in Comes a Shower of rain, but hope thro' favour they may fave the Bleffing beftowed upon us—Tell Jofy to fend a barrel of fhad to the ferry and a Line to let them know where to leave the money for it.   You may at any time fend any thing you wifh by yᵉ Stage.   The Stage to Weft Chefter runs twice a week from Thomas Calverts, North Fourth Street I fhall lodge my letters there as it is difficult any other way.

Thy Sifter
MARGARET WORTH

Dear Sifter

I have never received a line from thee fince I faw thee the Diftance is not fo Great, but that we might have more Communication, Neither is our immediate bufinefs fo pref-fing as to Deter us from writing.   I know of no excufe but Negleft, I often think of thee and fhould be glad to have thee near me, as it can't be many years that I fhall be in Mutability, and if it may pleafe the Great Author of our being to Prepare us for a Happy Eternity we will not care how foon.

I mifs my Dear Companion, but my Lofs is nothing to his gain he was favoured to Stay till he was found ready for the Chainge I believe it may be faid, it was Sorrow at Night but Joy in the morning with him.   Our brother Henry is very Earneft for my Coming to Derby to Refide but while I am favoured with the ufe of my Mental faculties

I fhall not leave a certainty for an uncertainty—at my time of Life to change my Habitation, would hurt my feelings much—I am favoured with the neceffaries of Life and that is fufficient—I intend to fit at my own table and fhall always be Glad of My Friend's Company

I wifh thee to Come here Soon When thee may be better informed of my Present State. Leaving thee to the Dispoffal of an All Sufficient God, Shall Conclude

Thy Affectionate Sifter

MARG: WORTH

To JOHN LADD ESQR NEW JERSEY

Philadelphia April 15th 1764.

Dear Uncle

Not till yefterday could my mother be prevail'd on to keep her Chamber notwithftanding fhe could not get up nor down without help, nor even in or out of bed or Chair when fitting, and then fhe would not have confented had she been able to fit up over ten minutes at a time, in the morning fhe tho't to have fat by the fire, but in raifing up to drefs like to have fainted away, yet fhe continued very cheerfull and ftill does as much fo as ever & I am almoft ready to think her Spirits higher—laft evening between 9 & 10 we tho't her going off, fhe was rouf'd by our going in to the room & faid fhe had been in a dofe, fhe refted pretty well & this morning feem'd very chearfull but more defirous of feeing Sally than ever, about Eleven I went into

the room when I was much furprifed at her change, and
tho't every breath was her laft, my Partner was juft going
to fet out for my Sifter who is juft come—1 o'clock, &
mother again feems more chearfull again—but fhe is fo extremely weak and changes fo often that I expeft her death
will be very fudden, efpecially as fhe is quite free from pain
or ficknefs at Stomack, her Cough this morning & laft night
has been very troublefome—I much doubt her continuing
twenty four hours

I intend to get fome of my relations to enquire of her
where fhe would chufe to be buried—Coufin C. Norris &
his wife was to fee her laft evening & was much furprifed
to fee her in the condition fhe is & alive—I heard Uncle
Parker intended up yefterday or very foon—Pleafe to remember her to Aunt in which Fanny Joins & in Love to
thee with Thy Loving Nephew

JNO. LADD HOWELL

To John Ladd Howell in Philad.

Darby 1772

My Dear

I am glad to heare thee is a mending and I hope it will
pleafe God to reftore thee to perfeft health—our Son got
home fafe thanks be to God—My deare it feems as if thee
had been Gone a weake from me already. If thee ftays
till Seven day I fhall think the time long, but if it don't
fuit thee to come fooner I muft bare thy abfence with pa-

tience. We are all middling well, thank God, Sister Nancy sends her love and thanks for the snuff

I am thine Affectionately

FRANCES HOWELL.

To FRANCES HOWELL AT DERBY

Philadelphia Feb 3rd 1773

Cousin Arthur Howell was at Woodbury Meeting on Sunday & hearing of Sally being married, next morning called to see her—She was pleased to see him—I have not seen Arthur since to speak to him, so that I know no more of the matter than when I was at Derby. Our Friends in Town are well. Clement Biddle's wife died the Day before yesterday in the afternoon.

I am, with my love to all at Derby

Your Affectionate

JNO. LADD HOWELL

To FRANCES HOWELL

Philadelphia 2nd Decem^{br} 1778

My Dear

I missed seeing Joseph Hugg but have wrote the inclosed Letter to him requesting him to let thee have Six Hoggs & three Quarters of Beef with Salt to Cure it, also some unrendered fat. The quantity of Fat thee must let him know. I have also desired him to inform thee when & where to send for the Hoggs &c.

Send the letter to him by fome careful hand

The Salt boᵗ of Ezra Jones thee will get by fending to Uncle Samuels—Coufin Nancy Howell was married the Night I was over with thee—to Aaron Afhbridge—the Old People feem much Troubled. The young ones are now at Chefter. Let me hear as foon as poffible Send thy Letters, for me, to thee Care of Coufin Samuel Howell. Uncle Samuel's Son. I fhall leave town this Afternoon Remember Me to Aunt &c.

I am Thy Affectionate
JOHN LADD HOWELL

———

To Joshua Howell, Jr. Burlington N. J.
Philad. Feb 12th 1779

Dear Joshua

Yefterday Afternoon on my arrival at Darby I was informed of Father Pafchall's being taken very ill, before I got to the Houfe he had expired, they propofed to bury him on Sunday. I am going over for your Mother. Would have you come down.

I am your Affectionate
JNO LADD HOWELL

———

To Johnathan Rumford
Elk May 20 1778

Your forwarding the enclofed letters to Col. Francis Wade and Mr Chalonor by firft opportunity fhall efteem a favor. On my return here yefterday found letters from

Chaloner that in confequence of the Enemy being about to leave Phil. our troops were fhortly going to the Jerfeys & orders from his Excellency for immediate and large fupplies of flour & provifions to be forwarded on for them. The want of waggons is now fo great, that any you can induce to enter the fervice and Send down here for Loading would be rendering at this time the moft effential fervice. Your real attachment to the Caufe affures me you will readily excufe my freedom in writing you on the fubject.

JOHN LADD HOWELL

JoshuA Howell, Jr. Mr. Thomas Powell's School Burlington N. J.

Cantwell's Bridge Decem. 21 1778

Dear Jofhua

I wrote the 13th Inft. and inclofed Sixty dollars £22.10. I hope you have received it and paid Mr. Powell for your firft Quarters Board & Schooling, inform me in your next. Yours of the 4th I received the 14th I am pleafed with the information you give me of Mr. Powell's attention to his School. There are three things to which I at prefent wifh your clofe attention, and are more than mere accomplifhments to the Man of Bufinefs as well as the Gentleman—Accuracy in figures, True Spelling and correct writing, for the firft pay a clofe attention to Your Arithmetic, for the two laft let your leifure Hour be employed in reading the beft authors as well for amufement as inftruction, & pay proper attention to what you read, Mr. Powell

will affift your Judgment in the choice of the Authors as well
as the Subject you may choofe to Study, let me as a Friend
advife my Dear Joshua to mingle Bufinefs with Pleafure.

> *January 5th 1779*

I wish you a happy New Year, & many of them. Yours
of the 26 Decem from Philad. I received the 31ft.   I hope
you croffed the River without accident.

> I Am my Dear Joshua
> > Your Affectionate
> > *JNO LADD HOWELL*

To John Ladd Howell Cantwell's Bridge

> *Philad Feb 8 1779*

Inclofed I fend the King of England's fpeech read and
profit therefrom, it is in my humble opinion sufficient to
reform the moft hardened Whigs or (which is the fame thing
in the Idea of others) to frighten us into a compliance with
their te:ms---it is laughable enough to hear our oppofitions
talk in the manner they do

> > Your Coufin
> > *SAMUEL HOWELL Jr*

Wm Govett Philad.

> *Cantwell's Bridge Jan 26 1779*

Info'm me of the ftate of Jofhua Howell, Jun. If you
have any news forward it.   The Rheumatifm in my hands
and th: Gout in my feet attacked me two weeks fince.   I
am no v about again but it is with difficulty I write there-

fore after prefenting my Compliments to yourfelf & Sally
you'll excufe my adding further for a few days than that I
am

Yours sincerely

J. L. HOWELL

A word on the times tho' with Pain The calling in the
Comiffions of May & April 77 & 78 has already been made
a means to raife the Necefaries of Life.   What think you
of Wheat £5 & Flour £18.   Formerly we were wont
to fay O ! poor old England, but now it fhould be—rare
times Old times forever.   Pleafe to fend forward the letter
to Jofhua it contains fomething of Confequence therefore
find a fafe conveyance

Yours as ufual

J. L. H.

———

To Joshua Howell Jr. & Frances Howell Burlington N J

Jan 26 1779

Dear Jofhua : Enclofed is one hundred & fixty dollars pay
Mr Powell Fifty Pounds & take a rect I have been confined
with the Gout for two weeks but have got out again—yet it is
with great pain I write which muft plead my excufe to Mr.
Powell—Show him this letter.   Do not be uneafy about
me, my ftay muft be longer than I expected—If you want
anything let me know.   As I imagine you will have fome
of the money that is called in & will not readily pafs I now
enclofe 112 dollars

Your Affectionate

JNO LADD HOWELL

JNO WILKINS ESQR
Woodbury July 2nd 1782 P. M. 4 o' Clock

Dear Sir

Your Letter of the 28th ult. I from the File at Col. Hillmans Just received—hearing you were to reap this Day, I intended tho' unaſked to invite myſelf to Dinner, & converſe with you on the ſubjeƈt, on which you wrote, not at the ſame time knowing of the Letter. That I have been a Delinquent I confeſs—the cenſures of illiberal & buſie perſons I deſpiſe—

Yet your duty to the Publick, ſhould & ought to direƈt to ſhow no partiality—

I ſhall reap, I expeƈt on Friday, & if I have not the pleaſure of your compy at Dinner on that Day before the 10th I ſhall call on you—

I muſt confeſs my obligations to you are ſuch—that I cannot conclude without a perfeƈt & ſincere aſſurance of my laſting Friendſhip

JNO LADD HOWELL

MAY 8TH 1782 TO THOS. JOHNSON
Gloucefter County May 8 1782

Sr

Shall I thank you for the performance or non-performance of your promiſe on the laſt Sunday—which—either or neither———

The Poſtſcript—I met with it in the city—to encourage

literary performances my Friend and old acquaintance Mr.
Ofwald was induced to add to the number of his fubfcribers
the name of your humble Servant

J. L. H.

To take on State
I'd ever hate
Even was mine a Manor
Tho yet forfooth
I muft in truth
This room call Hall of Candour

The effects of Gout make writing painful to the Wrift—
when you call here I fuppofe I fhall fee you——

Mr. Johnson

Gloucefter County Candor Hall May 9th 1782

Sr

If you have no objection—I invite you to a familiar,
friendly, fociable and literary correfpondence on any fubject, at all opportunities I fhall be glad of your Signature
Candor & filence fhould be the Motto

J. L. H.

Mr. Johnson

Candor Hall May 10th 1782

Sr

You perhaps may have heard of men riding for their
Lives, not that at this prefent moment I wifh you to think

I am on the back of my favorite Fly—yet returning home from one of the Vulcanian breed I received yours of this date—unfealed—in future feal Curiofity is an impertinent & predominant paffion—rather would I have my efcritoire opened—than my Letter——

I am much pleafed that you have fo readily taken the hint of a Correfpondence

J. L. H.

I have not room to rhyme
And nature faith I ought to dine.

————

Mr. John Ladd Howell Near Woodbury
*May 10th 1782 from Thos Johnfon recd fame Day at Noon
Johnfon Hall May 10th*

Mr. Howell
Sr

Living at the Hall of Candor—Candid you ought to be —the fault is but half mine—give the other to Jos—full of religion in the morning—of frolic in the evening. The poftfcript might have been at the Devil for him—You have been in town—You tell me no news—mark that—Ofwald deferves encouragement—I am glad you fubfcribe—literary merit fhould be cherifhed by the Literati.

Hog trials to morrow—H—— in the chair—mum— Johnfon Hall in the road to the Court houfe—you know you will be welcome to

Your humble Servant
THOMS JOHNSON

To the new hall of Candor
I hope foon to Wander
And politics talk over Toddy
But there muft be no rout
With your pain & your Gout——
Be cheerful in mind and in body

———

THE HBL. THOMAS JOHNSON SECTY

Candor Hall May 13 1782

Sir

Yours of yefter evening was put into my hands paft noon of this Day, not from the negleft of the bearer was the delivery delayed to that late Hour, but owing to the *Idiofixcrafy* of my conftitution about the time of Sol's appearance, I was taken ill—my Pillow was part of my fupport 'till one o'clock—when I gave *prefence*—that Fly would behave I did not doubt—the Salubrious draught I make no doubt exhilerated the Spirits & occafional convivial Mirth—Spelling I am no mafter but to *adulterife* the name Jofhua I fhd. think Jofh. or Joufh or Gawfh—not Jos——

In troth not much matter
As we mean each to befmatter

Upon receipt of copies, your preceeding one fhall be answered I am not yet starborn

tho' your Humble Servant

HOWELL

Mr John Ladd Howell Near Woodbury

Johnson Hall Novr 6th 1782

What is become of you my Lord? Are you dead or alive. If the former, immediately inform me, if in your power, what reception King Pluto gave to a Lord of the Federal Union. Has he depofed decrepid Charon, and made your Lordfhip Governor of Styx? for fomething either mortal or fpirit told me you had purchafed a Boat. As I look upon Charons office to be the moft lucrative in his Tartarean Majeftys dominions; on your fecretary's arrival, I hope your Excellency will appoint him Treafurer. If you are alive—'tis moft probable you are preparing for a Voyage to Kamtfchatka as the genial feafon now flourifhes in *that mild climate*

Whether on earth or below the Earth let me fee you or hear from you if Leave of abfence can be obtained or pen ink and paper procured for Love or Money. Suppofing you to be in the land of the Living the following Lines are humbly dedicated to your Lordfhip by your Lordfhips moft obedient Sec & Servt

T. J.

In lofty ftrains while Poets fing
Columbia's praife or Gallia's king
Of armies conquered cities won
The matchlefs Acts of Washington
My mufe attempts far humbler lays
She writes for pleafure not for praise

Content if you my Lord admire
The artlefs warblings of her Lyre
Nigh Delaware's majeftic flood
Placed in the Centre of a Wood
Whofe shades afford a fafe retreat
From all the turmoils of the Great
When penfive folitude remains
And mufing Contemplation reigns
A Dome appears nor great nor fmall
And by the Mufe named Candor Hall

Tho' near to this calm Seat refide
Strife faction hatred envy pride
You live at eafe and with your wife
Contemn the Village-vex'd with Strife
And quite my Lord from Party free
Can laugh at Party rage with me
And feated o'er the focial Bowl
Give loofe to all the Flow of foul
Like tuneful Horace pomp defpife
Be fometimes merry fometimes wife
Ee'r chearful and ferenely gay
Devote to Friendfhip every Day

LETTERS MILITARY

For Mr. John Howell Deputy Commissary.

Philadelphia March 1st 1776.

Sir

You being appointed Deputy Comiffary of Provifions to

the Second Pennfylvania Battalion under the Command of Colonel Arthur St. Clair now under marching orders for Canada. You will Pleafe to obferve to leave written inftructions at every Stage, Directed to the feveral Captains belonging to the Battalion that they fign two returns for what Provifions their Companies may receive from the Perfons you may Contract with, one of which to be delivered to you at Albany, & the other to be left with thofe who you have Contracted with & according to the feveral Returns delivered you at Albany by the Captains, (where you are to remain untill the whole Battalion arrive) you are to fettle with the Perfon you employ. If you think it necesfary to depofit a fmall Sum of money with thofe perfons you procure your Provifions from, you may do it, as many Perfons will be anxious to have a fmall Pledge for a Security for their undertaking.

You will provide as you go on to Albany for the whole Battalion which will confift of Seven Hundred Men, but you muft obferve to make a Contract with thofe Perfons who undertake to provide for the Troops that you will not pay for any more Provifions than what is Iffued to the Troops, as it is too accuftomary for many people to take advantage of Troops on their March.

As to Beef you had better not apply for any as you will have no Butcher with you to Kill, therefore give them Pork altogether.

The officers of the Firft Battalion did not draw their Rations on their March, I therefore allowed them for

their Breakfasts, Dinners & Suppers but with a Caution
against extravagance.

Should you be so fortunate as to go by water up the
North River, I would advise you to leave your Horse behind.

at your Arrival at Albany you deliver up the Troops to
the Commissary General of the Northern Department.

each Colonel draws 6 Rations

D. Col.	"	5	"
Major	"	4	"
Capt	"	3 (?)	"
Lt. Col.	"	2	"
Ensign	"	2	"
Surgeon	"	2	"
Mate	"	2	"
Chaplain	"	2	"

As to the Rout & different Stages where you are to make
Provisions you must be governd by the directions of the
Commanding Officer of the Battalion which I shall furnish
you with.

I imagine the Eleven Hundred Dollars you have been
furnished with will be sufficient, but should a further sum
be necessary for the service your Drafts on me shall be duly
Honoured.

  CARPENTER WHARTON Commissary.

To Mr. JOHN LADD HOWELL PHILADELPHIA.

  New York June 22 1776.

Sir
  Not hearing from you till the Day before yesterday when

both your Letters came together I engaged˙ an Affiftant in
my Office.   But if you are difengaged there is very good
Birth in the Quarter Mafter General'ſ Office.   Allowance
Capt'ſ Pay & 2 Rations.   If you should accept it & any
Thing afterwards offer in my Power you may depend upon
my rendering you what (?) Service I can.

I am Sir,

Your moſt Obed. & very

Hbbl Serv.

JOS. REED.

———•———

To Mr. Gustavus Risberg & Mr. John Ladd Howell.
Phila. July 14, 1776.

A Number of Troops from Maryland are expected in
Town this Evening and the Quarters which might ſerve a
ſmall part of them in the Barracks being infected with the
Small Pox, I have confulted the Honorable Congreſs, who
are of opinion that I ſhould make uſe of the Churches &
Meeting Houſes in caſe of Neceſſity.   Therefore (having
alſo their Opinion thereon) I hereby Order that you apply
for & obtain the Keys of the Preſbyterian Meeting Houſe &
Friends Meeting House both in Market Street, & there
Quarter the Troops which will arrive here this Evening or
To morrow, & when Neceſſity requires your making uſe
of places of Worship that you take them in turns without
partiality, & Only when the ſervice abſolutely requires it

Charging the Troops to refrain from damaging the Buildings in any way whatfoever.

CLEMENT BIDDLE

D. Qur. Mr. Genl.

OATHS OF ALLEGIANCE OF JOHN LADD HOWELL.

I DO hereby CERTIFY, That John Ladd Howell of the City of Philada Merch't. Hath voluntarily taken and fubfcribed the AFFIRMATION of Allegiance and Fidelity, as directed by an Act of General Affembly of Pennfylvania, paffed the 13th day of June, A.D. 1777. Witnefs my hand and feal, the fifteenth day of Auguft A.D. 1777

o........o   *JNO. ORD*

: L. s. :

o·······o   No. 1002

Printed by John Dunlap.

State of New Jerfey.

This may Certify Whom it may Concern That Mr. John Ladd Howell Hath Voluntarily taken and Subfcribed the Oaths of Abjuration and Allegiance According to Law, Given under my Hand this Tenth Day of October, Anno Domini 1778.

Gloucefter Sst.   *JOS. HUGG.*

Camp Valley Forge Jany 12tb 1778

To Mr. John Ladd Howell,

Sr. His Excellency having thought it neceſſary to order a Detachment from the Grand Army to be joined by a party of G. Pattens Brigade of Militia to proceed forthwith to that part of the County of Philada & Bucks lying between the Old York road & Delaware River under the Command of Col Stewart in order to Support and protect you and the aſſiſtant purchaſers of Live Stock ſent with you in driving & conveying ſuply to Camp as the fat Cattle Hoggs & Flour that you may purchaſe or the inhabitants can Spare allowing them a ſufficiency for their Support you are therefore required to proceed on this buſineſs and Receive and take from the Several Farmers all the Fatt Cattle Hoggs, Salt pork & Flour not wanted for their reſpective familys uſe and Load the Same to Camp under ſuch Guard as Col Stewart may furniſh giving the Owners receipts for the Same to be paid for at Such Rates as the Legiſlature of this State have or may by Law affix and giving them an aſſurance that all thoſe who do agreeable to his Excellys procl. thereto their Cropps and deliver the Wheat at Such Mills as you fix upon Shall have protection for the quantity neceſſary for their ſupport which you are to give them in writing & for the Qt deliv. at the Mills they ſhall receive in Ready money the price p Bl allowed by Law I am in behalf of C. C. Blaine D. C. G. of Purchaſes.

Prices affix'd by Law
Flour 35p p cwt

Wheat 12p p Bushl

Your moſt obedt.

JOHN CHALONERS A. C. of Ps.

On Publick Service John Ladd Howell Eſquire. Head Quarters.

the bearer Dr. Howell is going upon Publick buſineſs

Eph. Blaine D. C. G.

Camp Valey Forge 10th. Feby. 1778 from Ephm. Blaine.

Camp Valey Forge 10th Feby. 1778.

MR. HOWELL

Sir

You will immediately proceed to the Head of Elk and deliver Mr. Huggins his Letter requeſting him without a moments loſs of time to forward all the Indian Meal and ſalt Proviſions he has and Acquaint him how great our Demand is, the Meal is wanted imediately for the use of the ſick. from thence proceed to Dover and Deliver Mr. Mc. Garment his letter, and requeſt him to uſe Every exertion to forward all the proviſſions he has by Water and Waggons, the Meal and ſalt Proviſions being very much Wanted, beg you may Aſſiſt him to forward the ſame with the greateſt diſpatch, when you have done this buſineſs you will return to the Head of Elk and there aſſiſt to forward the Stores till I come which will be near the Same time, I wiſh you a good Journey and am Sir

Your moſt obd. ſervt.

EPH. BLAINE.

D. C. G. of Purchaſes.

FEBY. 19TH. 1778. INSTRUCTIONS FROM CAPT. LEE.

Middletown Feby. 19th '78.

To MR. HOWELL

Sir

By virtue of powers and authority to me committed by his Excellency Gen. Washington commander in chief. I do hereby authorize & empower you to superintend the appraisements of each & every article that may be collected at this post. You will keep just and regular account in behalf of the States, and furnish the respective farmers with proper certificates specifying the appraised value of each article. You will also coadjute Ensign Mc. Clane in the executions of orders to him delivered, to which you are referred. And I do hereby invest you with full powers to call on every subject of the United States to your aid & assistance. To arrange all the waggons in brigades, that may be sent to this post; To nominate & appoint all & every necessary officers, who are hereby commanded to be obedient to your orders and directions.

your most obt. servt,

HENRY LEE Capt. L. G.

From Capt. Henry Lee Dover Feby 20th 1778

To MR JOHN LADD HOWELL D. C. MIDDLETOWN DEL.

Sir

I transmit to you in this letter an order from General Cæsar Rodney to Capt Witherspoon. You will please

communicate it to the Captain and urge his immediate compliance.   He is to furnifh a Sufficient Guard for the Stores
collecting at Middletown which will be difpofed of as
yourfelf & Lt. M'Clane may Judge moft proper.   Acquaint
me of your fuccefs & how the people comply with our
orders ; whether there is much difcontent, from what caufes
it may originate.

Your moft obt Servt

HENRY LEE Capt L. G. U. S.

To John Ladd Howell D. C. Middletown Del.

Dover Feb 22. 1778

I wifh you had finifhed your bufinefs at Middletown as we
want all hands here.   When you Set off Select Some of
the likelieft youths of Capt Witherfpoon's Company—
mount them on the horfes you have collected, put them in
charge of my Sergt,   They are to do the duty of dragoons.

Your Obt Servt

HENRY LEE, Capt L. G. U. S.

To John Ladd Howell D. C. Middletown Del.

Dover Feby 25 1778

Sir

In anfwer to yours of yefterday I muft fay that the pro-
vender confumed by your horfe and the dragoon horfes
fhould be made in one account.   The diet & other expenfes
are all to be thrown together in one general certificate to be
given and paid by my order.   You will fee Mr Blaine at

Elk. A letter from Headquarters informs me he will be furnished with Cash to settle the accounts contracted by me. Defire him to Send a proper perfon with a Sufficient Sum of Cafh to me immediately as I wifh to be on my return & cannot think of leaving this Country till the people are paid off.

Your Obt Servt
HENRY LEE, Capt. L. G. U. S.

To John Ladd Howell Middletown Del.

Dover Feb 23d '78

Sir

Horfes may be got. I cannot fuppofe the reafon why we want them. Capt Wilkinfon is under orders to be fubfervient to our directions. He muft affift us. Whenever New Caftle is done with, we want all hands here. I am Sorry you muft go away, do if poffible finifh things where you are, communicate to me what may be left undone. I return you my thanks for your aid & will not fail to mention your Services at Headquarters

Your Obt Sevt
HENRY LEE

Middletown Del. Feb 25 1778

To Capt Henry Lee

Sir

I received yours this afternoon, five horfemen fet out for

the lower Dept. immediately. Some of the parties juſt there arriving—the evening of the 24 they were all out on Command. This morning in expeᵭation of a Large Drove of Cattle from below paſſing this place. I ſent out one of the Militia to Elk requeſtng Col. Hollengſworth to ſend a party to take charge of them with what might be colleᵭed here, Since which, am informed they have gone by the Red Lyon. Supt. Brooks has under his charge three horſes for the immediate uſe of your troop.

The buſineſs being now done here ſhall ſet out for Elk in queſt of Col. Blaine. The troops under Sergt Brooks I ſhall recommend to leave this to day, Enſign McLane propoſes to ſet out in the morning early to join you. At Elk ſhall have leiſure to take a Copy of the Acct. of Receipts at this Place & leave them with Col. Hollengſworth for you. It is poſſible I may remain at Elk a day or two for want of intelligence. I know of no diſcontent amongſt the Inhabitants but what might naturally ariſe from the nature of the buſineſs we are employed in—thoſe of the diſaffeᵭed excepted & whom we ſhould not need. One cauſe, & a juſt one, will be the want of Caſh—the people want to know where they may call for payment. If my Services ſhould meet your approbation & be thought of uſe to the Publick, ſhall be well pleaſed

I am Sir your Obdt Servt

JOHN LADD HOWELL

Dover 1ſt March 1778

Mr. John Ladd Howell
Sir

You will proceed to Middletown & there waite the arrival of a number ot Waggons from Camp, which have loaded with the Flour at Cantwells Bridge and the Mills about that, ſhould there be any of the Indian Meal left which Mr. Mc. Garmant had ground for the uſe of the Hoſpital, have it forwarded by the very firſt Waggons to Camp—at Mr. Canby & Stephens mill upon the Head of Saſſafraſs River there is near Six Hundred Barrels of Flour, and a large Quantity of Wheat & Flour Barrels, you will order Mr. Stephens to continue and exert himſelf in Grinding out his Wheat, for which he shall be properly ſatisfied, and have Craft immediately engaged to forward his Flour to Charles Town—direct it to the care of Mr. Patrick Hamilton of that Place. should you not be able to procure Craft in Saſſafraſs apply to Coll. Hollingſworth & Mr. Huggins for their aſſiſtance in ſending ſome from Elke for that purpoſe, and likewiſe to furniſh what waggons they poſſibly can ſpare for tranſporting the Flour & Wheat from Cantwells Bridge out of danger—the Flour muſt be the firſt object, after that the Wheat—I requeſt you may ſeize all Waggons which are paſſing and repaſſing with private property and load them all to Camp, firſt giving them an opportunity of Storing their Loading in ſome place of ſafety. This Buſineſs Compleated you will return to Camp where you may expect to meet me and receive further inftructions, pray ufe every exertion in the removal of the above mentioned Flour.

Mr. Mc. Garmant will afford you every affiftance in the execution of this Bufinefs.

I am Sir Your Obd. Hble. Servt.

EPH. BLAINE D. C. G.

Dover 1st Mar. 1778 From 1777 Ephraim Blaine rec'd at same time

To JOHN LADD HOWELL

Sir

In the execution of this bufinefs you will apply for the aid & affiftance of the Civil & Military authority who are requefted to fupport you.

E. BLAINE D. C. G.

what certificates you give refer the people to Mr. Mc. Garmant for payment.

E. BLAINE

Dover Mar. 2nd. Copy I re. from Geo. Read to Col. Mc. Donough dd. March 4th. 1778.

Dover March 2nd. 1778.

To COL. MC. DONOUGH.

Sir

Mr. John Ladd Howell the Bearer of this an officer in the Commiffaries Department of the Continental Army will be in the diftrict of your Battalion for fome time to come, forwarding Provifions for the ufe of *that* army, and for the more fpeedy and Effectual Execution of this Bufinefs he may want the aid of fmall parties of the Militia from time to time.   I muft requeft you to Iffue your orders for fuch aid, & know that they are executed, as no delay muft be permitted, if poffible to be prevented on our part.

this from yours &c.

GEO. READ.

———

On publick service To John Ladd Howell Dpty Com. at the head of Elk.

Wilmington 21ft May 1778 from Coll Francis Wade
Dear Sir

I was handed yours of the 20th——I am difpofed to give you every affiftance in my power Confiftant with my duty & have wrote to Mr Nealfon and fhall write to the Bridge this day——As to more Waggons for the preft from this place it is out of my power, for the want of bridles collars & almoft all forts of harnefs and drivers to drive teams——and not only fo, but have received orders laft night from the A. Q. M. G. to forward all affiftance in my power in Waggons horfes &c for the ufe of the Grand Army.   Thefe Confiderations will apologize for any relyance you can have of a farther fupply from me, I am

Deare Sir

Your moft Huble Servt

FRANCIS WADE

To John Ladd Howell, D. C. Elk, Md.

Newark Del. May 31ſt 1778

I arrived at this place this morng the diviſſn under Genl Smallwood having left Wilmington.   I urged Genl Small-wood to ſend back to you all the teams I furniſhed him to remove his diviſſn & he promiſed me he would—From the beſt Intelligence we can colleɛ, how the Enemy is or has laſt night evacuated Philad. great numbers of their ſhips full of men all down the River and parties have been plun-dering in the neighborhood of the Red Lyon, our Army is in motion towards the City.   I hope ſoon to have the pleaſure of congratulating you on their full poſſeſſion of it & that I ſhall once more enter my Habitation there.

Yours &c

FRANCIS WADE

To John Ladd Howell D. C. Elk

Newark June 6. 1778

I hope the ten wagons under Roſs got ſafe to Elk and will give you ſome aſſiſtance, the deſertions concealing horſes & waggons &c and the general diſpoſition of the people to avoid the ſervice makes it difficult to make a large Colleɛion of Waggons in this Country.

FRANCIS WADE

To John Ladd Howell Esqr. at Head of Elk recd
Aug. 11th *1778*
Philada August 1st 1778.

Dear Friend

Your Favor of 24th Ultimo came duly to hand, and you
might with juftnefs blaim me for Negligence, in not anfwering it before, could I not with sincerity affure you, that all
my time is taken up to tranfact Bufinefs in two extenfive
Departments in which I am acting in—I expect foon to
have them properly adjufted & to fpare more time for my
Friends, however you may depend on, it gives me infinite
Pleafure to hear from you & fhall embraffe every Opportunity by informing you of what happens here—

I have wrote Mr. Wiley requefting him to examine the
Bread at & near Wilmington and if any Store Houfes are to
be had, to Store all that is good as Veffels may as well load
it there as here & thereby safe the expenfe of Tranfporta-
tion, it being deftined for the French Fleet—

Colo Blaine left this about two Weeks ago and is gone to
eat mufh & Milk & Kifs his Wife twice a Week—I dont
expect to fee him here this 10 Days as White & Chaloner
wrote him that everything went all clever and that his
Prefence was not wanted—No Letters from him fince his
Departure—

Since our Army is encamped on the White Plains nothing Material has happened—Genl Gates with 6000 Men
under his Command had Orders laft Week to advance towards Kingfbridge

It is faid the French Fleet has taken 27 Prizes of which none is yet arrived at this Port altho' Many expected—The Fleet is failed for Rhode Ifland and we may fhortly expect to hear fome agreable News from that Quarter—The Enemy after their return to New York fent 1300 Men to that Place & our Great & Noble General has alfo difpatched a Body to reinforce Genl Sullivan, Prepare yourfelves therefore to be congratulated on the Surrender of that Ifland—You fee I wifh to guard you againft Surprife, altho' I know it would not do you any great harm—Have you any good Madira in order to celebrate the day—there is very little of it left here, & if you are well ftock'd fend us a few dozns.

By fome Prifoners who are lately Exchange we learn the Scarcity of Provifions at N. York—The Soldiery is oblige to put up with Rice inftead of Flour which caufes a great Murmour amongft them, particularly the German Troops who are not ufed to fuch living—It is confidently reported that the had revolted in confequence of it—

The continue ftill to defert When Opportunities offers, and lately 15 Jagers with their Horfes and Accoutrements in One Day came in to our Camp—A Gentleman juft arrived From France informs of Lord Chathams Death in May laft and that the Miniftry in England had employed fome fcribners to write a Pamphlet refpecting the Intereft of the Nation to declare America Independent & enter in a Treaty of Alliance and Commerce with us—

Col Jones our D. C. G. is now with me he is come to

ſettle his Accounts & deſires to be remember'd to you—

I incloſe you a few Papers to which refer for further News—

Believe me to be Dear Sir

Your very hl. ſervt

GUSTAVUS RISBERG

P. S.

Your Couzin Jacque gives his Compliments to you and is juſt ſetting off for Lancaſter—

This Letter has not been ſent off before the 4th for want of opportunity

---

Philada Novr. 2nd 1778 Ephraim Blaine recd. Novr. 5th.
1778

Philada. 2nd. Nov. 1778.

Mr. John L. Howell

Sir

You will immediately proceed to Cantwells Bridge and advertiſe the Country you will give conſtant attendance to purchaſe wheat on Acct. of the public, you muſt Confine your ſelfe to the under Mentioned Prices wheat weighing 58lb p. buſhel 25s and in proportion for what it may weigh above or under, ſhould you meet with any which is clear of the flye rather than Looſe it, give thirty Shillings, you will keep a lookout & diſcover every perſon who may be Engroſſing flour or wheat & report them to me, the Legiſlative Authority of the Delaware State will ſtop the Monopoly of all Kind of Proviſions, and make examples of

thofe concearned in that ungeneroufe bufinefs, the late refolution of Congrefs will I hope ftop the forrage Mafters from
buying wheat, you will however forbid them fhould they
attempt and report them to me, buy every bufhl. you pofibly can, and give four pounds five for good Flour you muft
clafs your wheat into three parcels, all the old wheat by it
felfe the good new and the ordinary the old wheat and ordinary let it be fent immediately to Mr. Evans and Tat-
nalls Mills, taking their receipts for the Different parcels—
and as you will be regularly fupplied with cafh Pay proper
attention to the people and Difmifs them in the moft
princely maner.

Mr. Williams whofe mill is near that Place will affift
you fhould you ftand in need at any time and you muft engage him to grind all he pofibly can, we will allow him as
Generoufe a Price as any other Miller in our Service, all I
have to fay is that large Quantities of wheat and Flour is
wanting, and that everything in your power muft be done
to Procure all pofible you can am with Efteem Sir

Your moft Hble Servt.

EPH. BLAINE D. C. G.

---

*Cantwell's Bridge November 11th. 1777. Copy of an Ad-
vertifement,*

Cantwells Bridge Novembr 11th 1777

ADVERTISEMENT

The Subfcriber begs leave to inform the Gentlemen
Farmers and others, that being Stationed at this Place for

the purpofe of purchafing Provifions for the American Army. Thofe who have Wheat or Flour may depend upon having a good Price and being punctually paid, for any quantity delivered at Cantwells Bridge, where he has taken an office, & will give Conftant attendence for that purpose.

The Subfcriber hopes an inclination to ferve their Country will be an inducement to give him a preference to any private purchafer.

JOHN LADD HOWELL
Affift. Commiffy. of Purchs.
Cantwells Bridge 11th November 1778.

MR. LAD HOWELL, COMMISSARY OF PURCHASSES FORWARDED BY MR. VDIKE.

N. Caftle March 20th 1779

Sir

I reced a letter from one Soloman Wright living about five miles from Church Hill in Queen Anns in the State of Maryland the contents in this Viz. : "I have yet unfold about 600 Bufhl. of Wheat fome very good & fome of my neighbours have alfo their crops on hand. I fuppofe about 4000 Bufhl. a line by the poft refpecting the price & a purchafes will Oblige &c." I faw Mr. Vn. Dike yifterday & he recommended me to give you this notice, you being Commy. of purchaffes. I am with refpect yr. Obedt. Hub. Servt.

Z. V. LEVENIGH

recd Mar 26th

PUBLIC SERVICE. JOHN LADD HOWELL ESQR ASSIST. COM-
MISSARY OF PURCHASES. CANTWELLS BRIDGE.

JOHN L. HOWELL ESQR CANTWELLS BRIDGE

Philada March 30 1779

Sir

Yours of the 27th. is now before us, in anfwer to which
we have to inform, that Col. Blaine directed us to inftruct
all his Affiftants refpecting the Purchafe of Wheat & Flour,
agreeable to advice that Congrefs might offer in Confequence of his applications to them for that purpofe.—We
have received no Advice from Congrefs on this Subject and
cannot undertake of ourfelves to direct in fo important a
Matter—We know that Flour is wanted—Congrefs know
it, & the very high price that the holders of it demand—It
becomes them to fay what we fhould do—and till then we
choofe to be filent on the fubject—We wifh you to afcertain the facts refpecting chopping of Wheat for Forage &
the Perfons names who practice it, alfo the Quantity of
Wheat that has been chopped & procured for this purpofe.
We are Sir

your moft obedt. Servants

CHALONER & WHITE A. C. of Ps.

SECTION THREE

CONCERNING JOSHUA LADD
HOWELL AND ANNA
BLACKWOOD HIS WIFE

Col. Joshua Ladd Howell

CHAPTER I.

JOSHUA LADD HOWELL.

Account of his death by Anna B. Howell—Letters—Extract from Samuel Mickle's Diary—John Ladd Howell, jr.

COL. JOSHUA LADD HOWELL, son of John Ladd, and Frances Paschall Howell, named by request of his grandfather, John Howell, after his great-uncle, Joshua Howell, merchant in Philadelphia, assumed the name of Ladd himself. He died January 10, 1818. As he was born in Philadelphia, September 19, 1762, it is safe to infer that his home was there till about 1781 when letters addressed to John Ladd Howell [his father] near Woodbury, N. J., and a bill from Samuel Mickle, of Woodbury, show that housekeeping and domestic matters were in full force at 'Candour Hall,' where he lived till 1805 when he built the house at Fancy Hill.

Col. Joshua Ladd Howell

Memoranda from his father's pocket Almanac, and tuition bills during the Philadelphia period of his life, give us a glimpse of the young gentleman's educational privileges. John Grimes is first mentioned as his tutor, in a bill dated March, 1773, though a memorandum dated February 9, 1771, sets forth that schooling for Joshua Howell, jr., was paid to this date. September, 1773, he enters Joseph Stile's school where he continues, possibly to the year 1778, when on September 27, John Ladd Howell notes in his almanac, ' Joſhua Howell, Jun., entered at Mr. Powell's ſchool ' in Burlington, N. J. Mr. Thomas Powell was to receive £140 per annum for board and tuition, but on January 9, 1779, wanted this increased to £160 so as to be able to meet expenses. A few interesting letters to him while at this school, from his father, will be found at the end of this sketch.

After leaving school, the date of which is not known, he assisted his father in the management of his large estate. On the 10th of February, 1786, he obtained from William

Livingston at Burlington, N. J., a license to
marry Anna Blackwood. The marriage certificate bears date February 16, 1786.

In 1793, he cleared out what is now known
as Howell's Cove, and began the shad fishery
then known as the Fancy Hill Fishery.
Hannah Ladd had refused permission to his
father to do this, having promised Deborah
West that she would not allow fishing in the
Cove, on account of supposed injury to West
Point Fishery. In 1811, Joshua Ladd Howell purchased the latter.

In addition to his interest in the fishery, the
management of the farms, ' Candor Hall,' the
' Fancy Hill,' one near Westville, now Vic-
toria, and one between Fancy Hill and Eagle
Point, devolved upon him. These farms,
together with immense tracts of land on which
were the primeval forest and tide meadows
above and below Fancy Hill, gave him abundant occupation. Later on he took up large
tracts of salt marshes along the Maurice River,
and with his sons and others, became interested
also in the smelting of iron at Ætna Furnace

at Tuckahoe on the Tuckahoe River in South
Jersey. These ventures culminated so disas-
terously in a financial way that it was found
necessary to mortgage Fancy Hill for about
thirty-five thousand dollars. This mortgage
was eventually cancelled, after a long struggle
with difficulties, by his wife, Anna Blackwood
Howell. His declining health and death are
certainly attributable to the distress of mind
incident upon these reverses.

He was a director of the old academy in
Woodbury, from whence have gone forth into
active life many ' good men and true ' among
whom were Stephen Decator and James Lawrence. The old bell that he was instrumental
in obtaining for the academy building, was
formerly in a Spanish Convent in Barbadoes
in the West Indies, and now hangs in the
First Presbyterian Church at Woodbury. He
was a strong Federalist, and took a deep interest in politics, but there is no evidence that
he ever held any political office.

Benjamin P. Howell was but a mere child
when his father died. Owing to this and the

reticence of his mother about his father's life, because of her affliction at his death, he did not have, barring one or two exceptions, any very clear memories of his father.

He remembered going to his father's camp at Bilingsport, in company with his mother, and noticing particularly the large tent or marquee of his father, in which they dined, and the dinner of roast duck which left a lasting impression. He remembered also seeing the evolutions of the soldiers on dress parade. This was about 1814. He remembered journeying from Fancy Hill to Columbia, Penn., with his father and mother in their family carriage. His father pointed out two Indians basking in the sun by the roadside. He remembered going to Cape May with his father and mother, a two days' journey, in their large travelling carriage fitted out for such journeys.

His impression of his father was that he was a tall, fine looking man, and displayed when laughing and talking his beautiful teeth.

Col. Howell was a member of the Gloucester Fox-hunting Club, formed October, 1766,

by twenty-seven gentlemen of Philadelphia,
subsequently joined by several Jerseymen.
The Jerseymen were Capt. James B. Cooper,
of Haddonfield ; Capt. Samuel Whitall, Col.
Heston, Col. Joshua Howell, of Fancy Hill ;
Samuel Harrison, esq., Jesse Smith, esq.

The club used to meet once a week, or oftener, for hunting.   Their most favorite fields for action were along the
banks of Cooper's Creek, four or five miles from Camden,
or at Horseheads, two or three miles from Woodbury in
Deptford, at Chew's Landing, Blackwoodtown, Heston's
Glassworks, now Glassboro, and Thompson's Point on the
Delaware.   The kennel of the club, which was kept at the
point by an old negro named Wetty, contained in 1778
twenty-two excellent dogs.   During the revolution most
of the members of the club were in their country's service.
The association was reorganized after the war, and continued in existence down to 1818, when the death of
Captain Ross, the boldest rider and best hunter of the company, caused it to languish and die.

So fond were most of the Pennsylvanians of their sport,
that they have been known when ice obstructed the crossing of the Delaware, to bring their horses over Trenton
Bridge, rather than miss the chase.   Mr. Caldwell, a Jer-
seyman, on one occasion plunged into the Delaware after a
fox which had broken through the ice.   Once the fox carried the pack in full cry to Salem.   It was a point of honor

not to give up until the brush was taken, after which there
ensued a banquet at the Ferry House at Gloucester Point,
kept by William Hugg, the rendezvous of the club.
The Gloucester farmers, suffering much from the great
number of foxes, were always glad to hear the horns and
hounds.   From tenth of October to tenth of April the
club had freedom of fields and woods and were often joined
by the farmers.

Of the attendants of the club, Jonas Cattell deserves
especial mention.   He was for twenty years grand guide
and whipper-in to the hunters, and was ' always at his post,
whether at setting out with the company, leading off, at
fault, or at the death. '   He travelled on foot with his gun
and tomahawk, and was always on hand for any emergency,
before half the riders came in sight.   His physical strength
and activity were almost incredible.   When about fifty
years of age he ran a foot race from Mount Holly to Woodbury, with an Indian runner of great celebrity, and came
off victor.   About the same time he won a wager by going
on foot from Woodbury to Cape Island [now called Cape
May] in one day, delivering a letter, and returning in the
same manner, with an answer, on the day following.   He
accomplished this extraordinary feat with ease, and was
willing to repeat it the same week, on the same terms.

The above account, taken almost verbatim
from Isaac Mickle's Reminiscences of Old
Gloucester, is not out of place here, in that it

serves to show the nature of the outdoor plea-
sures engaged in at that day. This club served
to bring together men of the prominent families of Pennsylvania and New Jersey, many of
whom were the life-long friends of Joshua
Ladd Howell, and were frequent visitors at
Fancy Hill.

Joshua Ladd Howell's military career
covered a period of about twenty-five years
during which he rose from captain to colonel.
His first commission, that of captain of a
company of militia in Gloucester County,
signed by Richard Howell, Governor of New
Jersey, is dated June 5, 1793. His second
commission signed by the same governor is
that of major of second regiment of militia in
County of Gloucester, and is dated February
19, 1794. His next commission signed also
by Richard Howell, dated November 12, 1796,
is that of lieutenant-colonel of second regiment of first brigade, first division of militia,
New Jersey. This commission he held till
1817 when on September 9th he was commissioned colonel of second regiment Gloucester

Brigade of militia, New Jersey, by Isaac Williamson, Governor, a rank he held at his death. During the war of 1812, about November 20, 1814, he was encamped at Bilingsport on the Delaware, and shortly afterward or about December 7th he was in command at Cape May. As we have very meagre information concerning Joshua Ladd Howell's movements during this war, all the letters found relative to that period, which show him to have been in active service, are published.

CHAPTER II.

ANNA BLACKWOOD HOWELL.

Her Revolutionary Reminiscences—Letters—Extract from her diary on death of John Ladd Howell, jr.

ANNA B. HOWELL, eldest daughter of Samuel Blackwood and Abigail Clement Blackwood, born in February 16, 1769, at Woodbury, N. J., in the house now the property of Belmont Perry, which stands on the south-east corner of Broad Street and Newton Avenue. Built by John Mickle, a brother of Hannah Ladd, some years previous to the revolution, it was owned by him during the residence there of the Blackwood family. It is a large handsomely built brick house. Samuel Blackwood, a native of Blackwood, N. J., settled in Woodbury; there is no date however to record his coming, or his removal from the Broad Street house to another property of the Mickle family—situated on the

Anna Blackwood Howell in Early Womanhood

east side of Delaware Street, owned at the present time by the Twells family. Here Samuel Blackwood died 1774. On this occurrence Abigail Blackwood, presumably desiring to return to and live among her kindred, made a home for her young family in Haddonfield, N. J. No light is thrown on the childhood of Anna B. Howell, but from tradition and and thro' her Revolutionary Reminiscences, she is discovered to be at that time a keenly observing, bright little girl of quick intelligence and surprising memory, qualities which were strong in her, and became her characteristics throughout her long life—failing her not even in the moment of her passing away.

Her opportunities for education were those which the excellent Quaker schools afforded. Springing from Presbyterian stock by her father's house and of largely Quaker descent on her mother's side, she inherited a claim to belong to those who were foremost and distinguished in the religious and educational movement of the colonial period. Her early years were spent among the Quakers of Haddonfield, a people of culture and refinement, and in the close companionship of a mother to whose admirable qualities of heart and mind her daughter bears testimony by earnest words and an exhibit of native powers and character so excellent that we may well believe she bore the clear imprint of such a mother. A supplement to this influence was her absorbing delight in books, and study of them throughout her life, to which faithful friends, later on, she turned her oppressed mind for solace and diversion when unparalleled loss and bereavement befell her.

Anna Blackwood on February 16, 1786, at Gloucester City, N. J., married Joshua Ladd Howell, by Friends' ceremony before her stepfather, Col. Joseph Ellis, who as Justice of the Peace, a high officer in those days, gave confirmation to the rites. The house where the wedding took place is torn down to give place to a more pretentious mansion. Col. Joseph Ellis and Abigail Blackwood Ellis gave the wedding party in the large, white frame house which stood almost directly on the bank of the river and fronting it ; its green doors and shutters, and rows of Lombardy poplars surrounding it, are within the memory of many.

Nineteen years of their married life were spent at 'Candour Hill' the Ladd Homestead. Those were years of serene home-life among her large family of children, most congenial to her turn of mind; there they entertained freely their hosts of near relatives and friends, and enjoyed life under easy and liberal circumstances. The property had come to them trim and fresh from the hands of the careful thrifty Quaker Ladds. In 1805 they moved their large family to the spacious new home at Fancy Hill on the Delaware River.

Here, as at 'Candor Hall,' father and mother united to spare no pains in the advancement of their children in every way befitting their position. In those days the Academy of Woodbury furnished teachers of no mean worth—also, tradition says, rigorous disciplinarians. At Fancy Hill a tutor was provided, the clever gentle-mannered Mr. Estey, of Morristown, N. J. The older sons were

prepared for college or business by the Rev.
Mr. Picton, of Westfield, N. J., and on the
marriage of Frances Howell to her cousin,
B. B. Howell, her younger sisters and brothers,
attending school in Philadelphia, made their
home with her, and received her care and over-
sight.   This was an age of repression for
children, but through a wise departure from
such methods, these children enjoyed an exceptionally genial companionship with their
father and mother—the latter especially, as
her early widowhood placed them solely under
her guardianship.   Her strong sympathetic
nature and earnestness, a judgment invariably
clear of prejudice and all narrowness, invited
the loving trust of her husband and children.
Ably fitted to be the safe counselor of her
husband in his busy life beset with many difficulties towards its close, she earnestly advised
against certain unwise speculations which,
when eventually undertaken, forced the mort-
gaging of their large property.   The troubles
which hastened Col. Howell's death seemed to
stimulate his wife to greater effort to save the

property—summoning for the occasion energy and a sagacity, that was extraordinary, she displayed a faculty for a business-like and judicious management of affairs, which slowly but surely turned bankruptcy into a complete redemption of her valuable property.

Anna Howell was not a member of the Society of Friends', possibly losing her *birthright* through her father, a Presbyterian, she wore the dress and used the language of Friends, accepted their orthodox doctrines and conformed to their plain usages, but with many liberal modifications. Her devout spirituality and love for sacred things, her eminently religious life gave her prominence amongst this Godly people; at the earnest insistence of the Woodbury Friends she sat with the elders in the gallery facing the meeting. Her fine stately presence softened by a gracious manner and speech, her benevolent face and earnest dark blue eyes, combined to present a personality so impressive and agreeable that it seemed the index of inborn worth. The tendency to lapse into sad reminiscences, so evident in her notes and letters, did not appear in her intercourse with others; naturally of a hopeful, cheerful temper, she possessed a strong sense of humor, and enjoyed it. Always, even in extreme old age, the interesting center of a group, her vigorous mind and delightful gift of conversation inspired all who drew near to her, with profound love and reverence.

Anna Blackwood Howell died suddenly when eighty-six years old. The day previous she had dined at 'Candour Hall' with her son, Dr. B. P. Howell, and his family—and her grandchildren, Margaretta Howell and Joshua H. Janeway. She was very bright and charming, and talked over the early times of her married life when the 'Old Place' was her home. As she drove away in her carriage, she buried her face in her hands, saying that every scene connected with her life there was so vivid. She died that night, in the arms of her beloved grandaughter, Margaretta Howell.

REVOLUTIONARY REMINISCENCES OF ANNA
BLACKWOOD HOWELL

My mother remembered well the appearance
of the Hessians as they passed through Haddonfield to the attack on Fort Mercer (or
Fort Red Bank) at Red Bank on the Delaware, being a mile and a half, or two miles,
below Fancy Hill. They presented a very
fine appearance, and were probably a picked
body of men numbering about twenty-five
hundred, under command of Count Donop.
They were in excellent spirits, as if assured of
an easy victory over the raw and undisciplined
troops of which a party of the small number
(about three hundred under Col. Nathaniel
Greene) which garrisoned that fort, consisted.
She used to describe their appearance, in
marked contrast, on their retreat, panic-strick-
en and completely demoralized. Two of these
soldiers entered the cellar of her mother's
house, in quest of food; finding there a pie,

My mother remembered well the appearance
of the Hessians as they passed through Haddonfield to the attack on Fort Mercer (or
Fort Red Bank) at Red Bank on the Delaware River, a mile and a half, or two miles,
below Fancy Hill. They presented a very
fine appearance, and were probably a picked
body of men numbering about twenty-five
hundred, under command of Count Donop.
They were in excellent spirits, as if assured of
an easy victory over the raw and undisciplined
troops of which a part, of the small number
(about three hundred under Col. Nathaniel
Greene) which garrisoned that fort, consisted.
She used to describe their appearance, in
marked contrast, on their retreat, panic-strick-
en and completely demoralized. Two of these
soldiers entered the cellar of her mother's
house, in quest of food; finding there a pie,

they quarreled for it, and in the struggle, it fell to the floor, and they stamped on it, and retreated in haste from the house, a Hessian officer having violently banged their heads against the door-post, as they made their exit ; upon which, Cousin Becky Harrison (niece to our great-grandmother) who sat with her back to a corner cupboard that contained ammunition, cried out, ' That 's a darling fellow ! '

As Count Donop and Lt. Col. Mingerode fell, mortally wounded, in the assault, Lt. Col. Linsing led the retreat. My mother remembered Count Donop's fine appearance and tall, elegant figure. My mother's stepfather, Col. Joseph Ellis, commanded the American troops stationed at Haddonfield, but at the time the twenty-five hundred Hessians under Count Donop, passed through Haddonfield, on their way to Red Bank, Col. Ellis and his command were not there. Count Donop pressed several persons, whom he found along the route, into service as guides, among them a negro belonging to the Cooper family, called Old Minch. Another negro, Dick, belonging to the gallant

Col. Ellis, and a white scoundrel named McIl-
vaine, volunteered their services as pioneers,
and at the bar of the Haddonfield tavern,
these two villains were loud in their abuse of
the Americans.   After the repulse of the Hessians, these two miscreants were immediately
seized and hung in Fort Mercer.   Old Minch
lived to tell admiring hearers how badly he
was scared in the memorable fight.   Resolved
not to bear arms against his country, and being afraid to run away, he got behind a hay-
rick when the battle began, and lay there as
flat as he could, until it was over.   'But Lord
massa, I guess I shuk as de dam cannon balls
come ploughin along de groun and flingin de
san in ma face, an arter de Auguster [British
war vessel] blowed up I tot fo half an hour
I was dead weder or no.'

After the slaughter of the Hessians, M. de
Maudeuit, a French officer, sallied from the
fort to repair some palisades, and heard a
voice from among the heaps of the dead and
dying exclaim in English, 'Whoever you are
draw me hence.'   This was Count Donop

and he was carried into the fort, where it was found his hip was broken, but the wound was not at first considered mortal. The Americans wished to give him no quarter. ' I am in your hands, ' said he, ' you may revenge yourselves.' M. de Maudeuit begged the men to be generous toward their wounded prisoner, and the latter said to him, ' You appear to be a foreigner, sir, who are you ? '

' A French officer, ' answered Maudeuit.

' I am satisfied—I die in the very hands of honor.'

Donop was first taken to the Whitall House, but was afterwards removed to the house of the Lowes, south of Woodbury Creek, where he died three days after the battle, saying to Maudeuit, 'It is finishing a noble career early, but I die the victim of my ambition and the avarice of my King. See in me the vanity of all human pride—I have shone in all the Courts of Europe, and now I am dying here on the banks of the Delaware in the house of an obscure Quaker.'

Old Mrs. James Whitall was spinning when the fight began and when a cannon ball whizzed through the hall showing her her danger she carried her wheel to the cellar and kept on spinning.

The house was used as a hospital after the action and the floors still show traces of the pools of blood that flowed from the wounded Hessians who pressed so close to the Americans that the wads from the guns were blown clear through their bodies.

In connection with this battle it is stated that a wounded soldier, a Hessian, came across the field to the 'Old House' for food and drink, and while slaking his thirst at the pump it was observed that the water ran out at a wound in his neck, the œsophagus or gullet having been opened by a ball.

Earl Cornwallis on leaving Woodbury encamped at Gloucester Point till he could collect large stores of provisions, and then crossed over to Philadelphia with them. While he was encamped at Gloucester, quite a brilliant affair took place. My mother remembered that about one hundred and fifty men of Morgan's Rifle Corps, under Lieutenant Colonel Butler, and an equal number of militia under the Marquis de La Fayette (who still served as a volunteer) were stationed at Haddonfield, and attacked with great gallantry a picket of these before mentioned troops, consisting of three hundred men, driving them, with the loss of twenty or thirty killed and greater number wounded, quite into their own camp after which they retired without being pursued. The Marquis, who was said by Gen. Greene to search for danger, was charmed with the conduct of this small detachment. ' I found the riflemen,' said La Fayette in a letter to Washington, ' above even their reputation, and the militia above all expectations I could have formed of them. ' My mother, then a little child of nine years, remembered a young French officer whom she always believed was La Fayette, and on whose knee she sat. He wore quite an amount of jewelry and was very polite and affable, and he appeared to be held in high honor and esteem by his brother officers. She remembered, too, Count Pulaski, the Pole. He was a very fine horseman, and was dressed in a handsome green uniform, tight fitting, and buckskin breeches. He frequently displayed his horsemanship by leaping his horse over a fence in front of her mother's house.

On another occasion a picked body of British Light Infantry was sent from Philadelphia, to make a night attack on the troops stationed at Haddonfield under Col. Joseph Ellis, who after the war married my mother's mother, Abigail Clement Blackwood. My grandmother had directed Mindy, the colored girl, to take the children to bed, with strict injunctions to take no light into the room, as information had reached her of the advance of the light infantry. Curiosity led the girl to disobey orders, and she took the light and put it in the window. In a few minutes the house was surrounded and filled with British troops whose approach had been heralded by a vidette named Chew, who swam his horse over Newton Creek, and thus reached Haddonfield in

time to give Col. Ellis timely notice of the
enemy's approach.

Not so fortunate, however, was Miles Sage,
another vidette.   He reached my grandmother's house to find it surrounded by
soldiers, whom he at first mistook for Colonel
Ellis' troops.   Seeing my Uncle John Blackwood, a boy of fourteen, in their midst, he
made inquiry about them ; John Blackwood,
then a clever sized lad, cautiously replied,
'They have gone.' Sage said, ' Where ? ' John
replied, 'Some one way and some another. '
Just then the burnished musket barrels re-
flected the light of a passing candle, and Sage
discovering his mistake struck the rowals into
the flanks of his mare and dashed along the
main street followed by volley after volley of
musketry.   When opposite the tavern at the
further end of the street, his mare fell, and
while he lay prostrate he received fourteen
bayonet wounds, when an officer interposed
with the remark, ' If the damned rebel has any
life in him let him live.'   Some of the kind
hearted ladies staunched his wounds and en-

treated Sage, in his critical condition, to be more choice in his expressions, which were not of the most pious character, in view of the treatment he had just received at the hands of the enemy. He persisted, nevertheless, to swear vengence on them, and that he meant to give them a shot in return for every bayonet wound he had received ; a promise he lived to make good, as my mother saw him after his recovery and remembered him afterwards as an aged man. Stirring scencs were these for the little Quaker maiden to participate in. She gleefully recollected her brother displaying to the British soldiers quarted in the house, his ciphering book in which he had drawn the picture, much to their mortified displeasure, of one redoubtable American putting to flight about a dozen of his Majesty's grenadiers.

Sir William Howe being relieved of the command of the British army in Philadelphia, Sir Henry Clinton assumed command and in expectation of a powerful French fleet under Count Destaing, off the Delaware Bay, Philadelphia was evacuated by the British June 18,

1778. It crossed the river to Gloucester Point and proceeded slowly through Haddonfield, Mount Holly and Crosswicks to Allentown which place it reached on the 24th. While at Haddonfield, where it halted two days, my mother had an opportunity of seeing this great army and its distinguished commander, Clinton, and his generals, Cornwallis and Erskine, who, I have heard her say, rode abreast as they marched out of the town. She often alluded to the splendid appearance of this army in scarlet uniforms, white kid gaiters, buttoned above the knee, white belts, and cross straps. The officers were especially resplendent in gold trimmings and facings. She was much impressed, too, with the appearance of the Scotch Highlanders, several regiments, she said, forming a body of fine, tall and powerful looking men dressed in their kilts, plaid and bonnets. The colonel of one of the regiments was quartered at her mother's with whom he frequently talked not hesitating to freely express himself as deploring the war. My mother, a bright and intelligent child, soon became a favorite with him, often sitting on his knee, and as often dancing about the room, having donned his blue velvet bonnet with its drooping plumes.

The army halted in Haddonfield several days. The officers and men were quartered on the inhabitants, and everything that was conducive to the aid and comfort of this large force was coolly appropriated. The horses of the army were turned into the standing grain, wheat at that time being ripe for the sickle. Every thing was conducted with the strictest military precision. After meals, pewter knives, forks, plates, etc., were washed and scoured till they shone and then packed away for instant departure.

BENJAMIN P. HOWELL, M.D.

CHAPTER III.

FANCY HILL AND LETTERS.

THE Fancy Hill property, for more than two centuries a part of the Ladd and Howell holdings, lies along the Jersey shore of the Delaware River, opposite the lower portion of Philadelphia. Here the river broadens into the ' Horseshoe ' or Ladd's, or Howell's Cove—a wide and beautiful stretch of water—its banks, rising into high bluffs, were well wooded with fine old trees, many of which are still flourishing. The good water view from this particular spot must have suggested this to Joshua L. Howell as the site above others the most desirable whereon to build the permanent home.

The house—a long brick structure, strong, substantial, built with a view to thorough comfort and in strict simplicity as regards its architecture—attests in its every detail the

Fancy Hill House, Facing Inland

painstaking care given by the owner to its
building. Large, airy rooms, with high, carved,
wooden mantels over the large fire-places, open
on wide high-ceilinged halls in the first and
second floors a broad, Queen Anne staircase
leads from the lower hall, by easy ascent to the
ample garret-rooms, the delightful store house
of old time things and the play room dear to
the recollection of those privileged ones
whose younger days were spent at Fancy Hill.
To those, whose happy chance it was to know
it in its halcyon days, each room was endeared
by association—none more so than the lower
hall for here in fine weather sat Anna Howell,
her arm chair placed near the river door, that
she might look on the scene she loved so well
—the great hall doors thrown open to the
sweep of air filled with the antique fragrance
of box, pine and cedar trees, the subtle odor
that wakes the utmost memories of the past,
her children and grand-children drawn about
her, for here was the great gathering place.

On the water side of the house was the lawn
familiarly known as the 'Water Lot,' through

the center of this, a path led from the western,
or river front, door to the river-bank. This
path was broad, and bordered by old-fashioned
flowering shrubs and fruit trees. It is one of
the many hallowed spots, for here have paced
back and forth ' through days of sorrow and
of mirth, through every swift vicissitude of
changeful time,' those who are identified with
Fancy Hill. East of the ' Water Lot ' was
the garden—Colonel Howell's special pride;
its fine fruits and vegetables, bee-hives and
lovely flowers made it famous. It may be interesting to know the fact that the tulips, jon-
quils, hyacinths and narcissus that bloomed so
long in this garden, were brought from England by the Ladds and planted at ' Candor
Hall' whence many of them were transplanted
to Fancy Hill by Anna Blackwood Howell.

Passing eastward from the garden, you entered the ' Spring House Lot ' where the
Spring House, or dairy, of rough hewn stone
stood encircled by the clear running springs,
and shaded by magnolias, willows and the
great hickory trees—a delightsome haunt.

From this, across the lane which led to the
Cabins of the Fishery, and to the river, were
the barn, stables and pertaining buildings—important adjuncts to such an establishment, for
the remoteness of Fancy Hill from desirable
points made a strong need for good saddle and
draught horses, vehicles of all descriptions,
chief of which, was the family travelling carriage fitted up expressly for the long journies
that were often taken thro' the Jerseys and
East Pennsylvania. About the house and
grounds, evergreen trees had been planted or
preserved, also oaks, walnuts and that tree beyond compare, the American tulip, many vigorous specimens of which are still flourishing.
The approach to the house on the land side
was through an avenue flanked by cedars which
spread into a half circle, thus forming two en-
trances.

An air of completeness and good taste char-
acterised the house and its appointments, and
held as a proof that the eye of master and mistress directed and regulated a necessarily large
force of servants. Generous hospitality and a

round of innocent pleasure marked the life at
Fancy Hill, before sorrow and reverse of
fortune brought their saddening influence.
Each and all felt the abundance of peace and
restful quiet which this old home gave to
soothe or delight her children and their guests
who come at pleasure to receive the 'kind
overflow of kindness' that charm-like was
thrown over all—an influence that has drawn
toward her with pathetic longing the hearts of
her children for five generations.

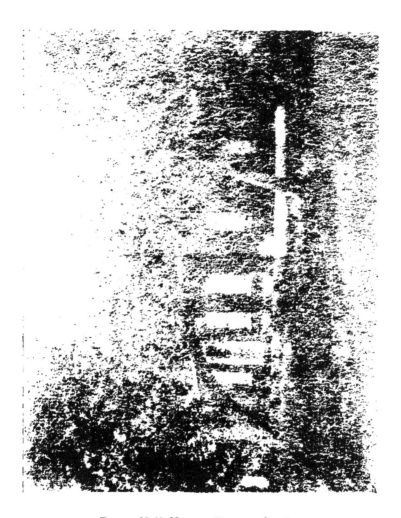

Fancy Hill House, Facing the River

AN ACCOUNT OF THE DEATH OF COL. JOSHUA L. HOWELL TAKEN FROM ANNA BLACK-WOOD HOWELL'S PAPERS.

About the 5th or 6th of November, 1817, I went to Maurice River to my beloved hufband who had been there for fome time fuperintending his bufinefs on the Salt Marfhes.

After fpending a week with him, I prevailed upon him to return with me I obferved that his ancles were confiderably fwollen and there was a purple fpot in one of them that he faid was very fore. I felt very much alarmed as I thought it indicated debility, and a bad ftate of the blood, I urged the neceffity of his living abftemioufly but his appetite was fo good that he could not give up to live on a low diet. The fpot on his ancle became very much inflamed and fo painful that he was obliged to confine himfelf to the bed. It became daily more painful and mortification fet in This however was foon checked and I flattered myfelf that it would get entirely well. But alas ! my hopes were delufions. A fimilar fpot appeared on the other ancle The fwelling increafed and every unfavorable Symptoms returned Moft unfortunately at this time Anna Maria was taken ill and her fituation appeared fo much more immediately dangerous than her father's that I feemed obliged to devote the moft of my time to her. Oh blindnefs to the future, I

can't in this inftance fay kindly given, I can never ceafe to
regret that any thing fhould have occurred to keep me from
him one hour.   On the 5th of Jan. in the morning he had
a flight ftroke of apoplexy.   On the eighth it returned and
every thing that was done proved ineffectual.   On the 10th
at half paft 9 o'clock at night he expired without a ftruggle
or a groan, in the 56 year of his age and the 32 of our
married life.   To defcribe my fufferings under this afflictive
difpenfation is fo utterly impoffible that I fhall not attempt
it.   I had not even the melancholy fatisfaction of giving
vent to my grief.   Anna Maria's life appeared fufpended
by fo flender a thread, that I was obliged to wear the fem-
blance of compofure when my heart was pained almoft to
breaking.   I am bereft of my companion and I feel that I
have loft a right hand that I mifs continually.   It is impoffible to convey the moft diftant idea of the painful void
that is felt in the mind when deprived of a beloved object.
Nearly three months have elapfed fince this forrowful event
took place and I am frequently almoft ready to doubt its
reality.

LETTERS TO AND FROM JOSHUA LADD HOWELL.

To Joshua L. Howell near Woodbury.

Dec 22. 1784

Dr Coufin

I heard the other day of the illnefs of your Father & have
been very anxious to fee him, the Situation of our own
family has prevented me & I am fenfible will fufficiently

apologife for my not coming. My Sifter Sally has been
extremely ill as alfo my Brother Arthur—they are now
nearly recovered—since which my Mother has been confined with the Quinzy fo my hands have been very full—
Your Uncle Armitt is much better—Pray let me hear from
you as foon as convenient and prefent my beft refpects to
your Father & Mother, if poffible I will fee him—

I am Dr Coufin

Yours Sincerely

JOSEPH HOWELL, Jun.

To JOSHUA L. HOWELL FANCY HILL

Philada. Aug. 23. 1797.

My Good Coufin

I have this moment rece'd your kind letter and invitation to your House During the ficknefs prevalent in this
City. Accept my dear Friend my thanks but my Situation, or rather that of my dear Wife, is fuch that I cannot
accept of the offer—My Hannah is ftill up how long it
will be I know not. I will wait on Coufin Nancy and
Polly of you wifh and inform you in a few days—do not
think the Fever is fo bad as reprefented believe me it is not
—how it may be God knows—the bearer is waiting—
therefore excufe this fcrawl and believe me as ever your
Affectionate Coufin

*JOSEPH HOWELL**

*The writer of this letter was Major Howell of Revolutionary fame, he was the
brother of Arthur Howell, the noted Quaker preacher, who wrote of Joseph Howell's death to Col. Howell. Benjamin Betterton Howell was his son by his first
wife, Rebecca Betterton.

COLL. JOSHUA L. HOWELL FANCY HILL

Philada 31 Octr 1800.

Dr Sir

I have great pleasure in congratulating you on your appointment by the Joint Meeting to be one of the Electors of New Jersey for President & Vice President and herewith send you a list of your colleagues

ADAMS & PINKNEY

William Griffith - - -	Burlington
Richard Stockton - - - -	Somerset
Thomas Sinnickson - : - -	Salem
Doct. Saml. S. Smith President of Princeton College - -	Middlesex
Judge Isaac Smith - - -	Hunderton
Mathias Williams Jun - - -	Essex
Joshua L. Howell - - -	Gloucester

carried thirty Eight Votes to fourteen—I now feel well pleased that you did not go to the assembly as this is of far more consequence, not only to New Jersey but to America; to have men that are firm and true to the Federal cause— Jersey will do her part is now not doubted and I hope that her firmness and Unanimity will encourage other States to follo v her example.

I am Dr Sir with great respect

Your Hble Servt

THOMAS HODGSON

MRS FRANCESS HOWELL KINGSESSING

F. HOWELL

Dear Mother

My not writing fooner has been owing to my being at Pens Neck for nearly 2 weeks—I got home laft fourth Day at night am done makeing hay have three flat loads yet to bring from there—have brought three loads |from there allready—as foon as I get the Hay up—fhall begin to dig the Celar of the new Houfe—have got the Hands engaged —and hope they will begin next week—I was in hopes thee had been to Brandewine and had enjoyed the pleafure of thy fifters fociety before this—am in hopes thee will yet have that enjoyment before thee returns to Jerfey—there is a talk of Anna Howells and my going to the fea fhore if thee has a wifh to go thee will let us know thee can go in the wagon with us—I fhould be pleafed with the Company of Uncle Benjamin to the fhore—if he would put his Horfe to the Chair we could change from Wagon to Chair fo as to make the journey agreeable to all—give my beft refpefts to Uncle B. and tell him ftarting is all that I have found it fo from my being frequently obliged to leave my family for 2 weeks at a time—if we go to the fhore it will not hapen in lefs than 2 weeks—pleafe to except of the beft Wifhes of thy fon

JOSHUA L. HOWELL

Mr Samuel L Howell at the Revd Thos. Pictons
West Field New Jersey

Fancy Hill Cabin June 1st 1806 Sunday 1 o'clock.

Mr. S. L. Howell

Dear Saml

While your mother is at meeting I have fat down to write to Benjn and you, and wifh you both to be here this Week, I have wrote to Benjn to come on as he is to go into the Mr. Lewifs Counting Room as you muft have feen in my letter of this Day laft, if you have got it, I put it in the Poft Office my felf, in it is a ten Dollar Note, as I expected you would want money by this time in your laft you expect to ftart by the 8th I wifh you and Benjn to be here this week as I expect to difcharge the Hands next, and want your affiftance————

Your mother and all are well, next Sunday I hope to have all my Family at my Table to Dine unlefs I fhould be difapointed in you and Benjn Frances has left Jaudon [Jaudon, a celebrated school of that day] your Grandmother is to come home to morrow from Derby

Your mother & my refpects to Mr. Picton, Mrs. P. was well on Thurfday, fo faid Mrs Barton Lautzinger in the city

Your affectionate Father

J. L. HOWELL

To Col. Joshua L. Howell
Frederick Co. Virginia Oct 17 1806

My dear Father

I am now feated in the delightful Valley of the Frederick
We reached this Paradife of Virginia on Sat. after a ride of
fixty miles on horfe back over Stony hills and muddy vallies more pleafant to behold than to travel over—I can fcarcely
with ftrict fincerity fay that it comes fully up to the exalted
notion I had been induced from my friend Meade's reprefentation to form of it. The Country is highly romantic
and altho' it is furrounded by the Blue Ridge mountains,
ftill when we compare its elevation with the plane of the
Ocean—It will itfelf almoft deferve the appellation of a
mountain—This is the Country which Mr. Jefferfon and
other modern philofophers fuppofe at fome former period
to have been inundated and to have formed an extenfive
lake. This fuppofition is grounded on the circumftances
of its being completely furrounded by high mountains and
of the vaft rupture in the loweft part of thefe mountains—
at the famous Harper's Ferry—where the Powtomack and
the Shanondoa uniting their waters appear evidently to
have forced themfelves a paffage thro' their great barrier,
leaving the fides of the mountain broken and ragged and in
fome places huge clifts impending quite over the margin of
the River—if this hypothefis be correct, we may without
any difficulty account for the fertility and exuberance of the
happy valley of Frederick. I find the people not only of
this neighborhood but of other parts of the State that I have

vifited furprifingly plain in their drefs, manners, living and equipage, as an example I will mention Mr George Wafhington Parke Curtis Grandfon of Mrs Washington and the fame little gentleman reprefented in the picture of the Wafhington Family—this gentleman whofe talents as a farmer and improver of fheep have gained him much celebrity in the Agricultural world was educated in Genl. Wafhington's family from quite a child, and in addition to a large patrimonial eftate received fomething very confiderable at the Genl's death. I had often heard Meade fpeak of his having married his Coufin Wm Fitzhugh's Sifter, and expected from the relationfhip in which he ftood to fo many great people and his mighty wealth, to have feen fomething remarkable, inftead of this when he came to Mr Fitzhugh's I was not little furprifed to find him dreffed in Clothes of the moft ordinary kind—having on, a coarfe woolen roundabout, an old weather beaten hat, and a pair of pantaloons and boots that I fhould not have felt comfortable in. Nor was his equipage inconfiftant with his drefs—he was mounted on an old fteed that in truth appeared to have feen better days but which now was almoft denied the privilege of feeing at all having under him a faddle to which our collection of old ones could fcarcely furnifh a parallel—a bridle which exactly comported with it—and armed on one heel with an old rufty spur *faying* with Hudibras That if one fide of his horfe went the other fide muft be moving. Thus tricked out you will not wonder at my furprife. But he is a ftriking exception to one of Chefterfields rules for

we are not to judge of his mind by his external appearance.
His talent may well be termed tranfcendently brilliant. He
poffefes a verfatility of genius capable of any thing which
will appear evident. When I tell you he is a farmer an author a painter and a mufician and in all of these poffefions
except the laft he may be faid to excel and in this altho
but a miferable fcraper on the violin if he continues to per-
fevere as he now does I fhould not hefitate to fay that in a
fhort time he will become a proficient. He has invited
me to vifit him after my return to Alexandria, and as I am
determined to avail myfelf of his politenefs I expeft to return to Jerfey replete with the knowledge of farming—
raifing fheep and making Virginia bacon I fhall continue
with my friend Meade till the meeting of Congrefs which
takes place in Nov. When I fhall repair to Wafhington to
witnefs the auguft fcene, I have not been to Mount Vernon yet tho' I am determined to vifit this facred fpot on
my return to Wafhington. I fpent nearly a week at Mr
Fitzhughs which was about ten miles diftant from it. but as
every day had its full engagement I found it impoffible to
gratify the earneft defire I have to fee this memorable place
Mr Curtis has very politely promifed to accompany me
thither on my return to Alexandria if his many and various
engagements will allow of it, which will be a very defirable
thing as there will be fuperior advantages in his company,
for having fpent many years of his life in habits of the
clofeft intimacy with Wafhington I fhall probably learn
from him many anecdotes relative more particularly to the

private character of this truly great man which perhaps are unknown to the many writers of his hiftory. I fhall be very glad if mother or yourfelf will write immediately on the receipt of this and inform me ;how my affairs are progreffing. they are fo intimately connected with the future that I feel very anxious about them. Give my love to Mother, Grandmother Frances, Pafchall and John Anna Maria and the reft—Be fo good as to inform me as to the ftate of the election in our County—likewife the probable refult of it in the State and how it has gone in Penna.

Yours my dear Father moft affectionately

SAM L. HOWELL

Mr Saml L Howell Student at Nassau Hall Princeton N. Jersey

Fancy Hill Decem 21ft 1806.

Saml L. Howell
Dr Saml

After leaving you we went on to Trenton and from there to the Wigwam where we arived between 10 & 11 oclock we did not leave Trenton untill dark, but drove very hard to the Indian Chiefs where we found him the Queen and Princeffes, The next Day the Captains Horfe was fo lame we where obliged to ftay and fpend the Day to the great fatisfaction of the Captain, Tewsday fet out for home in company with the Chief to Holly got there fel in with major Bird it was then propos'd to go and dine with Mr

Birzittah Newbold we went and found him wife and
Daughters at home, and very much pleafed to fee us,
went back to the Chiefs that night, next morn fet out in
two fleighs the Captn and Miss Lydia in one, the Chief
Caldwell and myfelf in the other for the City, left Lydia
there and brought the Chief with us to Fancy Hill, he left
Fancy Hill on Friday morn for the Wigwam—the family
are all well except Blackwood [Jofhua B. Howell] who
was very ill laft night with the chatarh   Your mother was
much allarmed   he is better to Day, we fhall be glad to
fee you and fome of your friends at Chriftmas if you can
prevail on Dr Smith to let you, fuppofe you where to try
it through Dr Hunter.   give my compliments to Dr Hunter, and thofe young Gentlemen that dined with you on
funday and fhall be glad to fee any of your friends at Fancy
Hill, you mother intended writeing but the Child has prevented, if you do not come down write foon

Your fincere Father

JOSHUA L. HOWELL

Mr Saml L. Howell Student at Nassau Hall Princeton
N. Jersey.

Fancy Hill Sunday Jany 4th 1807

Dear Saml

   Your Mother received yours of the 1ft laft evening.   I
am happy to hear you where agreeably entertained at Mr
Stoftons as you could not be with us at Fancy Hill   dis-
appointments fometimes are of fervice to us all, tho not

agreeable, I am in hopes to pay you a vifit with your Brothers and fifter before it be long, if there fhould be fleighing, your Grandmother is fomewhat indifpofed owing to taking cold but is about we are all well except Blackwood who has a fwelling under his ear fomething like the mumps, your mother and all your fifters and Brothers join in their love to you and Mr Estey his refpects, and wifh you a happy new Year, and that you may enjoy many is the fincere wifh of your father

J. L. HOWELL

write as frequently as you can, your mother will write foon, the Child prevents at prefent Mr Eftey's eyes prevents his writeing this morning

---

Mr SAMUEL L. HOWELL PRINCETON N, J.

Fancy Hill Sunday 22 Feby 1807

SAML L HOWELL

Dear Saml

I received yours of the 16th on Friday following am happy to find you are well, as we are all at prefent you wifh you could receive letters more frequent I fhould write oftener but bufinefs of Publick and private natures has prevented for fome time paft I have not given over my intention of Vifiting you before fifhing commences and if the roads fhould be good bring Francefs and Pafchall and perhaps more company, I have been getting out a quantity of fhip timber and Logs, but the Ice prevented my receiving money for it as they cant get it away, as foon as I can

get fome money I fhall fend you fome as I know you muft
be out, Pafchall has this morning taken Mary Clayton to
her Uncle Harrifons fhe has been here on a vifit for a week
or more, your mother has began a Letter this morning
which fhe intends finifhing this afternoon I have fettled my
fifhing buffinefs with Tatem he paying Bills to the amount
of $800 he will be indebted to me $100 I am going to
build another Cabin at home and have the Hands all under
my own Eye, and not be oblig'd to run up to the other
place, but let Tatem manage his own, and fell his own fifh.
Jeffy Sparks has engaged to be my Clerk, Benjn Esty and
John have gone to meeting, I muft finifh as your mother
wants the Pen and ink

    remaining your affectionate father

       J. L. HOWELL

COLNL JOSHUA HOWELL NEAR WOODBURY N. JERSEY.
  New York April 3d [*Probably 1809 or 1810*]
COLNL JOSHUA HOWELL
My dear friend

 Since the receipt of your efteemed favour I have been fo
much engaged that I have fcarcely had time to anfwer a fingle
letter, and truft that you will overlook my apparent neglect
in not anfwering yours earlier, accept my dear fir my fincere
thanks for your congratulations and kind offer and reft affured that fhould it be in my power to take a trip in Jerfey,
I fhall not forget my friends at Fancy Hill, fhould I be re-

moved from the Hornet, you muſt not be ſurpriſed if I take
you by ſurpriſe for there is not a man in the world I would
ſo ſoon travel a hundred miles to ſee as yourſelf. Mrs. L.
is anxious to accompany me but I am fearful will not be able
She was indeed to pay me a viſit in Boſton on my return
from my firſt cruize, and ſad to relate the poor girl *got
poiſoned.* She with myſelf beg to be affectionately to
the family. Mrs. H. and Frances are great favorites of
hers We often talk of the happy hours we have ſpent
under your hoſpitable roof, tell Benjamin I feel gratified for
his kind invitation and should I go to Philada will ſpend as
much of my time with him as poſſible altho' it will not be
in my power to meſs with him haveing relations who would
be diſappointed, preſent my reſpects to my Woodbury
friends and believe me ſincerely yours

JAS. LAWRENCE.

JOHN L. HOWELL TO THE CARE OF MORDECAI & SAMUEL
N. LEWIS. PHILA.

Boſton U. S. S. Hornet Sept. 4th 12

J. L. HOWELL
Dear Howell

We have arrived here after a long and unſucceſsful cruiſe
we have taken But a few prizes and burnt two of them
When we ſailed from New York I was in hope that we
ſhould have an opportunity of ſignalize our ſelves in the
cauſe of our country But was diſappoint however we may
have time yet The Conſtitution Friggate has taken the

pride of the Englifh Navy (The Guriere) who had a chofen crew to fall in with the U. S. Friggate President When he difcovered the Conftitution he told his men that there was a damned Yankee Frigate and he would only allow his men 20 minutes to play the Yankee and in 30 minutes he would give them Molaffes and water to drink But how was he difappointed when Capt Hull reverfed the thing precifely   When he (Capt d Acres) delivered his fword to Capt Hull he faid hear is my fworde and the firft Friggate in his Majefty fervice and wifh to know what kind of men there was on board of the Constitution for they was more like Tigers than men   The Geurier officers faid they never new nor heard like of a fhip that keep up fuch a fire in their lives   (Both the Geuriers officers and men wher eather in the battle of the Nile or traffelgar)   If all our friggates fired like the Conftitution (which they all can, for her crew was a new one) they did not know what will be- come of his majestys friggates.

We have heard fomething of a battle Between The U. S. Friggate Effex and the Britifh Friggate Maid ftone if it is true   We know which way it will end for they is not fuch a rotten crew in the U. S. Navy as the Effex has they are very near of equal————

My Beft refpect to your family togaeter with Capt Law- rence rember to my friend Sam Harrison tell him to write immediately   Have you chofen me a wife

Your fince Friend
B. COOPER*

————
*Ben Cooper's father was Capt James Cooper, a soldier in the Revolution.

JOHN L. HOWELL TO THE CARE OF MORDECAI SAMUEL N. LEWIS

U. S. Sloop of War Hornet Boston Sept 18 '12

J. L. HOWELL

Dear Sir

I had the pleasure this morning receiving a letter from your amiable hands—

You wish to know the circumstances Between the President & Belviderer we discover'd a sail at 6 a. m. and made sail in chase at 11 discoverd the sail to Be an English Frigate. at 4 Commodore commence fireing which was return By the Enemy at ½ past 4 discovering the Enemy to heavy our . . . Boates anchors, spars and everything that could lighting her in order to escape Commoder finding at this Time he was a droping her sheered and gave her three or four Braw fide in order to carry away her spars But a number of her shot fell short at ½ past 5 cease fireing on the Enemy But still in chase   The (Congress was second she fired two shots But Both fell short) we chased till 2 Oclock a m and then lost sight of the Belvir. this is as correct account as possible can Be given. all those dam'd Raschall that accues Com. Rogers of cowerdice any thing out of way in Regard in not caping the Belvidire if I hear

---

When a boy he (J. C.) was apprenticed to a man in Woodbury who locked him up in a room. He jumped out of a window and enlisted under Capt Henry Lee who was here recruiting at the time. He fought in the Carolinas with Marion and Morgan. J. Cooper was a staunch friend of Joshua and Anna Howell though much their senior. He used often to visit Fancy Hill and spin his yarns. He swore dreadfully and when he did so Anna B. Howell's face would lengthen but only for an instant as his fun was irresistable. He married a cousin of the family by the name of Morgan.

him he fhall give me fatisfaction (if he is a Gentleman) he fhall eather take my life or I his. Commodore Rogers is as Brave a man as ever ftept on Board of a fhip and a friend to his country. The Englifh has keep fix of the Naultys crew and they are a going to take them to England to try them for they fay they are english But we know two of them to Be American men. Commoder Rogers has taken 1 2 of the Geurier's crew and fays if thofe hang them, he will hang two for one. . . I received a letter this morning from Harrifon who informs, me of your courting a Butiful girl and fhe accepts of your courtship I shall anfwer Harrifon to morrow

Yours forever

B. COOPER

N. B. I cannot tell you when we fhall fail tho' we are now in under Commodore Bainbridge who has taken the Conftitution as Capt Hull is on fourleigh in our fquadron Conftitution, Cheefepek, Conftitution, a Hornet the Chesepeck will be ready for fea in a fhort time we are much the fuperior force of other two fquadrons Rogers & Decatur

B. COOPER

COLONEL JOSHUA L. HOWELL WOODBURY GLOSTER
COUNTY NEW JERSEY.

Newark, Oct 26th 1803

My Dr Jofbua

I have been attempting to write you for fome time—you

are all in Mourning and fadnefs of Heart has taken poffeffion of you & yours & you have great caufe for Mourning the beft of Mothers & the beft of Brothers have been taken from you in a very short fpace of Time But it is under the order and direction of that being who giveth & has a right to take when he pleafeth and who never does wrong.   .

I have faid [I believe a thoufand Times] that except my own Mother I never had thofe filial feelings for any other woman that I ever was acquainted with but Mrs. Ellis— There was fuch an overflowing of human kindnefs in her actions, words, looks and ,in her whole life & converfation that I became her child by election & fhall remember her with affection as long as memory remains.   All her family appeared to be related to me & I can truly fay I mourn the death of John Blackwood as I ought the Death of a Brother and friend.   His fifters & all his connections have received in the Death of this truly ufeful Man a great lofs—your county has received a great lofs & the State and Union have received a great lofs when a fenfible {prudent Man dieth. You will my Dr friends remember me With affection to all others as if named and nothing now remains but that I subfcribe myfelf with the fincerity of Friendship your Brother & unchangable friend. ,

J. N. CUMMING.

To Col. Howell in New York

Afhfield N. J. Aug 26 1814

My dear father

I have juft now received the alarming tidings of the

deftruction of our Capitol by the enemy—What is next to happen short of the demolition of Baltimore, Philadelphia and New York, for in the name of Heaven what is to prevent ? Where is now the martial fpirit of Americans where the patriots who were to facrifice their lives their fortunes —nay their *Sacred honour* too, in its fupport ! Alas ! they fly at the fight of the enemy—they retreat across the Potomack at the mere found of British Cannon and they referve their lives, fortunes & facred honour—nay even their fire too, for a fitter opportunity. Such is the fample we have given the enemy of our valour and at a time too when every incentive which could inflame a real patriots bofom is offered to excite it into action. The invading foe in the heart of our Country menacing our very homes and firefides. Emboldened by fuch daftardly conduct what will not Great Britain attempt.

It is high time fomething were doing for the protection of Philad—depend upon it—it is in Jeopardy and I tremble at the anticipated iffue.

There is a draft of Militia ordered by the Governor which extends to your regiment and to be made immediately—The particulars of which I will afcertain from John Clement (Major) and will apprife you. To change this diftreffing fubject to one far more grateful to your feelings— a domeftick one—We are all in good health and enjoying all thofe comforts which externally refult from our fituation and are now rated as far more eftimable by the apprehenfion that this may foon be interrupted. Mary is fitting by the cradle rocking her little Anna and Sally is enjoying the sweets of repose after a day of amusements. Anna Maria & the little boys are well. Mary sends her love to you all and hopes the enjoyment of your visit may n't be interrupted by the news from the South—I shall go to the City on the morrow—*Philad. Sat. 9th.* The people are in great consternation here—There is a report of a British fleet being in the bay of great force—God preserve our Country ! Nothing under Heaven, save the rising of the people en masse can save us from recolonization. You'll be obliged to return home e're long. It is time we were doing something in Jersey—will have a volunteer Corps or two organized against your return—The first Company of Washington Guards have again volunteered—The 2d Company, together with the City Fencibles—First troops of horse & some other Corps march this day for Kennets Square to be ready to act either on the Chesapeake or Delaware—We must all become soldiers or Independance is no more. My brother John & Sam Harrison were last evening appointed Sergeants in the first Corps of Guards. Yours affectionately

       SAML. L. HOWELL.

[Battle at North Carolina and Bombardment of Fort McHenry Sept. 1814.]

To be forwarded as early as possible.

To Col. Joshua Howell near Woodbury N. J.

            Philad.

Dr Sir

 The English have landed at North Point to attack Baltimore—Forces differently ſtated 5000 to 15000 men—they have undoubtedly been reinforced—When the mail came out yeſterday Afternoon the armies were engaged & the firing was heard by the paſſengers for ſeveral hours. 32 Sail of ſquare rigged veſſels were ſtanding for the town and bombarding the forts. We are all in great anxiety to learn the reſult which we hope to do ſome time tonight—Genl. Smith deſpatched an expreſs requeſting Genl Bloomfield to order the troops from here to his aſſiſtance which he however declined

Yours

B. B. HOWELL

———

[From Genl F. Davenport to Col Joſa. L. Howell with reference to the foregoing letter]

Col Howell

I do not See in the within anything that may immediately require the Jerſey requiſition under your Command to move—Why Genl Bloomfield has *declined* to march the troops under his Command in Philad.—we know not— The morning or poſſibly *this night* may let us know more. At preſent no official is ſent us

F. DAVENPORT.

———

Millville Sunday evening Nov 20th 1814

My dear Father

You ſee we are progreſſing toward the place of our deſtination. We marched fifteen miles today and as the three laft miles were fandy beyond even the tracklefs deferts of Africa our men were, many of them, worn down with fatigue, but we are all in good fpirits, and I believe anxious, to a man, for the novel and untried fcenes of *an affair* with John Bull's myrmidons—I have borne the hardfhips of a foldiers life without any great inconvenience and fo long as I retain my prefent appetite and there is no fighting to be done, I fhall not *die by foldiering.* We fhall not reach the Cape before Wednefday, when, if rumors are to be credited we may as well face to the right about and countermarch home again, for by this, it would appear that the enemy frightened no doubt by your approach, have quitted our waters thereby depriving us of the pleafure of driving them off fecundum artem—You fhall be apprifed of our progrefs, meanwhile believe me yours very truly and refpectfully

SAML L. HOWELL

Fifhing Creek 30th Nov 1814

My dear Father

This difmal day by interrupting the regular routine of Camp duty allows me time to give a brief account of our fituation and proceedings here

We arrived on the 24th and found the Coaft clear, on the 25 however, a fmall tender [fhooner] made her appearance ftanding up the bay and a barge about 6 miles ahead ftanding in the fame direction—Their apparant object was an outward bound brig which had juft before made

her appearance, but night following we loft fight of them.
The next afternoon ¦Major Strong and I rode to Cold
Spring where we learned that the brig had been run afhore,
we rode thither and found her to be the Union of Philad
the Supercargoes (young Negus and Rooverft, nephews of
Mrs. Woodruff) reported that they were run on fhore in
the preceding evening in a bright moonlight, owing to the
drunkenefs of the pilot and, I fufpect the treachery of the
Captain. The fufpicious looking fchooner ftill lay in the
offing apparently watching her opportunity to Catch the
brig when circumftances should favor her, induced Major
Strong to propofe that a company should be detached for
her protection during the night. Our Company was detached for this fervice and the line of march was taken up
with fo much filence that not half a dozen men in Camp
the fentinels excepted knew of our abfence. We reached
the Brig at one in the morning to find that they had got her
off at the preceding high tide and that the enemy had dis-
appeared we ftationed a ftrong guard at the beach. The
brig remained undifturbed during the night, we continued
at our poft till the 2nd day when we were ordered to repair
to the encampment I took charge of the company and
marched them round by Cape Ifland and difmiffed them at
Mother Hughes for a half hour where they had their own
merriment on the Strand, viewing the Ocean a curiofity new
to many of them. I am juft informed by Orderly Hugg
that you are now on your march hither and as this letter
may only anticipate our meeting a day or two, I will thank

you after reading it, to feal it again and fend it to my mother who will be pleafed to hear from me, and on the prefumption of her receiving it will fay a few words exprefly for her hearing. The night after my arrival at Cape May Court Houfe I vifited Mary Holmes nee Leaming now Confort of Robert Holmes of roguifh memory. Mr. & Mrs. H. were very pleafed to fee me and preffed me much to repeat my vifits during my ftay which I fhall be glad to do whenever I can obtain leave of abfence. While at Cape Ifland I vifited the feveral rooms occupied by our family party of 1803, the chambers have now the fame appearance which then impreffed my memory and I could almoft fancy that I faw their former inmates prefent before me. I muft conclude but firft dear mother let me requeft thee to fee Mary & my little ones as often as you can and whenever you can fpare my Sifter Anna her Company will be very grateful to Mary who muft be even more lonely than thou art

> Yours moft Affectionately
> 　　*SAML. L. HOWELL*

To Col. Joshua L. Howell Cold Spring
　　　Dennis Creek Monday Dec. 5. 1814

Sir

according to orders received from Majr Genl Shinn, Capt Armftrong is to remain at Cold Spring, Capt Swaine at Fifhing Creek, Capt Peterfon to be placed at Gofhen and Captains Bunt & Bowen at this place. I fend down to you two videttes for the purpofe of fending up to Port Elizabeth, where I fhall take my quarters tomorrow any information of occurrences that may take place on Cape May, and alfo the weekly returns of the troops, until further orders.

You will occupy any place, moft convenient to yourfelf from Cold ₁Spring to this Poft for the prefent, And if in your opinions the videttes are not neceffary, fend them up to me that I may difcharge them. The Quarter Mafter Genl will make provifions for their fubfiftence below. Major Seagraves will be ordered on to Cumberland or Salem and therefore the troops in Cape May will be entirely to your direction, fubjeĉt to fuch orders as you may from time to time receive from your

Humble Servant

EBEN ELMER Brigdr Genl

To the Officer Commanding the United States Forces
at Cape May
His Britannic Majefty's Ship Spencer Delaware, Dec. 7.
1814.

Sir

Having underftood from the Officer Sent by me to land the Mafter of the Schooner Moreau on the 1st inst. (whofe bad health and a wifh to make the misfortunes of War light, induced me fo to do) that you had four British Prifoners of War whom you wished to Exchange for an Equal Number of Americans; I have therefore Sent four of the United States Subjects and truft you will allow the Exchange to take place, and can affure you that I fhall at all times feel a

Olpha Bonny pleafure in meliorating the fate of War, on
Peter Lawrence Equal terms. The names of the American
Thos Dowers Subjects who are fent to be exchanged are
N¹ Anderfon in the margin.

I have the Honor to be Sir Your Moft Obdt Humble Svt Richd Raggett Captain and Senior Officer of His Brittanic Majefty's Ship off the Delaware

---

Cold Spring 8th Dec 1814 1 P. M.

Dear Sir

Having recd information early this morning that a flag was approaching the Ifland from the Enemy's Ship lying in the Bay I haftened to the Beach to receive & meet it.

Upon the landing of the boat the enclofed was delivered to me by the 3rd Lieut. of the Spencer—he was accompanied by a midshipman & four men—I informed him that I had recd orders yefterday to forward the Prifoners, to whom he alluded, to Philad. & that thofe orders as far as concerned me had been put in a train of execution—and in a mode to make their fituation as comfortable, at this inclement feafon, as could be adopted—The officer requefted permiffion and feemed anxious to procure butter and vegetables for the Commodore—This I of courfe declined granting.

I shall wait with anxiety to hear from you—the vidette that carries this will bring me your anfwer

[not signed]

To Col. Jos. L. Howell

Port Elizabeth Dec 9 1814

Dear Sir

I have juft received your letter of yefterday, with the enclofed communication from the Britifh Commodore in the Delaware by a vidette.   As General Gaines has directed the British Prifoners to be fent to Philad. we are not competent to make an exchange.   befides as the Commodore calls thofe in his poffeffion ' American Subjects ' it is not clear that they are real prifoners according to the Cartels— They may be non Combatants and not proper fubjects of exchange.   If the Commodore is willing to land thofe in his poffeffion, you can give a receipt for them Specifying in the receipt their names, places of refidence & manner of capture of each individual ; and the exchange referred to the Commanding Genl or Commiffary of Prifoners.   If confent is given the British Prifoners will be releafed. The Commodore may be affured that the American officers will be at all times as ready, and ufe every means in their power, 'To meliorate the fate of war on equal terms' with as much freedom as any of his Brittanic majefty's officers.

It may be proper for you to remain at your prefent Station for the prefent. Genl Shinn left orders for me to continue the Troops at the refpective pofts they at prefent occupy until further inftructions are received from Genl Gaines ; and I fhall remain at this place untill that time. The Horfemen, except a Sergeant and fix privates have been difcharged. The Sergeant & four have gone to Bridgetown to be mufter'd ; two of them I expect will be here today. When any urgent occafion should make it neceffary to fend up a vidette, he will be relieved and another fent down in his place.

I am Sir

Your Humb. Servt

EBEN ELMER Brig. Genl.

Mrs. Anna Howell Fancy Hill

Etna Furnace Sept. 9. 1816

My Dear Anna

I reached the Lake in the evening but took no cold after the wet ride—On Saturday laft went deer hunting got a young Buck had two fair fhots at him broke one of his fore legs and feveral fhots in his body, but he ran a mile to a mill pond when Jonas waded in and cut his throat—I am engaged this morning in raifing the Bridge over McNeals branch—I am fo well that I am fure I could walk from morn till night. I think the Furnace will be done this week. I fhall be engaged all this week in running roads, and hunting ore—and wifh to clear out the channel below

the wharf, and look up the navigation to the Grifcom Ore
bed   .   .   .

Nov. 1816

Arthur Howell arrived here laft night (reports letters to
come for me by the ftage) which makes a pleafant addition
to our family of bachelors

Did Anna Maria, Richard, Jos & Ben reach home fafely
—tell me every thing that you think will intereft me. I
wifh Griffiths to make me a warm coat—let it be *blue*—a
double breafted one, to lap over well. I have taken a
flight cold—if thee could fend it I fhould like fome of the
cough drops thee makes for me. Tell Sammel I am badly
off for a faddle horfe—we alfo need 4 pair of oxen I can't
go in fearch of them or any other needful thing for want
of a horfe to ride. Dams muft be raifed before we can get
into blaft, the laft bellows is going on—I can't fay when
we will get in blaft—I fend thee a draft of the prefent road
from Tuckahoe up to Woodbury—I do not recollect anything more at prefent—to fee thee would be the moft agreeable to me at prefent.   .   .   .   .   .

JOSHUA L. HOWELL

Mrs. Anna Howell
Etna Works N. J. Dec. 30 1816

my dear Anna

The Etna Works are done at laft—the mill wrights
finifhed yefterday I fent them to the poft this morning. I
will give thee Jofhua Haines and Captain Andrew Steel-

man's opinion as to the value of this property—they fay there is from 40 to 50 acres of Cedar Swamp, that is worth from $10 to $300 per acre that the Cedar Swamp and the Cedar railes on the property is worth the purchafe money. that the pine raw timbers and coating timbers are cheap at the price. So much for my firft days work—I would not take $4000 for my or our bargain. Stoby is to meet us on Tuefday to finifh running round it. We are in hopes it contains 600 acres, and fome likely places for ore—we know there is a large quantity of good ore. Haines & Steelman fay the Cedar rails on the property are worth $2000 as there are two or three acres from which Stewart fays he can clear one thoufand dollars per acre. I finifh this by Candle light—I am well and wanting my breakfaft--I wifh thee good morning and a happy New Year—as it is near and will come before I can fee thee my love to all my children

Believe me thine Sincerely

JOSHUA L. HOWELL

Etna Works Jan 17. 1817.

Am glad to learn from thy letter that thee and all our family are well altho' the weather I think was never colder in this country as is proved by its freezing the rivers & Delaware Bay—Captain Robinfon reports its being frozen as far as they can fee from our Bank and it is faid almoft acrofs from Cape May to the Light Houfe at Cape Henlopen.

The Furnace works as well as a Furnace can work, fo fays Beft, but the Grifcom Ore wont do I fear—I am fixing a place to burn loam & ftone—I have found that bed that Walker talked of it is almoft as good by the magnet as the Deal ore—it is very rich and a large bed of it. We *muft have it* and that *foon*. I write to thee that thee may fhow it to John & Benjm. as they may be there. . . . thee may conclude that it has ftormed hard as I have not been out of the houfe fince my coming—thank the All wife God it looks like clearing—at leaft the moon gives fome light throug the dimmer Clouds. I am thankful more particularly on account of the Poor Souls that may be too near our Coaft for we have had a tremendous ftorming day on Shore—it muft have been horrid at fea. I hope we fhall not hear of any accidents along the Coaft—tho' many would be glad to fee a fhip afhore in the morning—

Tell Hill to put on the White Oak plank on the boats. William ftarts early in the morning with fome long boards 35 ft long. Tell Samuel I feel under obligations to him for his Particular attention to my bufinefs and I fear to the injury of his own—I wifh thee to come down—come in the fleigh and will fend it back before the fnow goes—thee will ftay here awhile of courfe. Almoft 10 o'clock Good Night; I wish thee and our children many happy nights of reft and days of eafe and may you never know what want is. the wish of thine

Yours Sincerely
JOSHUA L. HOWELL.

COL. JOSA. L. HOWELL DIVIDING CREEK CUMBERLAND

Co. N. J.

Fancy Hill Dec 31 1809

Thy letters received with pleasure and to learn that thee continues well both on account of the badness of the weather and the danger thee would be exposed to at the raising of the Mill—thee knows very serious accidents sometimes happen at such places and the wealth of the Indies could not compensate this family for serious misfortunes happening to thee. Tomorrow is the beginning of another year I sincerely hope thee may enjoy many returns of it. We have lived together 24 years, it seems a little while to me but it is hardly probable that we shall live together 24 years more. I hope we shall live together in another and better world.

We have heard from the Brahmin, Paschalls ship, by Capt. Tallman, off Minerva 4 or 5 days sail from Malta and all well, that was little more than a month after she left here I cast my eyes over a list of departed Friends, which brought to my mind the mercy of the Almighty, in sparing us to each other and our children to this day while so many younger Couples have been separated—how sincerely my dear Joshua do I wish that we could be sensible of this great blessing.

[*ANNA B. HOWELL*]

COLL JOSHUA L. HOWELL ETNA FURNACE NEW JERSEY

Philadelphia Nov. 1st 1817.

COL. J. L. HOWELL

Dear Sir

I have not been unmindful of your request to purchase a racking Horse, having made much enquiry as well as engaged a number of your and my Friends to assist me—but without success. Horses of that description are remarkably scarce & dear—I shall continue my enquiries and think that the chance will be much better as Winter approaches, please advise me how high I may go—an old racking Horse sold a few days since for 130 drs & the seller wishes to purchase him again

I have once more made Philada my residence, say 118 Spruce Street where I hope soon to take you by the Hand, for which pleasure I am anxiously looking—

The weather prevents our landing the Iron for Dorchester arrived yesterday, some little has been landed & very much approved.

I was in hopes to have paid you a visit this Fall & still have some feint hopes of doing so—B. B. H. & myself have been unusually busy & hope to be kept so—perhaps I can blend business with pleasure & get down before you have shot all the Deer

I am dear Sir

Yours very sincerely

REEVE LEWIS

To Col. Joshua L. Howell Fancy Hill N. J

Philad 8 mo 10. 1798

Beloved Coufin

Thefe are to inform of the deceafe of my brother Jofeph yeftermorn abt. Nine was inter'd this ab't fame time & though many doubted of the propriety of an Invitation and that few would attend the ffuneral yet there was a refpect- ful Compy attended. I should have informed thee yefter- day of his removal and came home with the intention to write thee on the fubject—but on advifing with feveral per- fons & taking the prefent alarming fituation of our City into confideration believed it moft prudent to omit it. Not feel- ing Eafy to Expofe thee to Danger by coming out of pure into infected air—though I have no caufe to doubt thy feel- ing mind will affect thyne eyes on this occasion.

Dear little Benjamin inclines to ftay a few days to be equipped with Cloathes—after which dear Coufin thou'lt I have no doubt take him under thy Care & Supply the vacancy of a tender Father who loved him much & may the God of Abraham Isaac & Jacob be with him & thee and thine teaching you by his good Spirit the way you should go—that fo in Concluding and trying moments his Joy may be your Strength

I remain Affectionately thine

ARTHUR HOWELL

Col. Joshua L. Howell

Philad. 8 mo. 13. 1798
(Firſt Day Evening near Ten P. M.)

Dear Couſin

I wrote thee on the 10th which expeƈt thou receivedſt that evening by Jno Pew informing of the removal of my poor brother—I intended Benjm should have ſtayed to be new cloathed but by the cloſing paragraph of thine believed it beſt he should return by John Pew which [informed he was to be here tomorrow morng left his longer ſtay in the City might give uneaſineſs to thy Dear Mother & Wife in creating fears about receiving him—though at preſent there is no real danger—our Neighbourhood as alſo his Mother being Healthy & Clear of infeƈted perſons. Moſt of the caſes moſt tranſpired are traced to the ſpot where it firſt made its appearance viz. Ross' Wharf between Walnut St & the Dock where the putrified coffee was landed. One Caſe only has come to my knowledge of a probability of recoverry among all that have taken it in that quarter and tho' it proves thus Mortal no inſtance it is ſaid yet has occurred of others taking it from them—there is ſomething very Infeƈtious certainly in that Neighbourhood as its Baneful Effects have ſpread each way North & South from the Center—It has even reached ſo far South as Stanpens Wharf where a woman died laſt week and North to Teniſs & Aveſly's Store—the latter is now ill as is a ſon of Widow Hamilton an apprentice to Jas. Yard on Walnut St. Wharf—he is very ill and it's thought this Night will cloſe

the scene of Life with him, My family are yet with me—
though they intend to remove to a kind friend's in Beggers
above Germantown.   My Lot from preſt. proſpects will be
to remain in this City as thou knoweſt Dear Couſin when
a ſoldier in the outward Army is fixed at his Poſt by his
commanding Officer however dangerous it may appear to
him or others it's Death to him to deſert it & ſo my dear
Couſin do I view my preſent Situation & unleſs I receive
a Command from my dear Maſter & Captain to move therefrom—I dare not, however hazardous my ſtay may to myſelf or others appear—His power is the ſame it ever was
(it's not diminiſhed) Whatever the ſons of defeſtion may
think.   He preſerved Daniel in the Lyons Den, & Shad-
rack Meſheck & Abednego in the Fiery Furnace & he can
& I firmly believe will preſerve me & all thoſe whoſe truſt
and confidence is fixed on him—Glory to His Ever bleſſed
Name ſaith my ſoul in that he has redeemed mee from all
ſublunary enjoyments & my Soul from the Power of the
Grave So that to me Death has no Terrors—Neither believe I will the Grave have any Victory—which that it may
be thy caſe as well as mine & all mankind Univerſally by
a Steady attention to the pretious Gift of Divine Grace is
the Earneſt deſire of thy Affeſtionate Couſin

                                    ARTHUR HOWELL

   N. B. Dear Ben will bring Cloathes with him with
which thou canſt have him Equipped at Leiſure & Should
he bring his Deare Father's watch pleaſe take Care of it
until he arrives at ſuitable age to wear it—with love to thee

and thine including thy dear Mother I remain affectionately.

Thine

ARTHUR HOWELL

To Joshua L. Howell Fancy Hill

Philada 9 mo 6. 1801

Beloved Coufin

I have wifhed to fee thee for fome time paft and am forry
I did not know thou waft in this City a few days fince—
this convinces that a more frequent Intercourfe between us
would not only. be pleafant but profitable—was in hope
John Hallowell would have feen thee as I have had occafion to apply to him of late on dear Benjamin's behalf—as
I find from fome late movements of the Widow they are
about Applying to the Orphan's Court with their accts.
and to have Guardians appointed for the Children—it was
to have been done laft Court but fomething prevented—
previous to which I fpake to John Hallowell to attend the
Court in order to object to their appointing One for Benjamin as he is of an age to Chufe for himfelf. The Court
will be the third Sixth Day in this month and as I am
likely to be out of the City muft leave it to thy Judgment
and difcretion to act in the cafe. Will it not be neceffary
for thee to come to the City & bring Benjamin or to fend
him with a Letter &c to John Hallowell to act for him—in

thy or his own name. I expect Brothers Widow & Father will attend on that day to proceed in the choice of one for her fon. John Hallowell attended the laft Court at my requeft to object to any appointment of theirs, but they did not attend, their accounts not being ready. I have informed Sifter Hannah that Benjamin is of an age to chufe a Guardian & defires to do it for himfelf

Remaining with due regard thy Affectionate Coufin

ARTHUR HOWELL

N. B. My Love to All as if Named.

EXTRACTS FROM SAMUEL MICKEL'S DIARY.*

Francis Howell here before & from Meeting. Arthur Howell here from Meeting, came forward in lively teftimony.

5 mo 1804 my beloved wife and Frances Howell about to ftart for Salem in the Chair. In the evening I bro't Frances Howell [Joshua's mother] here in Chair to be in readinefs to go to Salem.

11 mo. 1804 this P. M. my beloved wife and Sarah Ladd went to fee Frances Howell fenr. faid to 've had a paralytic ftroke but on their return fay fhe is better of a bad cold and no paralytic affection.

1 mo. 1806 Anna, wife of Jofhua Howell & fon Pafchall and daughter Anna Maria Howell on vifit till abt. 8 P. M. & T^d [took tea]

5 mo. 1806 Arthur Howell in meeting favoured in teftimony and in fupplication, has returned from a religious vifit as far down as Maurice's River in Jerfey.

1806, 4 mo. In P. M. went with my dear wife to Jofhua Howell's having heard of his being very ill, found him better, and the next week my beloved wife and I rode to Jofhua Howells to befpeak shad & to fee his poorly [sick] wife,

*Samuel Mickle was a nephew of Hannah Ladd—in this Diary frequent mention is made of the members of Joshua Howell's family as above.

found her better, on our way home called at Candour Hall
to fee his mother Frances and took T.

1809, 1st mo. Sam L. Howell fpent y° even   here, alfo
his brother Pafchall fome time, and their father Jofhua
Howell.   Jofhua Howell's wife anna and daughter Frances
on vifit y° P. M.

1811, 8 mo. 5th In P. M. took Sarah Ladd with me
to fee Jofhua Howell's mother Frances who has been bed-
ridden moft of a year and continues fo, his fon Richard ill
with fever

22nd Jofhua Howell's daughter Rebecca Interred y°
P. M.

26th hear Jofha Howell's bound girl decd & Interred
this P. M.   Alfo hear Jofhua Howell's daughter Anna
Maria & bound boy are ill.

29th Pafchall Howell ill

9 mo 1811 1ft Hear that Jofhua Howell is ill & his fon
Pafchall decd y° eveng abt. funfet

2d attended at Friends' Burial Ground y° funeral of Pafchall Howell abt. noon.   A fmall company and I think not
one female, Jofhua Howell's daughter Abigail ill of the
fever at her brother Saml's farm ' Ashfield ' Jofha Howell
lies in a ftupor

10 mo 1811, 21ft This P. M. in Co. with Sarah and
her fon John Mickle Whitall went to fee Frances Howell
at her fon Jofhua's at Ladd's Cove, found her very low
with fever of which 3 of his family decd in 9 mo. laft   By
advice of Phyficians s^d Jofhua, his wife and surviving

children have all removed away for a time, fome to Benjamin Howell's in Philad & fome to 's fon Samuel's.

1812, 5 mo, 2nd About 3 y⁵ morning Frances Howell
widow of John Ladd Howell & mother of Jofhua Howell
deceafed to be interred tomorrow to meet a 3 P. M. at
requeft of faid Jofhua I notified y⁰ 3 fchools of the funeral.

1818 1 mo. 11th This morng recd an Invitation to y⁰
Funeral of Jofha L. Howell, to meet tomorrow 11 A. M.
Deceafed at 9.30 laft night.   I was wth him on a vifit at
his houfe 8 mo. 28, laft.   Thomas Saunders took me y⁰
P. M. to Jofhua L. Howell, Benj B. Howell informed me y⁰
deceafed was 55 years old in 9th mo laft

12th Attend'd at Frds Burl Ground in Woodbury, the
Funeral of Jofha L. Howell

18.   .   .   ⁻ Lot in m⁵ thought on y⁰ multitudes
of my Frds. & acquaintances gone to their long homes &
near or quite whole families extinct.   On y⁰ 2d inft the
fcythe of Death brufh'd me down, on its way to Jofh L.
Howell !

LETTERS TO AND FROM ANNA BLACKWOOD HOWELL.

Mrs Ann Howell Fancy Hill Gloster County New Jersey.

Newark, Sept 11th 1811

My Dr Madam I had yefterday written you a letter of condolence, mourning over your great and fevere loffes, I felt for you I am fame as a Brother for a Sifter, that he loves, yefterday I lamented for your lofs of a Hufband, a Daughter a Son, to Day have only to mourn for your lofs of Daughter & Son, being correctly informed that your Hufband is living, and I fincerely pray God that he may live, live long, a bleffing to his Dr wife, Family & friends, & may that God who has wounded you lonely, pour into your wounded Bofom the balm of confolation, which is needful for you—may he reftore thofe of your family which are fick to Health & fill your Hearts with Gratitude. My Harp was yefterday hung upon the willows today I rejoice. My Dr. Mrs Cumming almoft a ftranger to you wept for you. She with me on reading Wm. Stocktons Letter of yefterday from Philada & learning that the refidue of the Family are in a fair way of Recovery with me rejoices in

---

*Letter written at time of death of Paschall and Rebecca. J. N. C. was a friend of Josh L. and Anna as well as of John L. Howell.

which our Children join although unknown to you, all
being pleafed, that their father's friends are in a hopeful
way of recovery.   Make my moft affectionate regards to
your Dr Jofhua and may God in whom the lives of all his
creatures are, have your all in his holy keeping is the fincere
prayer of your

affect. friend

J. N. CUMMING.

To Miss Ann Blackwood at Mr William Hugg's
Timber Creek

Naffau Hall Feb 26. 1784

Dear Miss

With great pleafure I received yours of the 19th, laft
evening & fhall endeavor to give you a few lines in return
for the favour tho' I muft tell you that my head is at present fo full of Latin & Arith. that I am fearful I fhall be unable to give you any thing diverting

A few evenings ago the Senior Clafs of this Inftitution
pronounced orations on the public Stage & I think fome of
them were the moft curious I ever heard, there were fome
who acted the parts of lovers—fome fpoke on the advantage
of long nofes, others ridiculed them—but among them all
there were none more ferious than one who gave the relation of an old woman's dream, which was this, fhe thought
that all the people in Princeton were to be affembled in the
College Hall, together with the Students & that in the laft
day of this month the College and all Princeton indeed,

were to be funk further under the Earth than it is poffible
for any one to imagine, but after they had waited longer
than the expected before it came and it did not come, fhe
prayed to the Lord to fave her foul from lying at which all
prefent faid Amen ! As you defire novelty and do not like
too much of one thing or you are different from moft of
you own fex, it may be dangerous to throw any reflection
on fo refpectable & worthy a body as the females are
neither would I even caft one on them, as I fhould be very
unhappy to incur their difpleafure. Pleafe to write the firft
opportunity

Believe me to be your friend & humble Servt

WILLIAM HUGG, Jun.

SPINNING & CARDING

A NEW SONG.

1

If to fpinning and carding and breaking of wool
You with pleafure can liften and think it not dull
Attend with good humour an mirth to my fong
And fhould it prove trifling it fhall not be long.

2

A great Colonels Lady ftands firft in the Groupe
Commander in chief of this diligent troop
Her wheel with rapidity traverfes round
A few better fpinners in Jerfey are found

3

Then clofe at her fide there brifk Miftrefs Patty
A carding of rolls and moft wonderful chatty
And that both lefs fatigue from their working may feel
They exchange with each other the cards and the Wheel

4

Then next on the floor then fits Beautiful Nancy
A picking of wool with a flight you muft fancy
She culls it fo nicely and freaks it fo clean
That one who works better is fcarce to be feen

5

Good natured Prifcilla affifts at the toil
Whofe countenance alway appears with a fmile
With a laugh of good humour she lightens her labour
And tries all she can for to equal her neighbour

6

Little Beck is the next, and a fmile or a frown
Breaks out on her face as her labor goes down
When tired of working her fpirits to rally
She gets up and plays with her young fifter Sally

7

Nor yet muft the fong forget Polly to praife
Who with gravity reels but with fprightlinefs plays
And at work or at play thou think it a jeft
Ambition excites her to equal the beft

8

But now I your patience no longer will tire
And finish with what is my hearty defire
And that plenty and peace may crown Carding and Spinning
That joy unto them may be always beginning

J.

Miss Blackwood [direction]

THOMAS JOHNSON* of Gloucefter City N. J.

Samuel Howell near Woodbury.

Cape Ifland Auguft the 22d 1802

My Dear Boys

I include you all, Benjamin, Samuel Pafchall and John,
we arrived at port Elizabeth the evening of the day we left
home, very much fatigued and allmoft devoured with muf-
quetoes, it is quite a wildernefs, we travled many miles without feeing a houfe, or anything to induce one to believe it
was inhabited, except once in a while a corn field, but
neither houfe nor barn to be feen near them.

---

*The above is by ' Master Johnson ' the same that wrote so often to John Ladd
Howell rhyms about Candor Hall. He from other papers appears to have been a
school master.

'Johnson was an English gentleman reduced in his circumstances. He had frequent remittances from his family but not sufficient perhaps to support him entirely. His feelings were so wounded by a gentleman in Gloucester that he left
the place. He was very soon applied to by the people in Woodbury—he removed
there—but he never felt at home. He had become warmly attached to the inhabitants of Gloucester & his separation from them seemed to break an already
bruised spirit. He died in 17— and found a stranger's grave. I did not attend his
funeral & I cant recollect why—I deplored his loss in common with very many
others. '' By foreign hands thy dying eyes were closed. ' ''—*Anna Blackwood
Howell.*

Johnson was Anna Blackwood Howell's tutor.

George Whitalls wife went in company with us, fhe concluded they lookd pretty well, confidering they were alone it is neceffary for perfons coming to Cape Ifland to have ftrong Waggons, good horfes, and agreeable Company. there is fo little variety in a great part of the road it is intirely cheerlefs. The next evening we got to the fhore, poor little Richard was very diverting the firft day we travelled, but the fecond was quite too much for both the Children, they have been very fick indeed this is the firft leafure hour I have had fince I came here. Richard is afleep and Jane has Abbigail away, therefore you muft let one letter fuffice for you Boys. . . .

ANN HOWELL.

Fancy Hill March 1801

SAMUEL HOWELL PRINCETON N. J.

As fome of the inhabitants of the Manfion Houfe of Fancy Hill have gone to Michael Fifher's—I will devote an hour to thee—have but little to communicate but that little coming from home will be acceptable.

We received thy letter with pleafure and were entertained by thy account of the party at Mr. Van Horne's, I am obliged to Mifs Sufan Smith for lending her aid as it procured thee permiffion to join an agreeable party and a little relaxation from Study—I find it is neceffary to have an advocate when you afk a favor of the Old Dr. Capt. Whitall is with us and has gone with thy Father, Benjamin, Mr Eftey and Pafchall to M. Fifher's. We have a continuation of cold weather with flight fnows but the feafon is too far advanced to contemplate taking a jaunt to Princeton in the fleigh—thy Father ftill contemplates it, but I think when the weather becomes pleafant his bufinefs will come on fo rapidly that he will not attempt it. I told the children I was going to write to thee and afked them what they would wifh me to fay—Richard fays, ' Tell him I am well. ' Abigail with her ufual mildnefs, ' Tell him to come home and not go back again ' Rebecca, ' Tell him to come to tea. ' Rebecca's temper is juft the reverfe of Abigails—My little Blackwood is a lovely boy and if I may judge from his prefent appearance will be mild and placid in his temper—fo thinks the partial mother —Frances defires her love in which John and Anna Maria Join—Pafchall will write foon—he is a great Fine looking fellow and has grown confiderably. I know I may give thy Father's love—Good night my Dear Samuel ' may that peace which the world can neither give nor take away be thine '—is the wifh of thy Affectionate Mother

ANNA HOWELL

Fancy Hill. March 30th 1806

To Samuel L. Howell care Rev. Thos. Picton West-field East Jersey.

My dear Samuel

We have had the pleafure of receiving three letters from thee, and generally the day after they were written this fpeedy conveyance of letters, pleafes me very much—We

were diverted with the reception thee met with from Benjamin—I anticipated it—I was fure from meeting with thee fo unexpectedly his joy would be boundlefs. Benjamins going to India is not yet reduced to a certainty—it depends in E. Hallowell who has at prefent gone to the southward. I was pleafed with thy meeting with Col. Rhea and am exceedingly obliged to him for his politinefs to thee—thee attention of our friends tho' pleafing at all times is infinitely more fo, when we meet with it at a diftance from home—I am alfo much pleafed with thy reception at Mr Pictons—I hope thy fituation there will in every refpect fulfill thy expectations.   This is the third attempt I have made to write have been prevented by company.   Pafchall has been to Mount Holly to fee his friends.   Thy Father, J. Hampton and Pafchall are talking Politicks—to avoid attending to them as I write I find I have wrote more crooked than common.   Prefent my beft refpects to Mr. & Mrs. Picton and take good care of thyfelf in every fenfe of the word
    Adieu fays thy Affectionate Mother

ANNA HOWELL

To Samuel Howell Westfield

Fancy Hill April 20 1806

My dear Samuel
    We received thy letters with real pleafure as they inform us thee was well and perfectly pleafed with thy fituation. I did not suppofe thee would .have reafon to be diffatisfied

with Mr Picton—on the contrary, I believe him to be well
qualified to pleafe thee both as a teacher and companion—
I can't name one whom I fhould prefer to him; I never
felt the fmalleft objection to thy going except the diftance,
but if Providence favours us all with health—I fhall think
nothing more of that. Thy Grandmother [Frances Paschall Howell] is at prefent as well as ufual—She was here
a few days fince and defired me to give her love to thee.
All the family are well with the exception of thy father and
little Rebecca—they have fevere colds—thy father was
Bled today—I hope that will prevent his from continuing
long—he faid when he went to the Fifhery he fhould write
to thee—but I fee there has company gone there, and he
will be difappointed. Mr David Eftey [the tutor] has arrived—he came on Fifth day evening accompanied by Mr
Tucker who recommended him—I was quite alarmed to
fee fo fmall a man and but twenty years of age ! I had no
idea of fo young a man coming in the office of teacher—
but he appears fenfible and very grave in his manner—he
enters upon his new duties tomorrow—Richard came to me
after breakfaft as Mr Eftey left the table ' Mother, ' faid
he, ' Which of them is the fchool mafter ? ' ' The Small
one, ' I told him. ' Ah, ' says he, and fhook his head.
' He's too little to keep fchool, Why Mother is n't he a
boy ? ' Mr Eftey comes from Morriftown, about 12 miles
from Weftfield. I fhould like a more particular account of
Genl Cumming's family, and thy reception there than thee
gave in a former letter—Remember that everything that

concerns thee is particularly interefting to thy affectionate mother.

ANNA HOWELL.

To Samuel Howell Westfield N. J.

Fancy Hill May 4 1806

Thy Father has I prefume written to thee today perhaps he may not have anfwered thy inquiries in regard to the tranfactions of the different Fifheries. The weather has been fo very cold, that fifhing has been attended with great labour and little profit. The complaint is general, there is not a Fifhery on the River that has done well, the nets have been torn by becoming faft on the mud banks— Cold contrary winds and weather and every difficulty attending fuch a bufinefs have we contended with. Jeffe Sparks has charge of the West Point Fifhery. Pafchall attends to the Fifheries included in the Fancy Hill. Thee thinks thy Father more excufable for not writing than I, he is to be fure much engaged with his various bufinefs affairs, but I little lefs fo—my large family—and the conftant coming of near friends and other guefts meet me with fo many interruptions that I put off till night to write my letters, but amidft all my bufinefs, there is not the leaft danger of my forgetting that I have a fon at Weftfield. . . . . Mr Jaudon, Frances with feven of the School girls were here to fpend the 1ft of May—Sifter Nancy Blackwood came to fee me and defired her dear love to thee. Thy

Uncle Saml Whitall and Captain Murdock alfo fend theirs.
I have had, for thee, a fmall box of Timber Creek Baconed
Shad packed, I hope you will receive them whilft they are
good.   The children fend their love, little Rebecca talks
finely, fhe has been very unwell but it has not leffened her
fpirit of which fhe has a good fhare.   Farewell

                              ANNA HOWELL
                                 May 26 1806

   Thee need be under no apprehenfion of tiring us with
the frequency of thy letters, they will always be received
with pleafure, while they inform us thee is well.   Tuefday
next is Mr. Jaudon's Examination Exercifes, he faid, when
he was here, that he fhould give to Frances the Honours
of the Inftitution, but he would then leave it to us to determine whether fhe fhould directly home, or continue till
Auguft.

                    .   *May 26 1806*

To Samuel L. Howell

   I have fpent one afternoon with Mary Picton very much
to my fatisfaccton, and as thee predicted I was better
pleafed with her than ever.   A Weitfield polifh improves
very much—She gave me an account of your spinning vifit,
it's a curious cuftom, and the part thee and Mr Picton
acted in it was truly laughable—you made quite a difplay
of gallantry.   I fhould have no objection to fuch a vifit
once a year myfelf.   Anna has juft handed me a note for
thee.   I fhall fend it without correcting.—She has mentioned

Richard and Abigail—I will tell thee of Rebecca She is a
fmart engaging little girl—talks a great deal—and is a child
of the higheft fpirit I ever faw. Thy Uncle S. Whitall
and Capt. Murdock are figuring away among the New-
bolds—report says S. W. is courting fome one of them—
but I give little credit to it.   Thy Grandmother has gone
to Derby to pay her annual vifit among the Paschalls.

ANN HOWELL

———

Samuel L. Howell, Nassua Hall, Princeton N. J.

.   *Nov 30, 1806*

We had the pleafure of receiving laft evening two letters
from thee—After thee had been gone from home one week
I intended writing, but the cares of a large family and the
contiuual attention I am obliged to pay my little Blackwood
occupies all my attention Pafchall and Frances as thee
obferves are inexcufable—My little Blackwood [Jofhua
Blackwood Howell] is fo frequently unwell that I don't
perceive him to grow one bit—Pafchall has informed thee
of the Profpect of his going to Sea   Thy Father on coming from Philad. told him if he were ftill difpofed to go to
fea, there was now an opportunity thro' Mr Reeve Lewis
as he was going to launch a Brig, that She was to go to
Madeira this winter and return in the Spring—then She
would go to the Eaft Indies to be gone three years—and as
Pafchall was fo refolved to go fometime he gave his confent—Pafchall has concluded to ftay at home this winter
and learn Navigation and go in the Spring—it is very much

againſt my inclination.   I am much pleaſed that every letter mentions thy ſatisfaction with thy ſituation at Princeton.
I hope thee will be careful of thy eyes—it would make me
moſt unhappy to ſee thy eyes in the condition of poor Mr.
Eſtey's I will ſend an extra pillow and towels this week.
I think thee had better change thy mattreeſs for a larger
one which will be warmer for thee.   I was pleaſed with
your proceſſion to Church and ſhould love very much to
ſee you.   I am often with you in idea—it is near ten
o'clock—Firſt day night.   I ſuppose you all aſſembled to
prayer and altho there is more than 60 miles between us,
I ſee thee with my minds Eye and unite with thee in the
pious exerciſe.   Our family are differently engaged whilſt
I am writing—I hear the voices of half a dozen at once in
the Parlour, that thee may figure to thyſelf how we look at
home, I will name them: There is Mr. Woodruff [of
Trenton] James Pearſon [one of the Darby Paschalls]
Capt. S. Whitall, James B. Caldwell [son of the fighting
Parson Caldwell] T. Wilkins, thy Father, Mr. Eſty and
Paſchall, all laughing and talking, Frances, Anna Maria,
and myſelf in my room, the little children in bed and
aſleep.   A.M. and Frances give their love.   Thy Grandmother was here to-day.

[ANNA HOWELL.]

Fancy Hill Dec. 29. 1806

SAMUEL L. H. PRINCETON, N. J.

This is the third attempt I have made to write but a ſuc-

ceffion of company and houfehold matters have hitherto
prevented my finifhing a letter.   As thee may obferve
Firft day is my writing day to thee tho I am feldom at
leifure even on that day.   I had anticipated the pleafure of
feeing thee at home on Chriftmas day, without thinking I
fhould be difappointed, of courfe I felt it more fenfibly—I
am not very much obliged to the Old Dr. Smith, I think
for once he was more ftrict than neceffary.   We had
Benjamin and Jane Rowan, and Mifs Debeiton here two
days—they appeared to enjoy themfelves and we kept as
late hours as when they were here laft winter.   Thy
Company would have made a very agreeable addition to
me, and I believe, to all the party.   Thee was correct in
giving thy uncle Whitall credit for thy Father's vifit to
thee.   The " Noble Captain " as a certain perfon calls
him had bufinefs at Trenton and Mount Holly, he wifhed
thy Father to accompany him, as he feldom undertakes
anything but what he accomplifhes it, he perfevered until
he obtained his confent.   I knew it would be very pleafing to
thee, therefore what influence I had I used in favour of the
jaunt.   Dan Newbold came home with them, and *Lidya*
as far as Philad. where fhe ftill remains.   John S. Whitall
Saml. Whitall and James have fpent the evening here, and
to use their own words have been running the Capt. all
the time.   Thee mentions in one of thy letters that thy
eyes have been very weak, it has given me much uneafinefs—I defire thee to fpare them as much as poffible—remember that all the learning thee may acquire cannot

compenfate for material injury done them. The propofal thee makes for Pafchall to fpend a little time at Princeton I fhall encourage, and if there should be good sleighing, perhaps Frances alfo, but the hope thee exprefles of feeing me there I fear will not be realized—my little Blackwood continues so unwell, that I confine myfelf to home altogether. Aunt Morgan [fifter of Abbegial Ellis] was here recently and defired me to give her love to thee. Frances is at thy Grandmother's. Thy Father would have written but was prevented by Company.

Good Night my dear Samuel and may health, innocence and happinefs be thine is the prayer of thy

Affectionate Mother

ANNA HOWELL.

Fancy Hill June 1807.

Saml. L. Howell, Princeton, N. J.

The chief of the news I have to communicate will be like a twice told tale, as Pafchall's letter and thy Father's will tell thee all that has happened. We have had our Trenton vifitors two weeks, I fhould like to know their fentiments upon the occasion whether they have really fpent their time agreeably or not. Since I have been writing Captain James Cooper has gone on board his floop for another voyage to Charlefton. I prefume thee heard what a tremendous paffage he had out before, he looks as if he had experienced rough weather accompanied with anxiety of mind. The defcription thee gives of Mrs. E.

B. Hamilton anfwers precifely to the idea I had formed of
her. I was fure fhe muft have a moft excellent opinion
of her abilities, and be entirely unacquainted with every
feeling like diffidence or fhe never would be able to read
before fuch an audience.

I believe I have nothing more to tell thee only that we
are well, that will be as pleafing as anything. Anna
Maria is as healthy, Richard as flighty, Abbigail as mild,
Rebecca as fpirrity and Blackwood as lovely as when thee
left home. Pafchall, Frances and John are old enough to
remind thee of themfelves.

There is no perfon living as anxious for thy well doing
in every refpect as thy Mother.

ANNA HOWELL.

Fancy Hill, Feb. 1, 1808.

SAMUEL HOWELL, PRINCETON, N. J.

Thy long expected letter never came to hand till yefterday. Thy Father thinks thee need not complain of not
receiving letters more frequently from home. Thy Father
feels no bad effects from the accident of his horfes running
away—he had a very bad attack of the Gout which confined him to the fettee for two weeks. Frances has given
thee an account of our journey and intended vifit to
Princeton, which amounted to nothing more than a vifit to
the Wigwam [Mr. Dan Newbold's] and a difappointment.
"The Indian Chief" who is as abfolute as Bonaparte,
entertained us with the greateft hofpitality, but he would

not let us leave his house till he chofe. After I had overcome the great difficulty of leaving home and expected to
have the pleafure of seeing thee by 9 O'C. that evening, I
did not feel very willing to ftop half way. I am very
anxious that Frances fhould return to Philadel. to her
fchool at Jaudon's as foon as I can fpare her, we have
three or four of the family fick now—Anna is one of the
number, the others are Kitchen folks.

There is a curious anecdote going about Ann Whitall
and Buelah Hopkins, they told a number of their acquaintances that they were going to Baltimore to fpend the winter, but how they were going or with whom was a fecret
even to Sally Whitall—Ann's mother. John Hopkins
and James Hopkins, only were in the fecret. John W.
endeavoured to reconcile his wife by perfuading her that
his knowing any circumftance was fufficient. There could
be no danger of his agreeing to anything that would be improper. They at length fet off, and after a few weeks
abfence it was difcovered that they were in Philad. at Mrs.
Rivarda's boarding school for the exprefs purpofe of learning to dance—so much for *Monthly Meeting folks!* Mr.
Efty is about leaving us, the time for his taking lifcenfe is
approaching, his eyes are no better, and he thinks he fhall
derive more benefit from returning to Morriftown and
ftudying with fome young men who are ftudying Law.
He will refrain from reading entirely and ftrive to profit by
their reading to him. That John and Anna Maria might
fuftain no lofs by his leaving fooner than was expected, he

recommended his Brother, who came yesterday. He looks very young. This Charles Efty I am told is the reverfe of David in point of gravity. I prefume thee muft have heard of the failure of James W. Clement & Coats. Wm. & Anthony Buckley have also failed. War and Bankruptcy seem to be for awile the order of the day. The Brig Saunders was spoke at sea four days out, and all well, which is all I have heard of either. Poor boys, there is no knowing to what quarter of the world they may be driven or carried. It is said that Bonaparte has laid an embargo on all American property and its supposed he will capture it at every opportunity. Thy Uncle Michael Fisher* will pass meeting shortly. Frances says she shall not write till after she has been to the City when she will endeavour to satisfy thee upon every particular.

[*ANNA HOWELL*]

Fancy Hill Feb 10. 1808.

SAMUEL L. HOWELL PRINCETON, N. J.

I cannot as usual say thy letter was received with pleasure, the intellegence it contained refpecting the condition of thy eyes was by no means calculated to encourage me. Thy Father intended to have written to thee but has been prevented by business. He thinks thee should by all means leave college immediately and says if his going to

---

* Anna Howell's sister Rebecca Blackwood was Michael Fisher's first wife—at the date of this letter he was about to marry his second wife Ann Clement of Haddonfield, cousin to Anna Howell.

Princeton will be of real fervice in relation to thy leaving
he will fet off directly after hearing from thee.   There are
feveral of thy favorite friends here, and have been near a
week.   Hannah Howell, Mary H. Clayton and Sufan
Newbold.   Jane Rowan was with us two or three days
but the Arbitrary lady, her mother, fet the time for her return and neither wind nor rain could prevent her from
going, I fhould not cenfure either of them—the mother has
a right to command and the daughter ought to obey, but it
fometimes makes it very troublefome to their friends.

I am very much pleafed with my company, and they appear to pafs their time very agreeably.   " *Our New Mr.*
Efta," as little Rebecca calls him, plays on the violin, so
they vary the fcene frequently by dancing; they have gone
to Woodbury this evening—I told them I fhould write to
thee—they left feveral meffages for thee.

Mr. David Efty went from here the day after I wrote
laft, he appeared to leave us with the greateft regret.

Thy Mother
ANNA HOWELL.

———

Fancy Hill Jan 22. 1808.

Saml. Howell, Princeton N. J.

My dear Sam

I am greatly indebted to you for the good advice in your
laft letter and hope I fhall profit by it.   You will be much furprifed when you hear that Mother, Father, Anna and David
Ward as driver fet out for Princeton, but the wind proving

unfavorable they could proceed no further in the fleigh than Mr. Newbold's where they remained until they could procure carriages to bring them home. Capt. Harrifon's family, Judge Hopkins, Wm. Hopkins, Judge Caldwell and Capt. Saml. Whitall befides our family were placed in the fame fituation—a very good reprefentation from Gloucefter Co., I think I hear you fay.

Sifter

FRANCES HOWELL.

Fancy Hill N. J.

Samuel L. Howell Princeton N. J.

My letter to thee laft Firft day by thy Father he entirely forgot to give thee so much engaged was he with company. The letter directed to Benjamin I committed to the flames agreeably to thy requeft without feeling the leaft degree of curiofity to know its contents, it will always give me pleafure to be in the confidence of my children, fo far as is perfectly agreeable to themfelves, but while I have the same reliance on their prudence that I have hitherto had, I have not the fmalleft inclination to know what they do not wifh to communicate. I was very uneafy after receiving thy letter until thy Father returned for fear thee would have a return of fever. I feel very grateful to Meffrs Herbert and Meade for their friendly attention to thee, pleafe to prefent my refpects to them. We have received a letter from Benjamin on his leaving the Capes. He bids us a

very affecting and affectionate farewell, his grateful fenfible
heart is portrayed in every line.   I have never read the
letter without fhedding tears—I fincerely wifh he may be
fuccefsful.   I do not know a perfon more deferving to be
so—take him in every point of view I do not know a more
perfect character.   I am very anxious about Pafchall, he
seems crazy to go to fea, he has an offer from Reeve Lewis
for his new brig *Saunders*, and his father has almost determined upon his going.   I have thought I would never
oppofe his going again, but I believe I muft a little, for at
prefent I have more than common reafons for objecting to
it, befides the opportunity he will lofe of improving his
education, the critical ftate of affairs between this country
and Europe, makes it an improper time to go. . . .   Our
Friend Mary Clayton has not yet returned to the City,
when fhe does I will take the earlieft opportunity of calling
on her.   Thy Father and thy Grandmother defire their
love and unite with me in requefting thee to let us know
the condition of thy health and eyes.   Mr. Efty gives his
beft refpeÅ“ts.   Thine

                                    ANNA HOWELL.

————

Mrs. Howell Care Colonel Howell Woodbury N. J.

            New York September 4th 1809.
My Dear Mrs. Howell

It was my intention to have written you immediately on
my arrival in New York, but fcarcely had I time to con-

gratulate myfelf, on being with my friends, when James received orders to fail for France, fince then my fpirits have been fo depreffed, that my letters, even to my moft partial friends, muft have appeared dull and uninterefting, but it was my laft promife to James that I would write to you, and that alone, would be fufficient inducement, without the aid of that affection which I feel for you all—knowing the caufe, I hope *you* my dear Mrs Howell can pity, and forgive, the apparent neglect of your young and inexperienced friend in *every thing, but sorrow,* prefent my affectionate regards to Mr Howell and the Girls, tell Frances fhe muft never marry a Sailor, for her life will be one continual fcene of care and anxiety and tell your *rattle cap* Pafcal to turn Merchant immediately, if ever he expects to enter the *Marriage State,* for he never will experience happinefs if he goes to fea, to Samuel & the Boys give my compliments—& believe me with fincerity your affectionate friend

JULIA LAWRENCE.

P.S. When you fee Mr Cooper, tell him his letter did not reach here, untill fome time after Mr. Lawrence failed

———

Fancy Hill March 1817

To Col Howell Etna Furnace Tuckahoe

I received a very friendly letter from H. Hefton inform-

ing me of thy arrival at and departure from her houfe [Col.
Hefton, Glaffboro]. I am glad thee ftayed there, fhe is a
kind friendly woman and I am fure did everything in her
power (and with pleafure) that would contribute to thy
full comfort. Thanks to a kind Providence thee feems
quite well, fo John affures me—I wifh to imprefs upon thy
mind the importance of carefully avoiding everything that
has a tendency to impair thy health—Any violent emotion
of the mind is particularly injurious to a perfon in delicate
health and it is fo utterly impoffible for us to live without
meeting many little crofs occurrences, that we fhould ftrive
to regulate the mind fo as not to fuffer ourfelves to be agitated by them. Benjamin requefts thee not to permit the
line ditches to be cut until he fends the courfes from the
Deeds, when he will be glad to have them run by Jofhua
Haines, as there are many errors in Willif's Survey—all
the ditches but the *line* ditches may go on as faft as pos-
fible—Benjamin is on the eve of going into bufinefs in
partnerfhip with Reeve Lewis under as favorable terms as
he could expect and better than he could have
hoped . . . . . .

Aug. 4 1817

Col. Howell, Cape Island

I reached home Saturday evening without any unpleafant
occurrences or great fatigue by the long ride from Cape
May—I have to report a general fcarcity of money—there
is no fale of hay or lumber, or any poffibility of collecting

from thofe who owe.   I am forry I have not more agreeable intelligence to communicate, however, I hope the
times will change for the better, thefe are evils that we fuffer in common with many other perfons—thy farming
progreffes very well—there is no occaffion for thy immediate return—everything fhall be attended to—Benjamin and
Samuel will prevent thy having annoyances in thofe affairs
thee mentioned. I wifh thee to make bufinefs ferve
rather as an amufement—let the burden lay on younger
perfons.

ANNA BLACKWOOD HOWELL.

Fancy Hill Oct. 2, 1817.

Col. Josa. L. Howell

I am rejoiced that thee is fo encouraged about the Marfhes
I hope thy moft fanguine expectations may be realized—
and that thee may fucceed in getting the proper perfons to
till them.   I wifh thee could manage thy buffinefs fo as to
attend to it with more eafe to thyfelf, and feel forry thee
fhould be fo engroffed with it as to expofe thyfelf unneces-
farily. . A moderate fhare of exercife I believe in, but thy
anxiety to improve the Marfhes may induce thee to expofe
thyfelf too much—it is certainly defirable to have it in a condition to do fomething but I muft entreat thee to pay proper
attention to thy health—I intend vifiting thee and John as
foon as the bufinefs here will permit—but my prefence
here is abfolutely neceffary I am certain.   I feel very will-

ing to do all in my power to leſſen the difficulties that we,
like ſo many others, ſeem to have got entangled in.

The Mr Lewiſes are experiencing a very great change—
they have all offered their houſes for sale—and Joſeph a
great deal of his nice ornamental furniture.   They intend
changing their ſtyle of living entirely by going into ſmaller
houſes and reducing their expenſes.   Maud Lewis is going
to Antwerp ſoon.   Frances and Anna Maria called on Rebecca—Samuel's wife—ſhe ſpoke very freely upon the ſubject.   Thy daughters deſire their beſt love to thee and
John, the little boys alſo ſend their love, little Ben obſerved
the other day that it was a pity and he was ſorry his father
could not enjoy his health here.   David Wards deſires
thee to have 600 ft of cedar boards ſawed for him ¾ of an
inch thick and 20 ft long.   He ſays if thee will do ſo, he
will warrant thee ſome good hauls of ſhad in the Spring.
Whenever the buſineſs here will admit of it I intend going
down to Etna and ſhould the weather be pleaſant Frances
will accompany me.

Thine

ANNA HOWELL

EXTRACTS FROM LETTERS OF ANNA HOW-ELL TO COL JOSHUA L. HOWELL AT ETNA FURNACE TUCKAHOE

Fancy Hill Jany 22nd.

*   *   *   That troublefome animal, Michael is making a ftir in the legiflature about the fifheries. I have not heard the particulars, but he wifhes to fubject them to many reftrictions I hear there are copys of the Supplement to the Act fent down to the owners of Fifher-ies John will be able to tell thee more about it when he returns.

*   *   *   *   I fhall be glad to have thee at home whenever thee can leave Etna with an eafy mind prefenting refpects to Thomas and Debby Judge—I am very much pleafed with the attentive behaviour they mani-feft toward thee and John. Thee in particular John is young and hearty, and able to take care of himfelf *   *   *

Candour Hall Auguft 10th

I enclofed thy letter and fent it to Benjamin that he might impart what was neceffary for J. R. Coats to know —to him that muft feem productive of nothing but embar-rifments and vexation I really think if it were me, and

the thing was practicable, I would throw all the marſh
that was not paid for onto J. R. C's. hands He has not
fulfilled his contraƈt in any one inſtance, which·puts it out
of your power to reap any benefit from it and if the tenants
ſhould be diſcouraged and leave it, it will injure the reputation of the property ſo, that you will find a difficulty in
either ſelling or leaſing it, I don't wiſh to diƈtate and I
have leſs deſire to do anything to irritate—but I ſee neither
reaſon nor juſtice in your ſubmitting to ſuch ſerious incon-
veniences—that is, if there is any way of avoiding it.

We are buſily employed in preparing a few articles of
houſekeeping for John. If Benjamin can poſſibly leave
town he will accompany Anna Maria to Etna on Friday.
Frances deſires her love and hopes thee will not think its
for want of thought that ſhe does not write—her time is ſo
entirely occupied with her children, that ſhe finds no leiure—ſhe is ſeldom without one in her arms.

Abby deſires her beſt love—the boys are in bed. I
think of their going with Anna I ſuſpect John is not prepared to accommodate ſo much company—give my love to
him if thee pleaſes and accept of a long ſhare thyſelf

Fancy Hill Sept 2nd

Reeve Lewis rode with us from the croſs keys he was
very amuſing but I was too tired to enjoy his humour, he
is reſolved to viſit you again and then he intends to *mould*
I have not heard from town ſince Benjamin left here. It

was his intention to have gone to Delaware but the weather has been fo bad I imagine he has not gone.* * *

Tuesday evening Octr 2nd

I fend thy Camles wool ftockings there is fo much on the marfh that they will not be too thick. I am glad thee is in fuch fpirits about that property. I hope it may pay thee tenfold—but I entreat thee to be careful of thyfelf and avoid expofure as much as poffible. Thee fhould follow Brintons plan—attend to it, but nurfe thyfelf at the fame time, let others bear the expofure.

Col Joshua L. Howell

Etna Furnace Tuckahoe

Friday night 10 o' clock

My dear

If you have the weather as cold with you, as it is here you had need to force an irruption, of your tiny modern Etna, to warm the atmofphere, I think I never experienced a colder day than this has been. By our houfe, up the river is the high road to the city, the fleighs are going conftantly. This evening fome of the paffengers in the ftage came in to warm, their faces appeared almoft frozen. I expeét Samuel has written particularly on the fubjeét of boards—Dr Ward learned that inch boards were the kind that were moft wanted they will command, from 50 to 60 dollars a thoufand. Thofe long ones Hill wifhed the fame thickneſs of thoſe already ſent.   There is more than enough here now, for both thy boats.

I beg thee will give me a particular account of thyſelf by William, we are all well

Fanny joins with me in love to thee and John.   A. M. is in the city on a viſit to her friend E. W.

I am ever affectionately thine

ANNA HOWELL.

P.S.   I ſent a ſmall portion of ſand for the beſt reaſon in the world, I had no more   But as ſoon as the ſnow leaves the face of the earth N. J. will ſend a larger ſupply.

Trenton Auguſt 17th

My dear A. M.

We arrived in this famous City, about 8 o'clock this evening and are all as well as can be expected, conſidering the intenſe heat of the weather, I ſhall ſay nothing of Trenton as yet. It was ſo dark when we entered it that we could not diſtinguiſh one houſe from another. We met with a very hearty welcome from our *friend Herbert* and ſhall ſpend the night with him, of courſe, and I think it probable we ſhall reſume our travels in the morning. Thy Father appriſed Mr Woodruff of our being in town, and in *proceſs* of *time* he with the Dr his wife Suſan and Maria came to ſee us, they expreſſed ſome regret that we had not called at their houſe, hoped if we could not call in the

morning we would pay them a vifit on our return, Mrs
Woodruff was fick, and Sufan and daddy were going to
the mountains in the morning, fo thee may set thy heart at
reft about the trenton party. While the weather is fo
very warm, my dear Anna if it is not convenient to fend
the little boys to fchool, let them remain at home and make
them attend to their books unlefs thee finds they expofe
themfelves more by being at home than at fchool, give my
love to them, and accept of a large fhare thyfelf.

Good night my dear daughter and may the blefling of
Providence reft upon you all, both here and hereafter,
prays thy affectionate

Mother

ANNA HOWELL

Anna Maria Howell.

Cape Ifland Auguft the 27th 1809

My dear Anna Maria

Notwithftanding all our fears and anxieties, about coming by water, we had a very pleafant paffage, the weather
was fo fine there was nothing to terrify, and we all efcaped
fea ficknefs except Kiz [the colored nurfe] who was fick
about an hour. We arrived at the fhore on the Bay fide
at ten o'clock on Friday evening, and landed at a place called
new England, where a carriage and pair were in waiting,
to convey us to Mother Hughes Hotell. We got there
about eleven o'clock, the good old Lady had retired to reft,

and muſt have been partaking largely of nature's kind reſtorative, balmy ſleep; for it was ſome time before we could gain admittance, the delay, gave us time to contemplate one of nature's grandeſt works, the ocean appeared to riſe much higher than the land, and as the moonbeams played upon its agitated waters, it gave to it, the moſt ſilvery, and elegant appearance, of anything I ever ſaw. There is very little company on the iſland at preſent, and that not of the moſt genteel kind, ſo that we conform to no rules but our own, we paſs the time very pleaſantly, but a few of our moſt intimate friends would be a very agreeable addition to our party. I ſhould like to have thee, and ſome more of the children if it was convenient, but we muſt defer that pleaſure till another ſeaſon thy Father and Frances have gone to church I expeEt we ſhall return next week whether by land or water is not determined, I hope you will take good care of yourſelves, that I may have the pleaſure of finding you all well and happy when I return, which I ſhould be very willing to do in two or three days more if the ſtages went at that time, give my love to Grandmother and everyone of the children there is no pleaſure I can receive here, equal to what I ſhould experience by being at home with you

from thy ever affeEtionate mother

ANNA HOWELL.

Mr Samuel L. Howell Fancy Hill.

Dear Sam

My principal motive for going to church was to ſee

Mary Leaming as I thought, but judge my surprise when inquiring for her, I was told she was no longer M. L. but Mrs. Holmes, both her brothers are married also, you see I got some news by going to church

My love to all enquiring friends

FRANCES HOWELL

Samuel I wish you would inflict some punishment upon Frances for her carelessness in writing

I've got one of Mother Hughf's Tavern bills to write on I applied to her for paper and this is the kind I got.

———

[To Abigail Janeway]

* * * * * * * *

for the last 3 months I have been in one continual bustle and my vexations and botherments continue—In addition to the most discouraging season I ever knew . . . . . The 18th of April with all three of the nets, we had caught but *90 shad* and my expenses between 80 & 90 $ a day—at the end of the third week in April I must have been in debt between $2 & 3000 I saw no prospect of anything else than to borrow money to pay my expenses— I was often almost determined to stop fishing—but where was I to get money to pay the debt I had incurred? I strove all in my power to be resigned to my situation *come what would* but I found it impossible. The idea of a host of *people* coming to me every hour for their money and not have it for them almoft crazed me. At laft the bountiful giver of *every good* fent the fhad & altho in *very moderate numbers* the price was fo *high* that I did rather better than I did laft feafon—I can truly fay I never paid a bill without feeling thankful that I had the means.

But we had a fucceffion of ftorms to the laft hour—I juft made out to get my own fhad the day before we quit. The tempeft raged within & without the *Camp*, I can truly fay.

The Gill Netters have contefted the point with us continually, even laft Monday we were affailed, by between 25 & 30 defperadoes in order to recover a boat, which had been taken from them. They found none but women and children except my hired man and poor old Jofiah Ward. There were ftrangers among who took Jofiah for David. They carried him on board their boat, beat him, robbed him, and then threw him overboard to get home as he could. It was moft fortunate that David was not here or they would have murdered him, as fure as the world. It was a curious fcene and a terrific one but I was not much alarmed; I locked the doors and refufed to be feen by them. Sam's wife was fpokefwoman; fhe told them I was at home but would not fee them—they fhouted and fcreamed like a fet of favages—Rachel & Mary all here poor R. was frightened out of her fenfes almoft—fhe declared fhe did not know herfelf in the glafs—Anna, Mary, Margaretta Howell have been with me for the laft two weeks—Rebecca, Fanny & Ellen were here fome time ago,

R & Anna have the ftability of women of any age they are uncommonly fine girls. . . . . .

Rachel is very thin & delicate in health—fhe has a fweet baby but I fufpect thy Nannie would make two of it. .

MRS. ANNA B. HOWELL

[I brought this old letter down, for the purpofe of deftroy-ing but I found it recorded events of much importance]

———

MRS. ANNA HOWELL
CARE OF DR BENJ. P. HOWELL
PHILA.

—

New York June 13 1836
Evg.

MRS. ANNA HOWELL
My dear Mother

I recd on Saturday a letter from Benj giving us informa-tion of this outrage committed by the lawlefs wretches [gill netters] who have heretofore given thee fo much trouble and one from Mary fomewhat more in detail to Ellen came to-day.   I regret that I am fo remote as to be unable to render thee any aid at this juncture, but I truft there are enough near thee to fee that at leaft an effort is made to bring the fcoundrels to juftice—if indeed there is fuch a thing left us.   There is fome confolation in believ-ing that when matters reach a certain point they muft mend, and it would feem that they muft have got to that in thy cafe.   It would feem that outrage could hardly go further in a land where law was fuppofed to have yet fome influence, I fhall feel anxious to hear what fteps have been taken to bring the rafcals to punifhment and with what hope of fuccefs.   .   .   .   .

From Ben's letter I was gratified to learn that notwith-ftanding the difficulties and difappointments which met thee at every ftep through the [fifhing] feafon, the refult was on the whole profitable.   It only fhows how valuable the property would be could thee be allowed to enjoy it unmolefted.

We hear that Mr [J. H.] Jones has had a call to Phila. [from New Brunswick] and that his congregation are in confequence beftirring thémfelves to make his prefent fitua-tion more *defirable*.   .   .   .   .   .

When thee finds the children getting troublefome fend them away—tell Mary and Meg I fay fo—Mary's account of the Gill men was quite graphic—almoft equal to the fmugglers in Guy Mannering—I hope they all do what they can to affift and amufe thee in thy troubles.

Remember me affeCtionately to fifters Mary and Rachel, and believe me always thine

B. B. H.

EXTRACTS FROM THE DIARY OF ANNA BLACKWOOD HOWELL CONCERNING THE ILLNESS OF HER SON JOHN L. HOWELL IN 1828.

On Monday afternoon 30th of June I recd a letter from B. B [Benj. Betterton Howell] faying he had a letter from John in which he faid he was very much indifpofed. That for a long time, he had been fuffering from the effects of repeated and neglected colds. That the night previous to his writing he had ruptured a blood veffel—that he was much at a lofs what to do, but felt a great defire, to get on, as far as Princeton if poffible. .   .   .   .

July 1st.   .   .   .   a letter recd from S. F. [Samuel Fisher] convinced me that John muft be ill, or he would not employ another to write.

Thurfday I went to Princeton in order to be that far on my journey, if it were neceffary for me to go on, and to confult with Sam'l upon what I muft do.   .   .

.   .   .   In talking with Sam'l he moft *properly ad-vifed me* to go on by all means. He had fent Ben on, with inftructions & medicine.   .   .   .   The 5th at length, arrived and we commenced our journey, on our way to Brunfwick we paffed the Stages with ftrained and eager eyes.   .   .   We went on to N. Y that night—At the City Hotel I heard that Jo. was very ill, that he had been .bled 6 times. . . The next morning at 6 oclock we embarked on board the fleam boat for Newburgh. . We reached N B in fafety, and the next morning at two o'clock entered the flage for Cofhecton. . . . •

July 7th Monday evening between 5 & 6 oclock—we reached our deftination, with an aching heart and trembling fteps I walked down the hill to S. Fifhers, not knowing what awaited me there; before we reached the houfe I faw Ben, and with joy unfpeakable I faw him fmile, I faid to Arthur Howell, who was fupporting me down the hill,—Is it poffible Ben is fmiling? I went immediately to the room of my fick fon whom I found pale and emaciated, indeed, and fuffering great diftrefs, both of body and mind, he had been bled nine times and nature was much exhaufted, but I was fo rejoiced to find him alive and in the poffeffion of his reafon, that I exclaimed " Thee looks better than I expected to fee thee—He expreff'd his joy at my arrival, faid, that he feemed to have the care of himfelf, that thofe about him. did what they could, but they did not know how to nurfe. From this time he feemed a little better, owing to his mind being in a meafure relieved, but, I foon found that the difeafe was not fubdued, . . .

Saturday 12th, To my great joy Samuel came to us, oh, this was fuch a relief! I felt as if a mountain was removed from my mind, I took him into the room where his brother lay, I faw he was exceedingly fhocked at his appearance, and poor dear John faw it too. As the Dr fat counting his pulfe I faw an expreffion of defpair fpread over his countenance, he lay perfectly ftill for fome time, there was not a found uttered. My heart beat audibly— At length the Dr roufed from his reverie and fet about adminiftering to his fufferings—He made a change in the practice which, by the next morning, produced a moft happy effect. I fhall always confider Saml's vifit as an *efpecial interpofition* of Providence. From this time, John may be faid, to be recovering, but the progrefs of amendment, was very flow. The fever tho very much leffened, was yet unbroken, he gained ftrength, but it was by flow degrees. The Dr. remained with us till the 15th—16th Jofhua & E. K. [Eliza Kirkbride] came. This was an unexpected pleafure, and I think it was a fortunate circumftance—As the mind has great influence over the body, I think E's prefence, beguiled him of many a defponding hour. His reftoration to health was fo flow, as fcarcely to be perceived

Auguft 5. . . The march of improvement goes on fo flowly, that in fpite of all my efforts to the contrary I feel difcouraged. E. K. and myfelf have been making fome arrangements for moving whenever our patient thinks himfelf equal to the tafk.

7th, John this morning propofed moving, but as the morning was paffing away, his refolution feemed to faulter —he felt his weaknefs, and the journey fixty miles over a mountainous country was appalling—He feemed to fhrink from the tafk. This was a trying fituation for us all—we dare not urge and yet, we were fick with anxiety to have him moving homewards. At length he thought he would make the trial.

In an agony of mind not to be defcribed I commenced our travelling preparations. An open Wagon, with fome hoops erected, and fome muflin fheets drawn over them, was the vehicle in which we were to commence our journey with poor John who was fo debilitated, as to fpend the greater part of the time on the bed. The weather was intenfely hot, and the dread of our fuffering companion's being overpowered by it, almoft made me delirious. However, with the fupport of a kind Providence we got along admirably to Fofter's tavern, 5 miles from S. Fifher's. The next morning John was much better, and, in our grand carriage we crept on to White Lake a beautiful fheet of water 13 miles from Cofhecton. Here we remained till the next day. We had written to Monticello for a carriage to come to this place for us, and about 9 o'clock, to our great joy the carriage arrived, fuch as it was, a fmall Dearborn, into which we were packed, to travel over mountains and vallies, we reached a place, that evening called Mammy Kating Hollow. The next morning we recommenced our travels, and croffed the Shongs Mountain, a diftance of 4 miles to Bloomings Burgh. From thence to Montgomery here we were obliged to lay bye, it was fomething of a crofs as we were within 12 miles of Newburgh, but John was too much fatigued to proceed. The weather was exceffively hot and we did not admire the appearances of the place, or its inhabitants enough to induce us to ftay longer than could be avoided. But neceffity has no law, we could not get away, till the next morning.

Between 9 and 10 oclock Ben arrived, with a rough going Yankee Dearborn in which we journeyed on, to Newburgh.

How we might have fung for joy as it really feemed, like being on the "banks of deliverance" our travelling by land was nearly over. We feemed as if we might almoft reft from our labours, after having got fafely over, that *awful fixty* miles, our difficulties feemed to have vanifhed. In 24 hours more we fhould in all probability be 'n the bofom of our dear family. We arrived at New York quite late in the evening—were conveyed to the City Hotel where we refted, and were much refrefhed—the next day we took the 12 oclock boat. . . . . .

Aug 28th.

Thurfday I came to Princeton to fee John who was taken ill—the violence of the fymptoms had fomewhat abated. . . . . . Sept 11

Two weeks this day I came to Princeton I though that in four or five days John would be able to go home [Fancy Hill] There was a little excitement in the evening 12 John appears much better this morning—He has hitherto been fo changeable that I am afraid to flatter myfelf that it will laft. . . . .

[At Fancy Hill]   *November 1828*

Tuefday 25th   This day my fuffering fon John became fo weak that he with difficulty got upftairs.   Dearly beloved child oh, how I dread that a trying feafon is approaching I think this was the laft day that the dear fufferer was downftairs.

Oh blindnefs to the future, kindly given could I have known what was to be the refult, of this *fad* ficknefs, how, fhould I ever have been able, to have nurfed, and done as I did, for my beloved child—Yes, I efteem it a fignal bleffing, that there was all the time, a hope fpringing up in mind that enabled me to comfort and cheer him—and to contribute in fo many ways to his comfort.   .   .

Decr 30th   It is one month this day fince my dear dear fon departed this life—This is a moft trying difpenfation— fix months he was fick, but his appearance at times, was fo flattering that till within the laft week of his life, I entertained hopes of his recovery.   How blind I muft have been   But in fome refpe&s I efteem the blindnefs to the future a bleffing   Could I have known, that at fuch a time he would have been taken, I fhould not have been able to have done my duty by him.   Dear Sainted being, with what tendernefs he enquired "How is thy head Mother?" the day previous to his death I faw the change and I could not refrain from tears, he obferved fomething was the matter   I told him my head ached,   This was the cafe—I might have added my heart ached alfo.

Oh, may the Lord have taken him to himfelf

EXTRACTS AND COPIES OF LETTERS WRITTEN BY ANNA BLACKWOOD HOWELL DURING SEASONS OF AFFLICTIONS.

[Copy enclosing a pretty lock of hair endorsed:]

" A lock of my dear little boys hair." " Sacred relic The 10 of Auguſt 1800 at 11 o'clock at night my beloved Joſhua left this tranſitory world in exchange I hope, for everlaſting Life and Joy " " Father of Mercies receive his little tender ſpirit, take him to thy boſom, let him enjoy the tendereſt of thy mercies. Thou haſt lent him me for a while till it pleaſe thee to recall the precious truſt. How ſoothing to my heart is thy gracious promiſe that little children ſhall ſee thy face & that of ſuch is the Kingdom of Heaven

" Ceaſe fond nature, ceaſe thy ſtrife
And let him languiſh into life."

[On the death of Abigail Ellis, her Mother, Anna Blackwood Howell writes thus:]

On the 20th of May 1803 about 9 o'clock in the evening, departed this life my honoured and beloved Mother, Abigail Ellis. She was removed by aſtroke ſo ſudden as to deprive any of her children the melancholy ſatisfaction of adminiftering the laft fad offices to an expiring parent. Oh! my beloved Mother could I have been permitted to have been on the fpot, to have fupported thy finking limbs, and caught thy parting breath.   But it was the will of thy Heavenly Father that it fhould be otherwife, and I muft fubmit.   I feel it *fenfibly* that I muft fubmit.   Let me turn which way I will, I find it my duty to fubmit in humble thankfulnefs that I have been bleffed with her fo long and that I am favored with a lively hope that fhe is fafely landed in that Heavenly City, that fhe is one of the members of thofe bleffed inhabitants, not one of whom fhall ever fay I am fick.   But nature has her ties and they are fo ftrong they can't be fundered without pain. When I refleft that I muft never behold that revered and honored face, never liften to that tongue that always conveyed comfort and inftruftion to my heart.   Oh, what a lofs I have fuftained, but I live in the hope that my lofs is her eternal gain.   Never can I forget how expreffive of peace and happinefs was that beloved countenance even in the icy arms of death.

[Death of her brother John Blackwood:]

On the 6th of October 1803 on fifth day night, between the hours of 9 & 11 it pleafed the Lord to take from this tranfitory fcene, my beloved brother John Blackwood.   His difeafe [Bilious Fever] was of a nature fo flattering that he was not fuppofed to be in danger until the laft day of his life.   He was nearly 40 years of age, bleft with good natural abilities & a benevolent heart, he had made himfelf fo well acquainted with bufinefs, that he was uncommonly ufeful in public as well as private life. He has left in the deepeft diftrefs an amiable wife & feven children, befides a number of other near relatives to deplore their irreparable lofs. Thus we fee the uncertainty of our earthly comfort. Well does the poet fay " The Spider's moft attenuated web is cord, is cable to man's flender tie on earthly blifs, it breaks at every breeze."

Five months had not elapfed fince we loft beloved Mother. Afflicting indeed was that awful difpenfation of Providence, fhe was removed in an inftant."

[Another paper contains the following:]

What a change of fcene have I been fpared to experience, but a fhort time fince, I was rich with the moft valuable and moft beloved relatives, exclufive of the comforts I enjoyed in my non-particular family, I was bleffed with an excellent Mother, an invaluable brother, and three amiable fifters. In little more than eighteen months it pleafed the Father of Mercy to recall to himfelf my Mother, brother and two fifters.

May 6th 1864 on Firft day evening my fifter, Rebecca Fifher departed this life.

Dec 6th 1804 on Fifth day My fifter Sarah E. Whitall departed this life.

[The death of her children.]

On the 21st of Auguſt 1811, it pleaſed the Lord, to take from me, my dear little daughter Rebecca, a ſweet little cherub of ſeven years of age. I was ſick and denied the melancholy ſatisfaction of being with her, to ſoothe and comfort her on the bed of ſickneſs and death. I ſaw her once, juſt to take a laſting farewell. Her little heart throbbed with pleaſure at ſeeing me, even in the arms of death. She went to ſleep and reſigned her precious life into the arms of him who gave it.

On the firſt of Sept following, on Firſt day of the week, the Lord demanded another ſacrifice, my beloved ſon Paſchall, a lovely youth, not quite twenty-two years of age, cut off like a flower in the prime of life and health. When he was made ſenſible that the awful change was taking place, he ſaid, it was the decree of Providence, that death had no terrors for him, and that he was perfectly reſigned. He expired a few minutes after without a groan. The worthy Dr Pariſh of Philad who was with him in his laſt moments, remarked to one of his friends that " He died like a lamb.'' (Sacred to the memories of my darling children) Oh death thou haſt indeed robbed me of ſome of my ſweeteſt comforts.'' Inſatiate Archer could not one ſuffice, thy ſhafts flew twice and twice my peace was ſlain and twice ere twice yon moon had filled her horn.

Nov. 30th 1828 My bleſſed ſon John departed this life, after an illneſs of ſix months. This was a moſt try-

ing difpenfation—but my cup of forrow was not yet full.
On the 8th of June 1829 it pleafed the Almighty difpofer
of events to call from earth my dearly beloved daughter
Frances. Oh *this* has *indeed* torn my heart to pieces.
Never were children more dear to a Mother's heart. God
of mercies fupport me under fuch heart rending afflictions.
To this dearly beloved daughter efpecially, I looked forward as my fupport and prop in age, fhould it pleafe the
Almighty to fpare me. Oh! fhe was all the fondest
mother could defire in a child, kind, amiable and lovely,
and the moft refpectful and affectionate in her whole conduct to me, that ever mother was bleffed with. Oh *my*
children my *bleffed children!* my bereaved heart bleeds for
my children.

When fuch comforts are torn from us by death, we feel
our infignificence, I can truly fay I am humbled in the
duft

" Their fouls too good, too pure for earth's abode
  Have winged their way to realms of light & God."

[On the next page enclosing a long, beautiful tress of
hair, the following:]

This is all that I have left of my beloved, my angelic
Fanny, Oh Fanny my heart bleeds to think that we are
feparated forever, oh not forever, this narrow fpace is not
forever.

[Found on a scrap of paper of old date:]

I feel difpofed to live a reclufe life, there are fo few
people here that I defire to vifit, and my mind is fo unfit
for fociety at prefent that no one need folicit mine. I
think of my dear Pafchal [he was at sea at this time] with
trembling anxiety I can't enjoy any thing, notwithftanding the many bleffings I am furrounded with.   Whenever I feel difpofed to enjoy any good thing, the idea of
what may have been his fate dafhes the cup of pleafure
from my lips—I am almoft ready to fay with Burns:

" But what can give pleafure or what can feem fair,
While the lingering moments are numbered by care?
No flowers gayly fpringing nor birds fweetly finging
Can foothe the fad bofom of joylefs defpair.

———

[From another book:]

The hardeft grief is from memory, *deftroy* that and you
indeed minifter to a mind difeafed.   Were the cup prefented to you would you tafte it?   My own memory is
what I would the lateft lofe, even if the functions of reafon were perfect without it, and though it fhows me in its
unflattering mirror, fome heart-breaking figures—if Lethe
would chafe like the mufic of the immortals anguifh, doubt,
forrow, fear and pain, it would alfo deftroy what overpays
them all—the memory of joys departed and friends that
made even the remembrance of forrow *pleafing*.

How do *I* fit folitary, who was once furrounded by a fam-

ily of children lovely and oh fo ardently beloved. Deareſt
and beſt beloved haſt thou who fo lately waſt my other
foul, *no feeling* left that claims kindred with any thought of
mine? Can it be that the reunion of fouls, fo clofely knit
together is entirely fevered, by the diſſolution of the body
as to hold no communion. Oh it can not be.

Nov 11th 1830

In looking over fome papers today I found the fragment
of a letter written by my dearly beloved daughter Frances,
altho ſhe is never abfent from my mind, letters traced by
her dear hand bring her more diſtinctly to my view. It
makes my heart bleed afreſh when I reflect upon the fufferings of that idolized child. I believe ſhe had been a
long time aware of her dangerous fituation, and the mental
agony ſhe fuffered at the profpect of being taken from her
children aggravated the difeafe and caufed her days and
nights of anguiſh. Dear fuffering angel her whole life had
been a preparation for death. No one living knew the
real worth of my incomparable, my noble minded daughter,
except her huſband and myfelf, neither were we fully fenfible of it till ſhe was taken from us. Oh Fanny deareſt
child of my foul thee never knew how dearly thee was beloved—when by my lonely firefide I can weep my woes
uninterrupted and unfeen by any eyes fave his who has
feen meet to afflict me thus forely. I wiſh not to cloud
the hearts of my other children, by making them partakers
of my forrows. Dear cheriſhed invalid ! never do I go up

and down the ftairs [at Fancy Hill,] without thinking how
we ufed to affift her.   [Her youngeft brother Dr Benj P.
Howell was one of her devoted nurfes.]

I am here furrounded by her children, poor things they
feem very happy, *too* happy.   They little know the ex-
tent of their lofs.   Never again will her loved voice fall
upon my ears in the endearing language of love and of
"dear bleffed mother."   Oh Fanny thee was indeed a
cherifhed child—never in this world fhall I feel the ardent
clafp of warm affeftion.   Her love for me feemed fo
boundlefs that fhe was often at a lofs for words to exprefs
it.   The fymptoms attending every ftage of that awful difeafe [Confumption] is indelibly impreffed on my aching
heart.   I fufpeft few people have fuffered more feverely.
My afflictions are grievous but not unmixed with a firm
hope and belief that my great lofs is the everlafting gain of
my dear departed children.   I always contemplate them
as angels of light.

Nov 30th

Sore and fick at heart am I this day.   It is the anniver-
fary of the death of my dearly beloved fon John.   My
heart is almoft broken at the forrowful retrofpeftion of the
paft two years.   To think that fo much life, love and lov-
linefs fhould die.

[Relative to the death of her son Dr. Samuel L. Howell,
died Nov 1st 1835.]

Left my home Sat 28 came to Princeton, *sad sorrowful
Princeton* how my heart bleeds at the recollection of that
I have lost there—the clay—the mortal remains of my beloved son is more dear to my bereaved heart than anything
there.   He who was in truth the delight of mine eyes the
pride of my heart and the beloved of my soul—my mind
wanders continually in search of thee.

———

[Extract of letter written to his daughter Anna Howell
Dodge.]

"I suffer very much from the presence of strangers, I
feel as if I were expected to think or say some thing when
my heart and soul are wrapt in .one absorbing thought.
His crimson chair I shall never see without associating it
with its late beloved occupant.   I have his figure in my
mind at this moment as he looked the day after the decease
of dear William [his son].   Bowed down with grief, his
noble heart almost broken—Spirit of purity, I trust thy
dear sensitive soul will never know anguish more.   "Blessed
are the pure in heart for they shall see God.

———

Dec 13

This day six weeks my idolized son Samuel was trans-
lated from this world of care to the mansions of eternal
happiness.   His sensibility was so acute, that in his pro-
fessional duties he suffered more than anyone I ever knew—

which really made him a man of forrows and acquainted
with grief, every hour of his time was fpent in ftriving to
mitigate the afflictions of thofe with whom he had to do.
He was a faithful fteward in the exercife of all his duties.
My dear deceafed fon was no common man. No he was as
fuperior to the generality as light is fuperior to darknefs. It
is furely allowable to mourn for fuch a being. Oh! the
Lord has touched me in a tender fpot. It is the apple of
mine eye that the thorn has gone through.

Dec 20th

It is feven weeks tonight fince my beloved Samuel was
taken from this to a world of reft and joy that will be everlafting. How fhall I give thee up, How fhall I ever be
reconciled to thy lofs. The Lord gave and the Lord has
taken away—bleffed be his holy name.

Dec 29th

I returned to my comfortable home. I ftrive to feel
thankful that I have fuch a home, even in the hours of
blighted love—Here I can indulge in uninterrupted woe.
Can recall to my mind the beloved child and afk myfelf,
Oh! how often in the day is it poffible that my idolized
fon is gone forever—What agony have I fuffered during my
abfence by being thrown into company with perfons, who
could have no feeling in unifon with mine. This vifit to
Princeton feems to have been neceffary to convince me
that I have not been fuffering from a diftorted dream—but

a fad reality. Where ever I ufed to fee my precious fon, there I ftill looked for him—In the parlor, at the table, in the entry—I could not refrain from fixing my eyes intently—but all was vacant, defolation was ftamped on everything—I never heard the wheels of Woodhulls gig—but I was ready to fpring as formerally to fee the object of my idolatry, upon whom I ufed to gaze with untiring delight.

[Extract from a letter to Eliza Kirkbride Gurney.]

It affords me a melancholy pleafure to contribute all in my power to the comfort of the bereaved widow and children of my late idolized fon—When I ufed to be at his houfe he never left it, but I gazed after him till he was out of fight and I was always the firft to hail his return. I never faw him but with a thrill of delight, nor heard him fpoken of but with pride—This I am now convinced was too much adulation to pay to any human being—If we were not affured, a " fparrow falls not to the ground without the Father, I fhould fay that Samuel fell a victim to his fenfibility—His heart was broken by the death of William and when difeafe affailed him, his fyftem was fo fhaken that he had no ftrength to oppofe it. Poor Mary [his wife] fhe loft a great deal in the death of her children. Thomas the eldeft fon was improving in every refpect, he was kind and thoughtful to his Mother and fifters and was growing like his beloved father—fhortly before he died he expreffed his hopes of foon joining his bleffed father and dear uncles and aunt. Thee knows what a cherub dear little Fanny was [Dr Howell's youngeft daughter] during her illnefs fhe commenced finging a hymn "Rock of Ages" fhe begged her mother to help her as fhe could not proceed. The circumftances connected with the removal of this forely afflicted family has been truly moft touching.

***

Sept 25 1836

My grandfon Thomas C. Howell departed this life. About a year fince his brother William M. Howell died and a little lefs than eleven months fince the death of his incomparable father.

***

Oct 3rd 1836

Dear little Fanny was alfo removed to Heaven. She was angelic even whilft clothed with mortality. Surely thefe are no common afflictions. Poor Mary! fhe is left to deplore the lofs of her hufband and three lovely interefting children.

This is a moft awakening call to be ready for "We know not the day nor the hour when the Son of Man cometh."

March 1831

I have juft returned from Haddonfield accompanied by my endeared friend Eliza Paul Kirkbride. We heard a moft impreffive fermon from Hannah Backhoufe, an Englifh Friend. It is feveral years fince I have been to Haddonfield—a place that I never enter without pleafurable fenfations. It was the home of my childhood and many pleafant recollections are affociated with almoft every thing I fee there—and even at this time when I am mourning over fweet comforts blafted—dear departed objects which have left a void which nothing in this world can fill. My widowed wounded heart wanders through the dark vifta of time long elapfed in fearch of fome little funny fpot for the mind to dwell in and repofe upon that is lefs drear and defolate. Being at this place revived memories that have long flept. Like a beautifully diverfified profpect which gladdens my heart when I am withdrawn from the noife and petty works of men, I confider myfelf in the great temple which the Lord has built for his own honor.

A COMMON PLACE BOOK.

March 5 1832

I have led fuch a wandering life for the paft year, that it is defirable to have fome little memmoranda of the manner in which and the places where I have fpent my time.

I left home July 2nd 1831 went to Princeton and after fpending a week as pleafantly as my fore bereavments will ever permit me to. I went to New Brunfwick to fee Anna Maria—a vifit which comforted me much—from thence I vifited Rahway and remained with Abby fome time after the birth of her little Theodore. I then went to New York to Benj. B. Howell's—found Benj. and his dear motherlefs children well. It is impoffible to defcribe my feelings during this vifit. For fome time after entering the houfe I could not fpeak I felt anew the lofs of my fainted daughter, I could not fpeak to the children without being ready to burft into tears. I felt the want of the warm clafp of affection with which my angelic daughter always ufed to greet me—I miffed her every moment and felt difpofed to feek her in every place and would not divert myfelf of the idea that her purified fpirit was prefent with us. This heavenly minded child was intertwined in my very exiftence The more I contemplate her character the more I find to admire and I always came to the conclufion that fhe was perfect—fo far as humanity can be fo. After a fad vifit of two weeks I returned to New Brunfwick. In a few days Anna became ill I then had fome *caufe* for exertion and the depreffion of fpirits gave way to a fenfe of dread that by my want of refignation to my Heavenly Fathers will, He might vifit me again by removing other earthly bleffings whilft I was deploring my prefent lofs. I had ceafed to appreciate the fources of comfort ftill left me. Anna became fo ill—fhe had taken cold which feemed to threaten her lungs that I was in terror left confumption with all its horrors fhould be the inevitable refult. To me the idea of feeing another child languifhing and dying daily feemed infupportable—I was compelled to appear cheerful as if there were no caufe for alarm in her prefence, when at the fame time I was fo agitated that I could fcarcely walk fteadily—At night my heart beat fo violently that I could fcarcely keep my head on the pillow. We fent for her brother Samuel and when he came was fo alarmed that to enable him to attend to her clofely he defired that fhe fhould be taken to Princeton at once. This was done and fhe foon began to recover and improved fo rapidly that I felt willing to leave her. I reached my long deferted home the 31ſt of Oct. accompanied by Mary, Samuel's wife, who alfo paid a vifit to her father Thomas Clayton. I think it muſt have been the 5 of Dec. that Thomas Clayton died—I went in fearch of Mary not knowing where he was at the time. The day was bitterly cold, I reached his late dwelling in the evening in time to receive Mary after fhe had followed her father, a folitary mourner, to his narrow houfe appointed for all the human race—Mary loſt her father under peculiar circumſtances and painful—He fickened and died among ſtrangers, and by the Hickfite Quakers was denied a grave, fuch a tranfaction in a Proteſtant Chriſtian Country! To deny a fellow being ' fix paces of vile earth ' " Oh fhame where was thy blufh? " and where the benevolent fpirit of Chriſt? Poor Mary after enduring a large fhare of mental and bodily fuffering reached her home the 17 of Dec.

Feb 17

I came to Philad. made my home aſ Sifter Harrifon's, and vifited feveral of my friends. It is fo long fince I had mingled with fociety purpofely or with any view to enjoyment that its variety feemed to bewilder me. I met with characters fo totally diffimilar as to prove that Lady W. Montague with all her wifdom was miftaken in afferting " that of all the people fhe had ever met with—there were two forts" that was "Men & Women." Lo I have feen more than Lady M. W. M.—Characters as oppofite as the Poles.

Feb 24th

I croffed the river to Camden and made a very pleafant vifit to Richard's family.

Feb 25

Returned to my long deferted home thankful for the comfort and privacy of my own firefide—I had left it with an aching heart not knowing the weight of afflictions that might be pending over me—But thanks be to a merciful God my children were faved alive to Him be all the Glory —I have been forely afflicted—Oh how deeply have I drank of the cup of forrow—the lofs of my fainted daughter exceeds all loffes—the little Jofhua and Rebecca precious cherubs—my two noble fons Pafchal and John—How do I fit defolate! Why fhould I mourn as one without hope— my children are not dead—nay I truft they are living where there is no death neither forrow nor fighing.

I have always endeavored to imprefs my children with this fact that an accomplifhed character has fo many charms that really nothing need be faid to induce a young perfon to wifh and ftrive for its attainments. That refolution which is neceffary for every valuable purpofe of life, is the fruit only of an active mind and was never found with indolence and floth—determine therefore to conquer every tendancy to an inactive temper.

1832 Nov 19.

I parted with Lewis Howell—dear child, he has gone a long diftance from friends & kindred—I fincerely pray that his Heavenly Father may preferve him from the dangers of the wildernefs whither he is going, he will be in a land of ftrangers—perhaps exploring a tracklefs wildernefs, expofed alike to favage man and to ferocious beafts of prey.

April 7. 1832

This day the Weft Point Fifhery was fold at public fale —it was bought in by George Thomas for me. The profpect of reclaiming the property for my children which has been fo long in jeopardy affords me as much fatisfaction as anything of that nature can.

July 20th 1832

I left my home to pay my annual vifit to my children I am now at Princeton enjoying the fociety of the Dr's family—there is a fad alloy in the prevalence of the awful cholera which keeps the mind in a ftate of alarm and in *me* does away all inclinations to travel further—In New York it is prevailing with terrific virulence—where it will ftop or who are to be its victims is known only to Him who governs the Univerfe and in whofe hands are the iffues of life & death

July 27

I was fent for to Rahway to fee my dear Abby who was quite ill—found her fuffering with remitting fever. I remained three weeks with her and fuffered greatly from anxiety. The peftilence was prevailing with great mortal-

ity in places where I had objects of interest—Benj. B.
Howell's family in New York Samuel expofed hourly to it
during his vifits to the fick laborers along the canal [Del. and
Raritan] and my precious Ben [phyfician in charge] at the
Philad. Almfhoufe—there efpecially it raged with violence.

Auguft 31 1832

My Beloved Jofhua left me at Princeton—In a few days
he will return to the Weft—It wrings my heart to part
with Jofhua—May the God of Mercy preferve him from
harm of every kind—Keep him fafe through time and fit
him for a happy eternity—The everlafting hills will foon
feparate us, but there is an interchange of Soul that inter-
vening mountains cannot prevent.

Sept 24

I was taken ill, the following day my dear Ben came to
be with me—was fo much better that the next week was
able to go to New York, tho I ftill felt the effects of difeafe—the excitement of fociety, let it be ever fo agreeable
and exhilerating, leaves a nervous irritability

1832 Oct 17.

Again I have returned to my long deferted home after
an abfence of three months. How lovely the country
looks, I think I never faw the woods fo richly beautiful
brightened by the glorious funfhine.——

When I wrote the foregoing how little did I dream that
an overwhelming affliction—the death of my idolized
Samuel was before me—In fome bereavements there is
nothing for memory to dwell on that can foothe the pang

of feparation—none of thofe tender but melancholy circumftances, that can endear the parting fcene, nothing to melt
forrow into thofe bleffed tears fent like the dew of Heaven
to raife the heart in the parching hour of anguifh

1840

Years have paffed and I have ftill felt unable to record
this heart rending event.

Nov 14th 1832

My dear Ben went to the city today to commence the
practice of medicine. It is a new era in his life—God
grant that he may be fuccefsful in the moft extenfive fenfe
of the term.

Nov 19 1832

I am at home and *alone* for the firft time for a long
while—I require no fympathy for my folitude it is really
grateful to my feelings—I may be ftrangely conftituted, but
I am often moft alone when furrounded by company.
When I become weary of my own fociety I find in a book
a companion that entertains me agreeably without requiring
anything in return on my part.

The eventide with its fober fhades and meditative influence foothes my feelings after being expofed to the buftle
of the world—the experience of every day convinces me
that I cannot enjoy fociety as is called the world—one all
engroffing fubject ftill occupies my mind and the common
place topics that I have difcuffed weary me exceedingly

1839

This afternoon at Haddonfield I attended the funeral of

my coufin Ruth Wood—This event is calculated to imprefs my mind ferioufly We were children together and
were always warmly attached to each other.

July 19 1840

I had today the real gratification of fpending an hour in
company with Jofeph John Gurney.   After we had drank
tea, he addreffed himfelf particularly to me in a very touching manner—he appeared to have internal evidence of the
many deep trials I had paffed thro' and directed me where
and how to feek confolation—" In every trial with prayer
fupplication and thankfgiving make your requefts known to
God."   I review that little vifit as a funny fpot in my
life.

1840 Aug 5.

This morning my beloved Jofhua left me for his home in
the far weft [Uniontown Pa.]   To his God and my God I
fincerely commend him.

Aug 14

My dear Grandfon Henry W. Howell fpent the day
with me—I think it muft be 3 years fince I have feen him
—dear fellow he looks thin and careworn really fo changed
I fcarcely knew him—The weight of years feems to have
been prematurely brought upon him.

July 2nd 1841

My beloved Jofhua and his interefting wife Mary
[Lewis] and their daughter Anna came from their home in
the Weft to pay their annual vifit.

July 18 1853

I have juft returned from Red Bank where I accompanied my beloved fon Jofhua B. Howell preparatory to his returning to his weftern home, after a moft gratifying vifit of feveral weeks. I was utterly rejoiced that he has regained his ufual health and fpirits after the fore bereavement he experienced laft fummer in the death of his wife—never was there a more fincere mourner.

1841

Departed this life in the 67th year of her age my dear fifter Mary Blackwood Harrifon. Bleffed are the dead who die in the Lord. The whole life of this eftimable woman was a preparation for death For a number of years before her death fhe had fuffered many of the evils attendant upon limited circumftances brought about by lofs of a large fortune—fhe bore this with a perfect patience—I think I never knew a more beautiful character.

[Extracts from notes on her readings:]

No perfon in his fenfes can voluntarily prefer death to life. Our defires of exiftence are ftrong and prevalent they are born with us—our ideas of a future ftate are not fufficiently clear to make us wiftful of hurrying into Eternity; efpecially as eternity itfelf ever remains incomprehenfible to finite beings—Human nature has a terror and abhorrence of its own diffolution.

Dr Swift was deprived of his reafon for fome years previous to his death—He had not even a child's power of expreffion—Apparently he was referved only as an example to mortify human pride and to reverfe that fine defcription of a human being which is given us by Shakespeare in an inimitable manner "What a piece of work is man! How noble in reafon! How infinite in faculty! in form and moving how expert and admirable—in action how like an angel—in apprehenfion how like a God, the beauty of this world, the paragon of animals" Thus poets paint, but how vain and perifhable the picture The fmalleft thunderbolt from Heaven blafts it in a moment and every tint is fo effectually obliterated that fcarce the outlines of the figure remain.

89066163403

b89066163403a

CPSIA information can be obtained
at www.ICGtesting.com
Printed in the USA
LVHW081421010821
694263LV00002B/72

9 780342 361397